Prais

Awakening the

'Ankush Jain's new book is a must-read if you're a coach who's ready to 'go pro' and build a thriving, professional coaching business. While there are many great coaching and coach-practice books out there, Ankush takes you behind the scenes and gives you an honest, access-all-areas look at the aspects of growing a coaching business most people never see (and most books never reveal). This is what makes it a must-read; his authenticity and generosity in sharing his journey (warts and all) will allow you to take big steps forward in your coaching career. As I read the pre-release copy, I regularly thought of coaches I want to send the book to, because I can see how instantly useful and valuable it will be to them. *Awakening the Coach Within* is a gift to every coach who's ready to put their coaching and their clients first and grow a practice grounded in connection, possibility and service. Highly recommended.'

– **Jamie Smart,** *Sunday Times* bestselling author, speaker and coach

'Whenever I stumble upon a true hero's journey, like this book is, I first rejoice and let myself feel the inspiration. Then I look forward to reading it again to study and learn. Anyone wanting to create a successful career can save themselves a lot of time and misery by reading this marvellous book!'

– **Steve Chandler,** author of *Time Warrior*

'*Awakening the Coach Within* by Ankush Jain is a practical, no-fluff toolkit for creating real, measurable change. The raw, relatable stories pack lessons that stick with you. This book doesn't just teach—it transforms, unlocking new levels of awareness, compassion and mastery. A must-read for anyone serious about coaching or leadership.'

– **Chris Dorris,** author of *The Book of Mental Toughness Mantras*

'I have known Ankush for ten years as a friend and colleague. He is such a loving person and his love comes through in this book. What a beautiful and heartfelt way to guide us through the evolution of a coach. The book is filled with hope. Since Ankush writes about his personal journey with both his doubts and realizations, you can see yourself and the potential for you to develop your coaching business. Through Ankush's personal story you are given proven steps that lead to a prosperous practice.'

– **Mark Howard, PhD,** Mark Howard, Ph.D., Clinical Psychologist, Three Principles educator, trainer and consultant

'Awakening the Coach Within is a masterful invitation to remember what true coaching is truly about—presence, service and deep listening. Ankush Jain has written a book that transcends techniques and returns us to the heart of transformation itself.

'As someone who has been coaching leaders for over three decades, I found myself both engaged and inspired by the simplicity and clarity of his message. This book is not just about becoming a better coach—it's about becoming a more useful human being.

If you are serious about coaching as a calling, this is essential reading. Ankush doesn't just teach coaching—he transmits the energy of it.'

– **Stephen McGhee,** Leadership Advisor, author of *Climb to Freedom* and *Get Real*

'The real hidden gem in this book is the ability to witness an irrevocable shift in being that is possible for the reader as the story progresses. I have always known Ankush to be a man who would choose truth over comfort and take a journey that would transform the *entire* world, not only the world of coaching. This book is not just words on a page. It is an invocation for the reader to awaken into a willingness to change, to be changed and to lead others by example. What you hold in your hands is the map of an actual journey, not theory, not philosophy borrowed from others, but lived experience transformed into wisdom. Read it carefully. Read it slowly. Allow the words to transform you.

– **Gary Mahler,** the Mentor who creates from being, who works within the space where infinite stillness becomes creation

'I've sat in Ankush's rooms more than once and attended one-to-one coaching sessions many times. Every single time I leave steadier, clearer and more focused on what I need to do. I attended his school (AJC) three times in a row—because his coaching *works*. It's not tactics, funnels, or clever scripts; it's service, presence and real conversations that turn into real results. *Awakening the Coach Within* is the calm, practical guide all coaches need. In this book Ankush takes us on the journey from leaving his corporate job to becoming a top coach. It's simple without being simplistic, human without the hype and immediately usable; you'll put it down and go serve someone better. I recommend it wholeheartedly.'

– **Angi Scott,** author of *The Coaching Blueprint*, AJC alum × 3

'Success leaves clues! I've always loved this quote, and this book is a perfect example. *Awakening the Coach Within* is filled with priceless gems—life lessons and coaching wisdom that will inspire and guide coaches at every stage of their journey.

'Ankush leaves us with invaluable clues about what it really takes to be a successful coach—serving clients at the highest level with humility, presence and love. It's a reminder of what becomes possible when we truly fall in love with coaching and dedicate ourselves to growth. This book is both a gift and a guide for anyone ready to walk the path of coaching with courage and authenticity.'

– **Dr Rani Bora,** Holistic *Psychiatrist*, Coach and author of *How to Turn Stress on Its Head*

'Ankush Jain's *Awakening the Coach Within* is for anyone who is sincere about becoming a professional coach—especially if you are wondering if it's possible. Ankush's story is important because it shares all the vital elements *every* coach needs to know . . . that if you stay the course, if you get coaching and if above all else you are curious and willing, you can do this. Ankush demonstrates over and over again what's possible. He doesn't hold anything back. You'll be inspired, you'll be gently guided and you'll experience what's available in every single chapter. I highly recommend using *Awakening the Coach Within* in service to your growth and the growth of your coaching business. Ankush's dedication to coaches and to what's possible is on every page.'

– **Carolyn Freyer-Jones,** author of *What if This Is the Fun Part?* and *The Total Coaching Success Book*

'I first met Ankush Jain in Scottsdale, Arizona, in 2024, and from the first moment he spoke, I could sense something rare—a depth of soul and mastery of language that revealed not just a man sharing ideas, but a human being embodying them. Ankush articulated timeless truths about human potential, presence and service in a way that resonated far beyond professional coaching.

'*Awakening the Coach Within* goes beyond the art of coaching. It is a profound guide for living with purpose, integrity and service. Designed for coaches, leaders and anyone seeking to lead a more intentional and value-driven life, this book illuminates a path of authentic impact and meaningful contribution. Ankush illustrates through his own journey that the true measure of fulfillment is not transactional success, but the transformation that arises when we serve from love—even when no external reward follows. This is not a business strategy; it is a calling to elevate humanity itself.'

– **Olga Campora, Ph.D.,** Life Coach and author of *Saint Behind Enemy Lines*

Giving it all away!

If you are a coach who wants to grow your practice, this book is not only a must read—it's a keep-by-your-side book. Ankush shares frankly, holding nothing back about his early years as a Coach, and in doing so, normalises the full experience, with the ups and the downs, the highs, and the lessons. This book will not only help you grow your business; it will support you as a human as you do so. Leaving nothing out, in service for you, is exactly the Ankush I've come to know and love, and through this book, so will you.

– **Julie Brown,** The Leadership Shift - The Impact Of BEing In A New Era Of Leadership

'Ankush Jain isn't the loudest voice in the room. But it's his presence, his groundedness, and his conviction in the power of coaching that guarantee you'll be hanging on every word he says. Each nugget of wisdom he offers comes from his direct experience of building a thriving coaching practice, and this book is no different. He weaves valuable lessons into the tapestry of his own stories, offering the reader not a polished "how to" guide, but rather the raw, unfiltered truths of what it really takes to make it as a coach. His honesty and candour will leave you thinking that if Ankush can do it, you can too. And speaking from personal experience, if you apply the teachings contained within these pages, you'll prove yourself right.'

– **Shazia Govindji,** Leadership Coach, Speaker

'Ankush Jain has a reputation for helping coaches build sustainable and thriving coaching businesses, and for good reason. As you read this book, you'll notice how relatable the stories are and just how doable it is for someone like you to build a successful coaching business. Not only that—you'll also find countless practical gems that will serve coaches all the way from the first steps in business through to a six- or multi-six-figure revenue and beyond. The transition from employee to entrepreneur is a foundational, but highly nuanced, mindset shift and one of the many things I'm grateful to Ankush for is his gift for helping coaches navigate that transition and acquire the skills and experience to "turn the money tap on" at will. Essential reading for all coaches.'

– **Nick Bottini,** musician, coach, bestselling author of Just Play: The Simple Truth Behind Musical Excellence

'Coaching has become so saturated with quick tips, social media promises, and grand claims of overnight success that it's easy to forget what this work is really about. Ankush's book *Awakening The Coach Within* is a breath of fresh air—it cuts through the noise and takes us back to the heart of what it truly means to be a professional coach. For years, I wished I could be a fly on the wall and watch how real, thriving coaches built their practices. Ankush has given us that gift. He doesn't just tell his story—he opens the curtain on what it really takes to succeed in this profession: the doubts, the failures, the grit, and the moments of deep transformation that make it all worth it. Over a decade ago, I wrote a book to help elevate the world of coaching. Reading this, I felt both proud and inspired—proud to see how far our profession has come, and inspired to raise my own game once again. Ankush's book reminded me why I fell in love with coaching in the first place: because it changes lives, starting with our own. This is more than a book—it's a love letter to the profession of coaching and to the people we serve. Ankush has set a new standard for what it means to thrive as a coach with heart, integrity, and purpose.'

– **Amir Karkouti,** author of Lessons From My Coach and What the F**K Are The Three Principles?

'Ankush Jain's *Awakening the Coach Within* is a gift to any coach, regardless if you've been coaching for thirty minutes or thirty years. Walking through Ankush's journey on these pages, I found a depth of value that goes far beyond just the act of coaching. As a leadership and executive coach myself, I'm already sharing insights and lessons from this book with my own clients. It speaks not only to the heart of coaching, but also to the essence of leadership itself and the journey of becoming a truly great leader. Whether you're building a coaching business or a team, you will find massive value in this book.'

– **Deryl Sweeney,** Founder of the SCG Leadership Institute

'Ankush's book pulls you straight into the real journey of becoming a prosperous coach. He doesn't hide the doubts, the setbacks, or the moments where it didn't to work. He shows what it actually took him to build a successful and sustainable business rooted in service, depth, and real relationships. I have transformed so much through our work together, and reading the book still opened up many new insights for me. I consider Ankush one of the world's best coaches, and this book makes him accessible to everyone. No matter where you are on your journey, it is a powerful example that the path is possible, and worth walking.'

– **Dr. Johannes Metzler,** CEO Coach and author of *From Stress to Success* and *The 10X CEO*

'This exceptional book is a page-turner and is not just for coaches. It could have been titled *Awakening the Leader Within*. You can read it for yourself, whatever your background, as a thrilling adventure novel about what it means to follow your calling, in which the hero describes his journey with remarkable sincerity, authenticity, and honesty. You will be able to take inspiration from everything he shares and apply it to your own life journey. And if you are a coach, you have here an extraordinary powerful reference book to help you in growing your practice. You will also witness how Ankush embodies his vision and mission to raise the consciousness of the planet by up-leveling the coaching profession and you may even be inspired to join in and follow in his footsteps.'

– **Liv Brunet,** transformative coach, translator of Sydney Banks into French, author of *Transforme ta vie avec les 3 Principes* (*Transform your life with the Three Principles*)

Awakening *the* Coach Within

Dear Kellie,

Great to connect on LinkedIn and such a pleasure to be able to send you this signed copy of my book which I published a few months ago.

As you build your nutrition + lifestyle practice alongside completing your nutritional therapy degree, the lessons in here will guide you well.

I look forward to hearing what insights you gain.

Ankush

Awakening *the* Coach Within

Lessons for Building and Embodying a Thriving Coaching Practice

Ankush Jain

Awakening the Coach Within: Lessons for Building and Embodying a Thriving Coaching Practice

Published by Ankush Jain Publishing

Contact the author:
ankush@ankushjain.co.uk
www.ankushjain.co.uk

Editing and layout by Chris Nelson
Cover design by Jefté Nascimento

ISBN: 978-1-9192753-0-7

First Edition

This book is a true account of my personal experiences and reflections. In order to honour confidentiality, the names and identifying details of clients and some individuals have been changed. However, the names of mentors, public figures, and those who have given permission to be identified have been used as they are. In a few cases, composite characters have been created or timelines adjusted for clarity. Any resemblance to other persons, living or dead, is purely coincidental.

For my family,
my mentors,
and every coach called to make a difference.

Contents

Foreword: Becoming Through Learning xxi

Introduction xxv

1. Being a Professional Coach Is Simple but not Always Easy 3
2. I Already Knew My First Client 7
3. You Can Learn on the Job 10
4. I Was in the Closet as a Coach... 13
5. When Starting Out, Payment Was Less Important for Me than Experience.. 16
6. I Start to Learn About Service 22
7. The Three Principles 24
8. I Didn't Need to Burn My Bridges 27
9. Meeting My Future Mentor 30
10. Setting Up a Business 34
11. My Coach Training Was Impacting My Regular Work 36
12. My First Package Client... 40
13. Using a Script Wasn't as Helpful as I Thought 42
14. Landing the Dream Job and a Choice 45
15. People You Don't Expect can Become Clients: My Second Package Client 48

16. Expectation Versus Agreement.......... 52
17. Clients Don't Always Want a Discount.......... 56
18. Launching My Website.......... 60
19. You Can Only Give Away What You Have.......... 63
20. You Can Impact People Even When You Don't Know What You're Doing.......... 66
21. Signing Up for More Training.......... 70
22. Implementing Systems.......... 73
23. A Humbling Lesson.......... 76
24. Impact Your Clients Like No-One Else.......... 80
25. Getting an Accountant.......... 84
26. I Was in a Rush.......... 87
27. Attending Dicken Bettinger's Event with Chantal Burns.... 91
28. Increasing My Fee.......... 95
29. I Couldn't Coach Everyone.......... 98
30. I Started to Be More Direct.......... 102
31. I Started Working with a New Mentor.......... 105
32. Not Holding Back.......... 108
33. Becoming More Impactful.......... 111
34. Speaking with Steve Chandler.......... 115
35. Attending a Retreat with Elsie Spittle.......... 119
36. Being More Visible While Being Scared.......... 122
37. Bringing Jamie into Work.......... 125

38. Not Everyone Will Support You 130
39. Heading to Norway 133
40. A Referral that Never Went Anywhere 136
41. Starting My Podcast 141
42. Signing Up for the London Intensive with Rich and Steve 145
43. The London Intensive, Day 1 150
44. The London Intensive, Day 2 155
45. Not Taking No for an Answer 158
46. My First Event Didn't Go as Planned 162
47. The Importance of Commitment and My Calendar 167
48. An Insight to Quit My Job 171
49. The Birth of My Men's Work 175
50. How I Filled My Intensive 180
51. Talk to the Highest Voice in the Room 183
52. Getting Creative with Clients 187
53. Getting Prepared for Going Full-Time 190
54. People May Be More Open than You Realise 194
55. Referrals Come from Service, not from Asking 197
56. Three Steps to Becoming a Great Coach 200
57. Give It all Away and Stay Humble 204
58. Don't Let Social Anxiety Get in the Way 207
59. Problems Are Your Friend 210

60. You Don't Need To Rush To 'Close' a Client 213

61. Go Beyond What Other Coaches Do 216

62. Delivering Amazing Service as a Public Speaker 220

63. More Tips for My First Speaking Engagement 223

64. The Half-Life of Enthusiasm 227

65. Fill Your Calendar with Conversations 230

66. Is Coaching More Fulfilling than a Day Job? 232

67. Coaching Is About Possibility 235

68. Crossing the Line to More Unfiltered Service 238

69. Understanding the Value of My Work 241

70. Flourishing Outside of Your Comfort Zone 243

71. Coaching Is a Two-Step Process 249

72. Learning from Other Coaches 252

73. The Ultimate Coach 255

74. Filling My First Immersion 259

75. I Didn't Need to Take This Seriously 262

76. The Seed of a Book 265

77. The Website Myth 268

78. A Business, Not a Hobby 270

79. Stacking the Cards in My Favour. 273

80. The Power of Preparation 277

81. Unexpected Connections 282

82. Reaching Out 286

83. A Lesson in Coaching Styles 291

84. Momentum 294

85. Tools, not Rules 297

86. Embracing Inner Peace: My Conversation with Sebastian Eck 300

87. A Client Who Drove Seven Hours 303

88. Freedom from Fear 306

89. Mastering the Art of Enquiry 309

90. The Fundamentals of Performance 312

91. Speaking from the Heart in Romania 315

92. Meeting Arthur Peters 318

93. Clients Don't Pay for Me 322

94. The Gold in Challenge 325

95. Possibility, not Affordability 329

96. Taking People off the Pedestal 333

97. Launching the Coaching Group: From Frustration to Service 336

98. The Lesson in Being Bold 339

99. Rewriting My Money Story 342

100. Breaking the Money Spell 346

101. Only Have Questions 349

102. The Power of a Simple Invitation 353

103. Filling My Second Immersion 356

104. Have Fun, Make Money 359

105. Coaching Is an Active Investment 363
106. Serve, Even if They Don't Sign Up 368
107. Share Your Story.. 373
108. What Are You Waiting For?... 377
109. Interviewing My Coach for the First Time 381
110. Falling Even More in Love with the Profession 386
111. Just Coach 391
112. Event-Action 395
113. Day 3 In Chicago 398
114. The Gift of Slowness 401
115. The Ashram Talk 406
116. A Collaboration That Brought out the Fun in Me............. 409
117. The Proposal 412
118. A Full Practice Takes Years, Doesn't It?........................... 416
119. I'll Meet You There 419

Further Resources 423
Acknowledgments.. 427
About the Author 431

Foreword

Becoming Through Learning

'I think that a life properly lived is just learn, learn, learn all the time.'

~ Charlie Munger

When I first met Ankush Jain at Steve Chandler's ACS training programme for coaches, two things immediately struck me.

First, here was someone with no pretence whatsoever. His manner was so open and genuine that I found it both refreshing and disarming. I quickly discovered that I could, without hesitation, simply be myself and connect with him on an honest, deep level. This is a priceless gift he still has. He's an extraordinary human being and coach who genuinely loves others and cares about making a profound impact on our world.

Second, Ankush and I could not have been at more different places in our lives and along our coaching journeys.

I was married, had two adult children and was still struggling to gain traction as a professional coach after years of trying.

Ankush, on the other hand, was younger and just starting his coaching career. He was aiming to leave his first profession to step fully into coaching, and was willing to do whatever it took.

That willingness has defined his journey, and it forms one of the most vital lessons—among many—that this book offers. The factor that most impacts the growth of yourself and your practice is *how you choose to engage with the process of learning.* Will you lean in with openness and honesty, with a willingness to be vulnerable, to be shaped by experience? Or will you hold back, trying to get it 'right,' needing to look like you have it together or clinging to an exit plan for when things feel uncomfortable or take longer than you hoped?

Ankush chose openness. *Awakening the Coach Within* illustrates how he learned from anyone and every experience that would teach him, and how he turned that learning into results. It will show you how to do the same thing and inspire you into action.

One of the main reasons Ankush gained traction so quickly is that he was fully committed to learning. He didn't hesitate or make it mean something negative about himself that he needed support. Instead he actively sought it out—including not taking NO as an answer when he initially tried to hire Steve Chandler as his coach (as you'll read about in this book). Nor did he wallow in self-doubt or get lost analysing imagined shortcomings behind what he thought was a lack of progress. He got strategic.

Ankush attended conferences where he didn't know anyone. When offered coaching by participants, he welcomed it and put their ideas into practice. He invested in himself by hiring great coaches (something he emphasises all outstanding coaches must do), and he became more and more coachable over time.

The results were remarkable. Early on, he launched *The Relationship Series* podcast, which is filled with valuable content from experts in the field. Through this work, he didn't just serve others with useful resources; he built deep, lasting friendships and partnerships with many of the professionals he interviewed. It was a powerful way to learn—surrounding himself with the kinds of people he aspired to become.

Like Ankush, if you get bold and creative in how you approach your learning, you'll see results you can keep building on. Your personal approach may look entirely different from his—you know how you like to learn, or you will *learn* along the way what you like and what works best for you. You will also learn where your edge is.

If you are open to it, my suggestion would be to go toward the places where *you'll grow*, where things feel a little uncertain, maybe even scary—but where they are also full of possibility. This will allow you to create yourself and your coaching practice in ways you may never have imagined.

As I say, you won't do it exactly the way Ankush did—your path and timing are your own. But by exploring alongside him, you'll benefit tremendously from his inspiration, his practical learnings and his insights. Over time, Ankush's business flourished with long-term clients and powerful coaching groups, including his *Men's Immersion Group* (which has sold out for twelve consecutive years). He also started his now much-sought-after *AJC Coaching Career School*, which teaches coaches the power of service in growing their businesses.

It's important to note that Ankush's business grew because *he* did. He became the leader, husband, father and friend he wanted to be—and he did it the same way you will: by taking action even when it feels uncomfortable. That stretch comes with the territory when you're learning and growing. It's not a sign to stop; it's a sign that you're doing the work that leads to real change.

So dear coach—wherever you are on your path—this book is for you.

For me, the deepest lesson you can take away from it lies in seeing who Ankush was being as he learned—namely, someone willing to ask for help, to proceed when uncomfortable, to create opportunities to serve, and to be unstoppable. This book recreates his journey in real time, allowing you to explore, in the context of living and practice-building, the kinds of questions that most coaches will immediately find familiar: How do I get paying clients? Serve? Set my fee? Market myself? Do social media? Transition from my day job? Enrol a group?

Let Ankush's story inspire you to rise to the challenge of being yourself as a coach. Ankush started with small steps, unsure at times, but he kept going and carved his own path. So did I—and so can you. This book will help you find your way, your voice and your own expression of service to yourself and to others.

That's how you awaken the coach within.

Melissa Ford
Chicago, Illinois
October, 2025

Introduction

When I finished writing my first book, *Sweet Sharing: Rediscovering the REAL You,* I thought I'd move straight on to the next one. That was back in 2019. And here we are.

This book has taken much longer than I anticipated, and I'm glad it has. I didn't want to rush the process. I wanted to create something that I know will be genuinely useful. Not just inspiring, but grounded in real-life experience. That meant diving into old notes, listening again to recordings of trainings I attended, rereading years of Facebook posts, and pulling together stories and insights that helped me grow a coaching practice from scratch.

But from the outset, let me be clear.

This is not a prescription.

I'm not offering you a perfect system or a step-by-step plan. This book is a collection of lessons, stories and perspectives from my own journey—and from the many coaches I've supported privately and through my AJC Coaching Career School.

Please don't read it as gospel.

Instead, treat it as inspiration. Let it spark your own thinking. Use it to test what feels true for you. Experiment, reflect, and most of all, trust your inner wisdom.

That might be the most important message I can offer you.

Right now, we're living through the beginnings of the AI revolution. It's already changing industries across the world. With it comes a lot of fear and uncertainty. One of the biggest questions I hear is: what role will humans play when machines can do so much?

To me, the answer is simple. AI can replicate knowledge, structure, even insight. But it cannot form a real relationship. It cannot love. It cannot see into another human being and hold space for their transformation. That is what coaching is. At its highest level, coaching is a deeply human act.

And the impact of that act is bigger than most people realise.

Coaching doesn't just change the client's life. It transforms their world—their relationships, their leadership, their way of parenting. It impacts their children. It can ripple into generations that haven't even been born yet. Coaching, when it's grounded in love and presence, has the power to shift entire family lines.

That's why this book matters. That's why this profession matters.

After nearly 13 years of coaching, I still see so many brilliant, caring coaches struggling when they don't need to. They follow advice that doesn't fit them. They chase models that disconnect them from their values. Meanwhile, the most joyful, profitable and impactful coaching practices I've seen—including my own—are built on something much simpler: service, presence and real connection. One relationship at a time.

The stories in this book cover the early years of my journey, up until the start of 2016. I chose that window on purpose. These years laid the foundation for everything that followed. This book is intentionally autobiographical, because I learn best through stories—and I believe many others do too.

As I wrote, a mission became clear. To raise the consciousness of the planet through transforming this profession. I don't believe we've even come close to what's possible for us as human beings. Coaching helps people access capacities they didn't think they had. I know, because I've experienced that transformation myself.

I know what it's like to lie awake at midnight, scrolling through another expert's 'proven system,' wondering if you're just not cut out for this. I know the weight of all that conflicting advice—the strategies that feel like putting on an ill-fitting outfit. Maybe you've wondered if coaching is really a sustainable career, or if you're missing some secret that everyone else seems to have figured out.

Here's what I want you to know: you're not broken.

In those early years I write about in this book, I discovered ideas that changed everything. I didn't need to become someone else to succeed. The coaches I've watched build the most joyful, profitable practices follow a simple blueprint—service—but they implement it in their own unique way, showing up as who they really are, even when it feels terrifying.

If this work is calling to you, if you feel it in your bones even when your head is full of uncertainty, then you're already closer than you think.

You don't have to get it all right.

You just have to trust that who you are is not only enough—it's exactly what the world needs.

Let's begin.

Ankush Jain
August 2025

Awakening *the* Coach Within

1

Being a Professional Coach Is Simple but not Always Easy

When I was nineteen I stumbled across the self-development world. At the time, I was enrolled in a university degree programme at Aston University in Birmingham, England. Like most students, I was trying my best to enjoy all aspects of university life. But I was also deeply insecure. While appearing confident, the opposite was true. I was desperately looking for friendships and a girlfriend to change how I felt about myself.

One of my first discoveries was that my personality wasn't fixed, and that I could change things about my behaviour that could result in better relationships, more confidence and even better grades. I wrote about this in my first book, *Sweet Sharing: Rediscovering the REAL You.* Suffice to say that up till this point, I had thought that my personality was just my personality. I was stuck with it and with who I was.

But after being introduced to personal development through a friend of mine, Abdul, I found that this wasn't true. One example—

around eye contact—seems simple but it had a big impact. I used to walk around staring at the ground, just a few feet ahead of me. It was an unconscious behaviour. However, after reading about the importance of making eye contact with people I started to experiment with staring directly ahead when walking around campus. It felt scary and exhilarating—and to my surprise nothing bad happened because of it. I didn't die or spontaneously combust, and I occasionally even had people smile at me.

What a shift! This led me to really delve deeply into the self-help world once I graduated, and throughout my twenties I was obsessed with anything that could 'make me better'. I listened to audiobooks on my morning commute, watched personal development videos at weekends and was always reading something to improve some aspect of myself. I even enrolled in courses overseas, seeking the best mentors and coaches who could help me have a better life and ultimately feel better about myself.

As I approached thirty, I constantly thought about what my true purpose was, how I could live my passion, what my ideal job was . . . and related questions. At the time, I was working for a large building materials company and earning a good living as a procurement manager (a job I enjoyed). I got to negotiate large deals, push my comfort zone and was on a respectable and well-paid career path. But deep down I knew that if I had a blank paper for my life and could design my profession any way I wanted, I would certainly be doing something else.

After two years of trying to figure this out without success, I set aside one weekend to find the answer. I would do nothing else but think about what my passion and purpose really were. After much soul-searching, thinking and testing, I came up blank. On Sunday evening, I gave up. After two days of intensely trying to work out what I wanted to do, I put it all to one side and just got on with life.

The next day I went to work. While not happy at my lack of an answer, I felt like I was no worse off than when I had left work on Friday. However, that evening, while cooking some vegetarian fajitas, I had a eureka moment: *I should be a life coach!*

It made sense: I loved self-development, I loved to help others and I knew people made a living doing this work. So it was feasible and something that I would love to do. That moment of realisation started my journey into the world of the professional coach.

I thought it would be fairly easy to switch careers once I made the decision to do so. I simply needed to commit to the decision. I started a year-long coach-training programme and believed that I would quit my job and be coaching full-time in a matter of months.

It quickly became obvious that things weren't going to turn out that way. Despite my best efforts, it took over two years before I was able to leave my day job and coach full-time.

What I didn't know back then was that this was actually pretty fast, though it felt anything but at the time. All those programmes littering the Internet that promise commercial success in a short time are not representative of what I have seen in my own journey or the journeys of my colleagues around me.

The good news is that for those wanting to coach full-time, this profession is simple—including the process of making money in a sustainable and ethical way. In the following pages you'll find steps to follow—not as prescriptions, but as guides—that will help anyone wanting to have success in this work. These are the same lessons I share in my AJC Coaching Career School, which I have run for several years, and which helps coaches learn how to sustainably grow their income. You may find that these lessons are often the opposite of what is taught in other business-building programmes for coaches.

I will not sell you the dream of high fees, dream clients and little work. That would be doing you a disservice. If you are truly passionate about helping others, willing to put in the work and willing to invest in yourself, then this book will provide a roadmap via the story of my own journey. My hope is that as you read what I've learned and how I grew my coaching practice, you will find lessons that you can apply to your own practice and journey, whether you're a new coach or have been coaching for some time with an established business.

Someone once told me that the world does not need any more average life coaches. I agreed. There is, however, a desperate shortage of *great, high-quality* life coaches—who seem to be a rare breed indeed. This book will help you become one of them.

2

I Already Knew My First Client

I started a year-long training with a coach called Jamie Smart. I knew of him through work I'd done with mentors and coaches who spoke very highly of him.

I didn't take this decision lightly—I researched many different options for training as a coach, from a $300 online certification programme to a master's degree in executive coaching at a prestigious UK university. However, there was something about my conversations with Jamie that had me decide to enrol in his Inner Circle programme.

I signed up in September 2012, just a week or so after my insight while cooking, and the first module consisted of three days with the sports coach and author Garett Kramer in a large, four-star London hotel near Heathrow Airport. Garett and Jamie introduced me to a body of work called the Three Principles, which has gone on to form the basis of my coaching. I'll share more about these ideas soon.

That first weekend challenged so much of what I thought I knew about how the mind works that it had huge implications for the rest of my life and coaching career. However, at the time I was really just scratching the surface of what I would later come to understand (you can learn more about that in my first book: *Sweet*

Sharing).

As I was in London, I decided to meet up with my good friend Abdul for dinner. We visited a great little vegetarian restaurant, a favourite of my father's, that was close to my hotel. Abdul had introduced me to the world of personal development over ten years earlier when we were both studying at Aston University, and he was curious about the course I was taking.

I was excited about what I was learning, so I shared the ideas as best I could about the mind and our feelings, and even drew a diagram on the back of a napkin. At the end of my twenty-minute explanation, Abdul pulled out a £50 note and said that he wanted to pay me. I was astonished and told him I couldn't take the payment for a conversation with a friend, but he insisted. He said he felt that he had really learned something new.

I assumed Abdul was just being kind and paying me to encourage a friend on a new career path. However, years later he confirmed to me that the payment was genuine, and that he gave it to me in return for what he felt was very valuable information.

I had created my first paying client.

My second client followed soon after. I attended a networking event organised by my former university the week following my training in London. There I met several alumni and current students, including a young lady called Fahima, who was studying for a Ph.D. in biology. We struck up a conversation about a friend of mine who had also graduated from the same university, studied a science degree and now worked in industry. I offered to introduce the two of them to help Fahima see if this was a career path that could work for her. I've always enjoyed connecting people I know where I see it could be beneficial.

After Fahima spoke with my friend, she was grateful and asked if there was anything she could do in return. I saw an opportunity to test out my coaching and offered her a couple of sessions free of charge, which she accepted. Again, despite my being very new at this, we met a couple of times in a hotel lobby and I coached her as best as I could. It was a great experience that really confirmed for me that this was the path I wanted to follow as my new career. I remember walking out of the hotel lobby to my car feeling like I was walking on air, thinking how incredible it would be if I could do this as my day job. After the two sessions, she insisted on paying me. I had no idea what to charge but she offered me £100 for the two sessions, which was in line with what I had received from Abdul, so I accepted.

I smiled to myself, thinking this coaching business was pretty easy. Within the first few weeks, two people had paid me without my even asking them to. I imagined handing in my notice at work within months.

I was naïve and perhaps a little cocky. What I didn't realise was that it would take me another seven months before my next paying client signed up, and there were many lessons I had yet to learn. Some of those lessons were hidden inside how my first two paying clients came about, but they were lessons I wouldn't see or understand for quite some time.

3

You Can Learn on the Job

I continued my training as a coach with Jamie Smart, and in those first few months I learned more and more about the how the mind works. I was opening up to a new understanding around the nature of thought and how it impacts my experience of life, and this in turn was leading to huge insights. I started to see that whatever I was feeling in a given moment was a reflection of my thinking in that moment, and not a reflection of my circumstances. This is the fundamental understanding that arises from the Three Principles.[1] It allowed me to stop getting so caught up in my angry feelings, to stop procrastinating at work and to quiet the constant noise of overthinking in my head.

I started to look for opportunities to test out my burgeoning Three Principles knowledge and hone my coaching skills.

Before I had done the first module with Jamie Smart, I told my manager's boss that I was enrolling in this programme. He was sceptical and advised me to be careful about investing my money in it.

[1] If you're not familiar with the Three Principles, don't worry. Throughout this book I will keep referring to them. They were first articulated by Sydney Banks, a Scottish born author, philosopher and lecturer, who passed away in 2009. They are believed by some, including myself, to represent a fundamental new paradigm in psychology.

But when I came back to work after the first module, I passionately shared my insights with him, and he was convinced that what I was learning had value. He encouraged me to continue.

I took this as a sign to share with other colleagues and offered a coaching session to my immediate manager. We coached about how the mind works and how his feelings were not an indication of his circumstances. He wanted to apply this understanding to his personal life, and in our second conversation he shared an insight he'd had around losing his temper when his young daughter hadn't eaten the lunch he had packed for her for school. He realised after he had gotten upset at her that his angry feelings weren't caused by her not eating her lunch, but rather by his *thinking* about her not eating her lunch. Based on this, he had gathered his senses, gone up to her room and calmly spoken with her about being concerned about her health. Then they hugged it out.

He saw enough value in what I was sharing with him that he was open to me delivering a half-day training course for the team.

We sat down and I suggested I could talk a little about how the mind works (that's all I knew at the time; I had about an hour of content), but I was also open to whatever he thought would be most useful. He said he would really like me to deliver a workshop on stakeholder management—that is, how to develop strong relationships with our internal customers and get their buy-in to our projects, which was critical for the team's success.

I told him no problem, but at the same time I had no idea how I would do this. Thankfully, I wasn't so arrogant as to not ask for help from those around me. The next time I went down to London for training, I used the opportunity to ask Jamie how he might approach this workshop if he were giving it. He advised me to start with 'best practice' ideas, things that were already well understood, and to then lead the attendees into what I wanted to share. It was great advice. I then spoke to other colleagues in the room, such as Chantal Burns, who had coached within corporations. This was one of the benefits of attending a group coaching programme that I hadn't at first realised: the connection to other coaches who were further ahead than me, and who could help and support my own growth.

My material and format started coming together. I even reached out to Cheryl Bond, a corporate coach whom I had never met before; I had heard an interview with her and Jamie Smart. She was incredibly gracious, giving me an hour of her time and helping me further develop my content and slides for the workshop.

I would love to tell you that the workshop went swimmingly. However, my team were challenging. They asked questions I hadn't anticipated, and they certainly didn't take it easy on me. Consequently, I was expecting mediocre feedback and was shocked when a colleague told me he thought it was one of the best workshops he had ever attended. He felt it should be rolled out to the entire company. I took from this a vital lesson that I still live by today: it's possible to throw yourself in at the deep end and learn on the job.

So, my skills were improving, and I was growing more confident in my abilities as a coach. But paying clients still eluded me.

4

I Was in the Closet as a Coach

While I was being very open in my day job about the coach training I was doing—and which was leading to opportunities—outside of work I was hiding. I had huge insecurities about what people would think of me, of all people, becoming a coach—the younger me wouldn't have believed it possible either. I was afraid of being ridiculed and scoffed at. It wouldn't have surprised me.

I was a painfully shy and insecure teenager. Even though my confidence grew in my twenties, I was still hiding my insecurities below the surface. I was part of the 'fake it until you make it' brigade, except that I never seemed to make it. I deeply wanted other people to approve of me, thinking that if they did I would finally feel 'enough'.

So while I was looking for opportunities to coach, I was also holding back from telling most people that I was even training to *be* a coach. What typically happened was that after meeting or speaking with someone for a while, they would ask me how things were going and what was new with me. I would then talk about everything *except* coaching—which was crazy, because it was the biggest thing going on in my life. I had invested thousands of pounds, a lot of energy and countless hours in changing my career. Yet, I didn't want to tell people about coaching because I thought they might judge me negatively unless I was a 'successful' coach—whatever that meant.

My hiding was as pronounced on social media as it was in person. This may come as a surprise to many who interact with me online now, because it's clear from my social media profiles that I'm a coach, and I have no problem being visible online, sharing what I know and do for a living. However, back then I didn't want to open myself up to people I thought might be trolls, doubters or naysayers. So I didn't even try.

If I could travel back in time, one thing I would tell myself would be to be more visible on social media. Not posting content in order to get 'likes' on Facebook but simply to share my journey of starting my coach training, the lessons I was learning and even the books I was reading. This is something I encourage all the coaches who attend my coaching school to do, as it not only makes them more visible and relatable to potential clients, but it helps cement their own learning when they share insights from their journey.

Behind my hiding I held a deep-rooted belief that coaching wasn't a proper job or career. It wasn't as prestigious, stable or respectable as my job as a procurement manager (which I also believed wasn't quite as good as an accountant, lawyer, doctor or investment banker). I was fearful that my new calling wasn't something I would ever earn a lot of money from. At best it would be personally fulfilling. At worst my pursuit of coaching would prove that I had finally lost my mind and needed professional help (and not of the coaching sort).

I justified to myself that once I had 'made it' then 'they' couldn't ridicule me. Ironically, I hadn't yet picked up that my insecure feelings about being judged as a coach were not based on anything other than my own thinking. I hadn't seen that even if someone judged or ridiculed me, it wouldn't have any direct bearing on how I felt (no matter how much it might look that way). Only my thinking had the power to make me feel anything.

It would take time and experience for me to see through my misunderstandings around this.

5

When Starting Out, Payment Was Less Important for Me than Experience

My friend Arnold ran a very successful, award-winning small business in England. Within two years of buying the business he had doubled its profitability and revenue. However, he was feeling burnt out from overwork and stress. A few weeks after I started my coach training, Arnold, two other friends and I went on holiday together to Marrakech in Morocco. Arnold and I were close, and I had sought his counsel after I'd had my 'eureka' moment about becoming a coach and before I had signed up for my coach training. He had encouraged me to follow my gut and was one of the few people who knew I was learning about helping people through coaching.

We stayed in a beautiful riad[2] in the old part of Marrakech, with the four of us sharing two rooms. Arnold and I were bunking together, and one evening he shared that he was incredibly stressed and working ridiculously long hours. He wondered if I could share a technique or strategy that would help him get more done and reduce his stress levels. He confided in me that he had once worked thirty-six hours straight, and he knew this was unhealthy and

[2] A type of Moroccan house built with an interior garden/courtyard.

unsustainable.

I had brought along a writing pad on holiday and suggested we take an hour together on the three-and-a-half-hour plane ride home. He agreed, as our other friends weren't interested in discussing personal development and how the mind works while they were enjoying drinks in the sun.

However, Arnold was open and coachable. He desperately wanted his life to be different, but he felt stuck. We spent an hour on the flight home talking about his feelings not being a reflection of his circumstances at work. When he was feeling stressed, this wasn't an indication that things were bad. Rather it was a reflection of his stressful thinking in the moment. Arnold hadn't yet seen that when he got caught up in his stressful feelings he could take a step back, take a breath and allow his thinking to settle down on its own (which it always does when we leave it alone).

One seeming source of stress was his staff and (in Arnold's mind) their inability to use their initiative or do their work effectively. For example, Arnold shared that his staff were not buying products that they sold effectively in their retail arm. They would order items that they liked as opposed to looking at what was selling and making the most profit. When Arnold blamed his feelings of stress, worry and anxiety on his workload and incompetent staff he would naturally speed up his thinking, because he felt he was struggling with other people's behaviours and things that were out of his direct control. This was the exact opposite direction to go in if he wanted to regain his bearings and make decisions from a calm, relaxed place.

A few weeks after our conversation, he told me that while he was still working hard, he was at least stopping work by 9:00 p.m. each evening, which was a huge step in the right direction compared to his regular sixteen-hour days.

A couple of months after this he told me he felt the next step was to have his staff learn about what I had taught him about the true origins of stress. As he felt that his staff were the cause of much of his stress, he thought that if they were trained by me, they could start taking more initiative and get things off his plate. We discussed the possibility of my coming to his workplace to train some or all of his twenty staff members.

This was exciting, but it also felt like I would be way out of my depth, given where I saw my abilities as a coach at that time. So I leaned on Jamie (with whom I was still training) for advice. The three of us jumped on a call together, and I listened while Jamie asked Arnold some questions—and went deeper in his questioning than I had gone. Jamie asked Arnold a mixture of coaching questions like:

- If there were a miracle tonight and you woke up tomorrow and everything in your business and your life was the way you want it to be, how would you know a miracle had taken place? What would you see, hear and feel that would let you know things have shifted?
- What's your theory about the cause of the high levels of stress you've been experiencing? What do you attribute them to?
- (In relation to his goals, objectives, aspirations) Why are your goals, objectives and aspirations important? If you achieve them, what would you have that you don't otherwise have?

Jamie also listened deeply to Arnold's answers instead of jumping in immediately to provide a solution he felt would help him (which is what I had been doing). He questioned things that Arnold was saying rather than taking them at face value and gleaned valuable information by doing so. For example, he would ask, 'What do you make of that?' 'So what?', and 'Who says?' to some of his answers.

Over a couple of calls, Jamie helped Arnold realise that training his staff wouldn't have the biggest impact on his business. The better leverage point, Jamie suggested, would be for Arnold himself to have a coaching experience to learn how to better manage his own stress and have greater mental clarity. Jamie pointed out that if Arnold could see how he was creating his experience of life through his thinking, he could slow down his racing mind, become more centred and have a bigger impact on his business.

Arnold saw how much sense this made, and Jamie suggested that he could help him via one of his four-day intensives. When the call was over, Jamie and I discussed whether it would be possible for me to sit in on the intensive, and he was fine with this as long as it was okay with Arnold—which it was.

So now, while I wasn't getting paid for training Arnold's staff, I was getting something much more useful at this stage of my career. I would sit in on a coaching intensive given by someone much more experienced than I was at the time. I knew this would be helpful, not least because I had no clue what to do with a client for more than a session or two.

Watching Jamie deliver the training to Arnold was far more useful than I could have imagined. Those four days opened my eyes to what Jamie really did. For starters, I asked Jamie how he was going to prepare for the intensive; he basically said he *wasn't* going to. We had already had a couple of calls with Arnold, so Jamie knew what a successful outcome would look like. I didn't really believe

Jamie, but I got to witness firsthand his being relaxed, building rapport and taking his time with Arnold. He simply relied on his training. And on the first day, Arnold had a shift deep enough to justify the whole intensive.

He wasn't the only one. The experience was, as I suspected it would be, invaluable for me too, because while Jamie hadn't done anything he wasn't already sharing with me through his training course, it was completely different for me to see it up close and in action. This experience was worth its weight in gold, and it helped me to see that the kind of preparation I needed to have for clients was already within me from all my previous training and learnings. When I was coaching with someone, I could rely on the right questions or exercises or insights to come to me at the right moment. And if something didn't quite land with the client, I could simply adjust and try something else in the moment, just as Jamie had done.

The bigger lesson I took from this experience, was to always be learning from other coaches, mentors and practitioners. I didn't need to reinvent the wheel, but could instead learn from their years of experience to shorten my own learning curve. Instead of comparing myself to them or envying their success, I could incorporate what I learned from them into my own practice in whatever way made most sense to me.

I incorporate this approach into my school for coaches by actively encouraging coaches to support each other rather than fall into comparison or envy. I built the school with the value of compersion rather than competition. Compersion is a word you don't often hear in business. It means wholehearted joy in the success of others.

I've seen, again and again, that when coaches operate from a place of competition—that is, when they view the profession as a zero-sum game—they unintentionally limit their growth. If a potential client chooses another coach, they feel they've lost. But this mindset keeps their energy contracted, guarded, and stuck in scarcity.

The most prosperous coaches I know don't play that game, and while I wish I had got this deep into my bones earlier than I did, I am glad that in this early example with Jamie I saw an opportunity to create a win for all of us rather than trying to sign up 'my' client.

6

I Start to Learn About Service

As I mentioned in Chapter 3, I found other coaches to be incredibly supportive of my own growth, so I started networking like crazy. There were a lot of coaches on Facebook, and I reached out to many of them. One of the coaches that Jamie had interviewed was Rich Litvin, so I sent him a 'friend request' and he accepted.

The first thing I saw on his profile was that he was just about to publish a book called *The Prosperous Coach* with another coach named Steve Chandler. The subtitle was 'Increase income and impact for you and your clients'. This, I thought, was exactly what I needed in my life at the time—especially the income part. I had a feeling that this new resource would enable me to take everything I was learning from Jamie and his colleagues—which was already having a profound impact on my own life—and start helping people while getting paid for it.

One day, two months after I connected with Rich, he posted that the book would be released any day, but that anyone who was really keen could message him and he would share an audio of him and Steve Chandler sharing some insights from the book. I immediately commented on the post and soon received a link to an audio about the book and the lies that coaches tell themselves.

In sending that link, Rich was modelling what he and Steve

would describe in their book: service.

I took two key things from that audio and the interaction with Rich. Firstly, if a potential client said they didn't want to work with me because they didn't have enough money or that the coaching was too expensive, I simply hadn't served them enough yet. This was the complete opposite of what I had been thinking. I had assumed that I needed to be a better salesman, more influential and persuasive, and also more outwardly impressive as a coach. Rich and Steve were pointing to something different, and it was a paradigm shift for me: *I had to make a difference in the person's life to such an extent that they would want to pay me to continue doing so.*

Secondly—and this was something practical and simple in terms of service—I could send prospective clients a little gift (just as Rich had done with me). It didn't need to be something I had created, which was a relief, because at this point I didn't have any of my own material. I immediately put this idea into practice and sent a gift of a free e-book to someone I knew it would help (I had permission to share this resource). I also sent a signed copy of Jamie's book to another person who seemed interested in what I was learning in my coaching training.

I didn't know it then, but these two insights would help me start signing up my next few clients. They have stayed with me as foundational in how I enrol clients to this day. This was the beginning of my ongoing journey into learning what service really means.

7

The Three Principles

When I originally signed up for the year-long coach training programme with Jamie Smart, I had assumed it was simply about how to coach a client based on standard 'best practices.' I had never heard of the Three Principles and I wasn't particularly interested in them. Jamie had described them as the best personal development approach in the world, but I quite arrogantly thought I'd learned enough personal development techniques in the previous decade. As far as I was concerned I didn't need to learn more personal development material for me in order to coach people; I just needed to learn the 'how-to' part about helping people change and creating an income doing so.

What surprised me very soon after signing up was just how significantly I started changing. My productivity at work shot through the roof. That was something I had struggled with for years and could never really master—my to-do list never seemed to end and I felt like I was always playing catch up, no matter how hard I worked. I had listened to audio books and attended training courses on time management but they'd had little real impact on my productivity. Within a couple of months of my introduction to the Three Principles, I was blasting through my tasks and even running out of things to do, which was completely unheard of in our fast-paced, target-driven department.

This change arose from an insight about anger rather than productivity. It had always seemed to me that any anger or frustration I felt in a given moment was a reflection of the stupidity of the person I was angry with or the unfairness of the situation in which I found myself. The new understanding I was gaining from learning about the Three Principles showed me neither was true. I had it all back to front. This was news to me.

My anger had everything to do with my own thinking. At first, I resisted this idea and tried to poke holes in it, but as I started to test it out for myself, I saw the profound truth that I had been missing. It was humbling.

This new insight led me to not stay angry for long at work. For example, when what seemed to be an unhelpful email came in from a colleague, rather than ruminate over it, share my feelings with my colleagues and work myself up further, I found myself observing the angry feeling, watching it pass quite quickly—and then getting back to work. This saved huge amounts of time.

This was coupled with a further insight that the things I was avoiding on my to-do list were not tasks that would actually cause me discomfort or boredom. I wasn't putting off these tasks because they were difficult, but because I was misinterpreting my feelings about them. This made complete sense to me when I ended up *having* to do a task that I had been putting off, often because there was a deadline looming—and it was never as bad as I had been imagining. So I would always wonder: Why did I put this off?

And yet I never seemed to learn my lesson. Now that I had a better understanding, however, I stopped acting out the same pattern over and over. I simply did whatever was the most important task on my to-do list without overthinking it.

This didn't only affect me at work. My relationship with my

parents and siblings changed significantly too. I realised my arguments with my parents had everything to do with me and not them. For example, every day my mother would talk to me about meeting a girl and getting married. She told me she worried about me. I used to think this conversation was causing feelings of anger and frustration to arise. I saw that this was a misunderstanding; my mother was simply acting like a concerned and loving parent. She was doing the best she could given the thinking she had.

I started to apologise when I got upset with a family member, and this helped deepen those relationships. I had been very reluctant to apologise in the past because I'd always had the excuse that the other person had caused me to become upset. When I learned I was simply feeling my upset thinking, apologising came more easily. I became nicer to be around and didn't take things so personally (because they *weren't* personal). I really felt as if my family relationships had become like a Disney movie in their simplicity, ease, and grace.

The strange thing about these changes coming into my life was that I still didn't fully understand the Three Principles. I *thought* I did, but if I tried to articulate them I felt clumsy and uncertain of my language. This seemed the opposite of what I had previously learned in my personal development journey. With other ideas I'd learned earlier on, it seemed that the greatest benefit from learning something came after I really understood it and incorporated it into my life; until then the impact had been marginal.

With the Three Principles, though, I was seeing bigger changes than ever, and yet I knew I was only scratching the surface of how this new understanding could play out in my life. I was starting to see that the Principles were not concepts or ideas, but a profound truth that applied to everyone.

8

I Didn't Need to Burn My Bridges

In January 2013, with barely four months of coach training under my belt, I flew to Las Vegas to attend a week-long success workshop. I had attended the same workshop a year earlier, and as an alumni of the event I got free attendance, so I jumped at the opportunity to go back. So much had changed for me in the previous twelve months—not least my embarking on this new career called 'coaching.'

I asked the organiser, Johnny Epstein, if I might do a short presentation or talk about what I had learned over the past twelve months. He agreed and I was given two hours to speak to the group. What I really wanted to do was to share how much I had been impacted by the workshop and encourage attendees to really pay attention and implement what they were learning—because it worked. Second, I hoped to show how my introduction to the Three Principles understanding had helped as much as the workshop.

I winged it. Looking back I don't really know what I spoke about for two hours, other than my own experience. I didn't use flipcharts or PowerPoint but simply spoke about what made sense to me. It wasn't polished or refined but several people told me later that they enjoyed it, and they sensed I was talking from a place of really knowing something to be true. A couple of years later, some of the people in the room that day would turn into clients.

I listened to all the other speakers and coaches who presented that week, and one in particular stood out to me. His central message was to burn your bridges. His approach was to ensure he had no safety net, no way to go backwards. His system for ensuring his own development was to have only one direction: forwards.

I felt inspired by this talk. I was committed to coaching but still unsure I could make it or that it would work out. Perhaps I needed to hand in my notice at work and just go into coaching full-time. It felt scary and exhilarating all at once. I had always played it safe when it came to decisions that would impact me financially, so perhaps I had to just go all in.

When I flew back to the UK, I told Jamie about what I had heard and my desire to 'burn my bridges.' Jamie responded that this was certainly one way to proceed, but he preferred to have the next bridge in sight before burning the previous one.

This was great advice. Over the years I would go on to witness so many coaches quitting their day jobs to go into coaching full-time before they had really developed the skills needed to enrol and deeply impact clients. Often these coaches have the best of intentions, but because they have given up their main source of income they fall into the trap of being needy for clients to sign up. This in turn puts off potential clients from working with them. They end up having to go back to their day jobs. Staying in *my* day job would allow me to continue investing in my development until my coaching business was able to provide me an income *and* pay for my continued personal and professional growth.

Steve Chandler and I would tell coaches years later (and I repeat this when enrolling coaches into my school) that if you need a client to pay your bills, you don't need a client—you need a job. Whenever any coach asks me about whether they should quit their day-job and coach full-time, I let them know that this is a wonderful profession and it can be as well-paid as any other. However, I ask them about their financial situation; that is, how long can they live without creating clients, and what is their experience to date in client creation, getting referrals and having clients renew? It is a balance, but I often find myself advising coaches to slow down, perhaps get a part-time job or reduce their hours so their main expenses are covered, rather than going all-in. Now if a coach is running out of time to coach all the people who want to work with her, then it's obviously time to quit. But for most coaches I speak to who are early on in their practices, that's not the case.

9

Meeting My Future Mentor

Jamie would occasionally invite other coaches or teachers to deliver part of his training programme. In March 2013, I got the chance to meet Dr Keith Blevens for the first time when he delivered a three-day workshop for the group on the Three Principles as a new paradigm in psychology.

Jamie spoke very highly of Keith, who had mentored him in the Three Principles understanding. But what really had me sit up and listen was Jamie telling us all a story of Keith reviewing a draft chapter of his book a year earlier.

Jamie had been teaching NLP for over a decade. Many of his clients had suggested he write a book about it, but he'd never felt there was another NLP book that needed to be written (or, at least, not one he felt inspired to write). But when he started to understand the Three Principles, he knew he had found something worth devoting a book to. He felt he would spend the next twenty years of his life teaching the Principles, and he dropped the NLP material.

Jamie had actually been introduced to the Three Principles in a book many years earlier, in 1999, but at the time he felt like he already understood what he was reading and so didn't pursue it. It wasn't until nearly a decade later that he saw how powerful this understanding really was. He became convinced it represented the future of psychology. Finally, in 2012, he decided to write the book he wished he had read when he was first introduced to the Principles.

When this new book was a month away from publication he sent a chapter of it to Keith to review. By this point, Jamie had been studying the Three Principles for some time, so he was confused when the chapter came back covered in red ink. He thought he had understood what Keith had been pointing to when he had him speak to his groups and had assumed Keith would love his chapter. What became clear was that he hadn't understood what Keith was pointing to as deeply as he thought. This led Jamie to shelve his book for a while and hire Keith for additional mentoring. Through his own coaching with Keith, Jamie came to a much deeper understanding of the Three Principles. The process had a profound impact on Jamie's final version of his book as well as all his subsequent work.

This was intriguing to me, because in many ways I felt like Jamie had before hiring Keith. I felt like I 'got' what I was learning in Jamie's course. I had heard many times that our feelings are a reflection of our thinking and not our circumstances. This led to many insights and realisations which had practical implications in my life.

However, I also knew that when challenged, my foundational understanding of this work wasn't as solid as it could be. It certainly wasn't as deep as Jamie's. I knew this was limiting me in my ability to really create and impact clients.

Keith shared with the group how he saw the Three Principles as a completely new paradigm in psychology, just like Antoine Lavoisier presented a new paradigm in chemistry when he wrote the first modern chemistry textbook in 1789 and laid the foundation for the periodic table of elements.

Keith clarified that Thought (all mental activity) is a constant, which is why it is a Principle. We are always living in and with Thought. Therefore the Three Principles aren't a model of achievement or somewhere to 'get' to. They are something to comprehend more deeply, because as you do this you naturally become less judgemental and a better communicator, and you start dropping your ego.

Keith suggested that there are times when any one of us can go 'outside-in,' when we forget that our thinking creates our experience in the moment. This happens to all of us more than we would care to admit—even to people who have a good grasp of the Three Principles. When we grasp this, we end up having more understanding of others and less judgement.

This was a profound shift for me. I was more judgemental than I cared to admit—both of myself and others. It hadn't occurred to me that this was a reflection of my not understanding how my experience was created, or of understanding it only from a more intellectual perspective rather than a lived one. It didn't make sense to judge others for their behaviour and actions when I went 'outside-in'—that is, when I forgot where my experience was coming from and therefore acted from my misunderstandings.

It reminds me of the proverb, 'People in glass houses shouldn't throw stones.' Why should I judge a colleague for acting out of insecurity when I often feel insecure and act accordingly (not realising my insecure feelings are a reflection of my thinking).

Keith further elaborated on the fact that the Three Principles aren't a method to teach yourself to have better thinking, to have more good thoughts and fewer bad ones. They aren't even about having more healthy thinking and less unhealthy thinking. He explained that when he understood this, it really helped his clients, because they were no longer trying to get somewhere—that is, to a place of better thinking. When you realise and accept that you don't know what you'll be thinking in thirty seconds time, never mind in a day, week or month, it takes a lot off your mind; you no longer have to try to control your thoughts.

As I listened to Keith talk my mind started to get quieter and quieter. What he was saying was so simple and yet so profound: learning and understanding the Three Principles is different from every other psychological or coaching modality because there is nowhere to get to and nothing to do. The Principles instead provide a north star, a reference point which helps us recalibrate when we have gone outside-in—when we succumb to the false belief that our feelings are telling us about our circumstances in the moment. They never are.

Our feelings—that is, our felt experience of life—are only reflections of our thinking in the moment, nothing more and nothing less.

The implications of this were huge for my own life, but I also knew it would help me tremendously in my client conversations. I realised that few people knew what Keith was pointing to here, and that when looking at the world through this new paradigm, many problems that people (including myself) had would just fall away. I knew I had to continue my study of the Three Principles and keep uncovering the hidden blind spots that were holding me back from being a better coach and a better man.

10

Setting Up a Business

I had committed to making my coaching business work by investing thousands of pounds in training, which included a commitment to travel to London once a month for a year. I knew in my heart that I wanted to be a coach more than anything, yet I still had some fears and insecurities around whether I could make this wish a reality. Spending time every month with other coaches ensured I didn't get sidetracked by my insecure thoughts. However, despite investing money and time in my training, I still hadn't set up a formal business.

It seemed like a huge decision, and one with many implications. First, I felt I needed a cool name that would make me stand out. Some of my colleagues had picked really creative names for their websites and their businesses. I didn't think I was as creative as them. I was toying with 'Kush Coaching Limited' until someone pointed out that in the United States, 'kush' refers to a strain of marijuana. I felt that might not have quite the connotation I was looking for when I said, 'Hire me and you'll get high on life.'

I took my dilemma to Jamie, who helped massively. He told me that the only place my limited company name would appear would be on my invoices. I could actually legally trade as any name. He also suggested I just call my business my own name, because my business was me. This further simplified things. After that it was only another few weeks of procrastination before I finally filled out the documentation and formed Ankush Jain Limited.

Like so many things it wasn't as difficult a process as I had imagined. I had to fill in a few pages of questions online and pay a small fee, and sooner than I anticipated my business was formed.

This was a huge step for me. I knew that, speaking purely financially, it might have made more sense to wait until I had more clients under my belt to prove that it was worth registering a business, because I was now obligated to file accounts and other documentation. But this was a declaration of my continued commitment—not least for myself. I was showing myself that I was really serious about this business, and I was going to make it work (even if deep down I still had huge doubts and fears).

Looking back, if I had waited a year or so longer, I might have fallen victim to my insecurities and been tempted to give up. Instead, I pushed forward—even though I had no clients at the time. Creating the business then also showed me that taking action towards what I wanted to create, no matter how small the steps, was a practice that would serve me well in all aspects of my life, no matter what thoughts or emotions came up. I didn't need to repeat my old habit of simply waiting until the time 'felt' right, because I knew from experience that such a time would never come.

I simply had to act.

11

My Coach Training Was Impacting My Regular Work

While I was undertaking my coach training and trying to create clients, the company I worked at was merging with a competitor. This meant that there would be cost-cutting and efficiency drives—which was code for some people losing their jobs. While my long-term vision was to coach full-time, I wasn't quite ready to leave the safety of a regular salary until I had started to consistently sign up clients and could see the income from coaching replacing my corporate salary.

It was only sensible for me to start talking to recruiters (as my colleagues were doing) and start applying for roles similar to what I was already doing as a procurement manager.

I landed an interview for a job I really wanted with one of the largest retailers in the UK. Our former procurement director had moved to this particular company, and I was told that working for this firm would look great on my CV.

I had a story I'd told myself for many years about interviewing: namely that I was good at my job but I interviewed badly. I knew now that I didn't need to pay attention to any thoughts that came up around this story (which was itself just a thought), regardless of how often they appeared or how much they seemed to be rooted in reality.

The interview was early in the morning and quite far away, so I stayed at a hotel nearby to minimise the chance of getting stuck in traffic and being late. In the morning I set off early, thinking I had plenty of time. I was in a relaxed mood and felt confident.

In fact, I felt I had so much time I stopped off to fill my car with diesel and even treated myself to a McDonald's breakfast. I then found that I'd just make it on time . . . until my satnav took me to a residential street rather than the actual corporate address I was supposed to go to. (This used to be a problem when using postcodes on early navigation devices.)

I started to feel a little tense, but I put in the actual street name, set off again and soon saw a sign with the logo of the retailer with whom I was supposed to interview. I thought I'd made it. I turned into the car park but all the parking spaces had cones in front of them except the first one. I turned my car into it and then—CRUNCH!

What was that noise?

Well, it turned out there actually **was** a cone there and I'd driven over it. The parking attendant came over none too pleased. I quickly reversed out of the spot; luckily there was no damage to my car. The attendant told me to park across the road.

At that point it was 11:05. My interview was at 11:00.

What else could go wrong?

Well, for starters, I walked into the building and realised it was the *wrong one*.

The correct building was nearby. I started running down the road and eventually found it. When I signed in at reception, completely out of breath, it was 11:10.

I sat down in the reception area, thoughts racing through my mind: *I might as well leave, They'll never hire me, It looks so bad that I'm late, I'm an idiot, I always mess things up* . . . and so on. I thought I should make up an excuse and start apologising profusely as soon as the interviewer came out.

However, thankfully, I realised in time that this was just my thinking. I became really still and realised that the best thing I had going for me in that moment was my clarity and my understanding. There was nothing I could do about the circumstances in which I found myself. I relaxed.

And after another ten minutes the interviewer came out and said, 'Sorry I've kept you waiting.'

He had no idea I had been late, and he was actually running behind schedule. If I'd given into my panic I would have been flustered and probably would have blurted out something about being late myself. Instead, I was in a great place to give my all to the interview—and the interviewer had no idea what had been going on inside me.

Funnily enough, I ended up impressing the interviewer but turning down the role, as I caught sight of some red flags in how he managed people. If I had been sped up and lost in my thinking as normal, I would likely have missed those signs.

Once again, I saw that my growth as a coach was not isolated from the rest of my life. In my training, I was learning that when we get panicked or worried, it's because of our thinking in the moment. And now I'd been given a real-life lesson. Not only did I see what happens when our thinking speeds up too much—I also saw that it will often stop immediately once it is recognised for what it is: just thought.

My growth as a coach was directly correlated to my growth as a person. Later, I realised that this was always the case, both for me and my clients. For example, coaches sign up for my school because they want to make more income, but the feedback I often get is that in addition to business growth, their marriage has improved, they've started to finally shed the extra weight they've been carrying or they've found a peace of mind that had been eluding them their whole life.

12

My First Package Client

A few weeks after the workshop with Dr Keith Blevens I had a conversation with Stephen. Stephen had reached out to me around the time I'd started my coach training with Jamie. He had heard through a mutual friend that I was looking to become a coach, and he wanted some guidance. We spoke a few times and I did my best to help him, not thinking he would ever be a client. This was in part because when he first reached out to me, I had suggested he read Jamie's book and he commented he would buy it when he could afford it. I thought if he was struggling to purchase a £10 book, he wouldn't be willing to pay for coaching.

However, I had time in my calendar to talk to people and he seemed like a sincere and genuine person. We spoke a few times, and through our conversations he became intrigued as to what I was learning about the Three Principles. He started asking more questions about this understanding and how it differed from other modalities and paradigms. I shared some audio resources with him, suggesting that they would help him understand what I had been learning. I invited him to listen and see if he could hear how to apply them to his own life.

After the third conversation, I made a proposal to him for a package of eight coaching calls, and he agreed. He requested we split the payment into five payments, with the bulk up front, and again I agreed. Even though I had heard coaches talk about requesting the full payment upfront, it just made sense to me to be flexible with the terms and sign up my biggest client to date.

Even so, I had some fear in the back of my mind. What was I going to do with him over eight sessions? I had never coached anyone for more than two sessions, and even though I felt like my understanding of the Three Principles was deepening every month, I wasn't sure of myself.

Suddenly an inspired thought popped up in my mind. Stephen had bought Jamie's book by this point, and I noted that it contained twenty-four chapters. I did some quick maths and suggested the book would serve as our curriculum. I requested that Stephen read three chapters before each coaching session, and then we would discuss the material on our call.

This gave me a structure to work with, and I reasoned that even if I wasn't great at coaching him, Stephen would still get something from the calls through reading the book. He readily agreed and was excited to get started.

Interestingly, however, we only followed this structure for the first call. By the second session, we went off script, and I simply asked Stephen what he wanted to discuss on our call. He came up with his questions.

I realised that despite what I thought, I didn't need a curriculum or structure to coach clients over several sessions or months. I simply needed to show up, listen and ask questions. I could share my thoughts when and where it was appropriate to do so—but in truth, my clients weren't hiring a Three Principles teacher. They were hiring a coach. My role was to facilitate their creating a better future for themselves, whatever that meant for them.

13

Using a Script Wasn't as Helpful as I Thought

I was struggling to create as many clients as I wanted, so I asked people who seemed to be more successful what they were doing and how they were signing people up.

One person I asked was a colleague on Jamie's course who worked for a marketer specialising in helping coaches create clients. Amongst other things, he had a script with twenty or so questions which were designed to have clients say 'yes' to a coaching package after just one call. He kindly shared it with me and said that if I used these questions I would create clients who paid me good fees.

It seemed almost too good to be true—and as it turned out, it was for me. I used the script verbatim once, but it didn't feel right. There were some good (if familiar) questions in there, such as ones asking the client how things were right now, how they would want them to be in the future, and what they felt was in the way.

But there were also questions which felt like they were designed to tap into a person's insecurity, like, 'What would be the worst thing that could happen if you didn't make this change?' I couldn't quite articulate it at the time, but this kind of question didn't feel aligned with how I wanted to create clients. I see now that while any of these questions *can* be useful, the script was designed around convincing a potential client to hire me after one short conversation, so it was less a mutual exploration of whether coaching together would be a good fit and more of a pain-point kind of sales technique.

I had the script in front of me a few more times in calls with potential clients but found myself deviating from it more and more—until I just stopped using it. I could see why it worked for some people, but in my experience it was so rigid and structured that it didn't give the potential client an experience of what ongoing coaching with me would look like. I wouldn't have a script for every session, and if I did it would be boring.

What I loved (and still love) about coaching was that I was working with *people*. They weren't robots. This wasn't a computer game. Coaching calls were fun, spontaneous and unpredictable because they involved real people. I didn't know where the conversation would take us, and I could be guided in the moment as to what questions to ask or stories to share—not by a script, but by my own gut instincts and common sense.

The only good thing about having that script was that it motivated me to try it out on people, and this by itself got me into conversations I might never have had otherwise. The script was a comfort blanket which I quickly let go of and realised I never needed in the first place. The experience led me to see why Jamie refused to share scripts, coaching questions or too much structure with us. It's also why I don't share scripts in my coaching school. These things weren't really needed and could easily turn into crutches.

If you're wondering how to get comfortable having an enrolment conversation without a script, I wish I could share some magic tip or technique that provides an answer. However, as mundane as it might sound, the answer is simply: practise. The more I spoke to potential clients, the more comfortable I became in having those conversations. Learning to get better at conversations with potential clients on enrolment calls is no different from learning *any* new skill. It takes some time, and at the start you may fumble or make mistakes, but this is part of the process. I will say that some guidance from a more experienced coach can be extremely helpful. I eventually hired a coach who would review these conversations with me, but I will expand more on that in later chapters.

14

Landing the Dream Job and a Choice

A few days after landing my first package client, I got a phone call from a recruiter I had reached out to. As I mentioned above, my day job was at risk following the merger of my company with a competitor. So, I was seriously looking at the job market for the first time in many years. At this stage I didn't know if I could make coaching pay, and even if I eventually could, I didn't know how long it would take to do so.

My research told me there were three companies in the UK that would be ideal next steps for me were I to stay in my corporate field. One was a global pharmaceutical company; the other two were global energy companies. I had been diligently pestering this particular recruiter, whom I knew could get me an interview with one of these three companies because he provided external recruitment services to them. I was told if I got a job with any of these businesses, recruiters would fight over my CV if I went back on the job market in the future.

This sounded like a solid backup plan, so I was delighted when the recruiter called me up about a procurement role he had found for one of the energy companies. It's worth noting that before starting my training with Jamie Smart and learning about how my feelings simply reflect my thinking in the moment, I wouldn't have even applied to this company. My insecure thinking would have risen up—*You are not good enough for this role, You won't get the job anyway, Why bother?*—and I would have interpreted that thinking as telling me not to apply. However, I now knew that whatever I felt about the role was not based on reality but rather on my interpretation of my circumstances—in other words, on my thoughts about them.

If the recruiter thought I was good enough for the role, then I guessed I had a good shot at getting it.

I flew through the whole process. Within two weeks of that first phone call, I completed a telephone interview, a face-to-face first round interview, and a follow-up telephone interview with my potential new line manager. They even offered me the salary I was looking for, which was a big step up from what I had been earning at the time.

However, I had a choice. My current boss, with whom I had a great relationship, told me that he'd secured his role and would be keen to retain me. He also knew I was keen on coaching and so he was prepared to put forward an option where I could do my day job four days a week and coach the team for the remaining day. It was an incredible opportunity for a new coach, and yet my gut was telling me to take the new role at the energy company instead—which I did.

Looking back this seems a bit odd for someone so committed to being a coach. Yet at the time it made complete sense. For years I had felt like I wasn't playing at my full potential and was instead always taking the safe option, especially when it came to my career. If I was going to become a coach, I wanted to give the dream job a go. I wanted to be able to say I could have had a great corporate career but I *chose* to coach—not that I did coaching because I couldn't succeed at anything else.

So I made the choice, and I was excited by it. It would mean moving to London, something I had wanted to do since graduating from university. I had no idea what the future held in store.

In the moment, I simply made a choice—which is something we can always do.

15

People You Don't Expect can Become Clients: My Second Package Client

A few chapters back I shared that in March 2013 I'd attended a three-day workshop which Jamie Smart had hosted for Keith Blevens. What I didn't mention was that I had missed a day of the workshop because I was the best man at a friend's wedding. As such, I had a couple of key responsibilities: firstly to look after the ring and secondly to give the best man's speech. This was clearly something that had to take precedence over the workshop (though I left as early as I could to be back in London for the final day with Keith, Jamie and my colleagues).

During my short time at the wedding, I spoke to Bruce, a friend of mine and the groom's. While we didn't speak often, I had known him for several years, and we had even been on a group holiday together with the groom and a few other friends. He asked me what was new.

This time I didn't avoid bringing up coaching, and this may in part have been down to my knowledge that he was into personal development. My first coach, whom I had hired back in 2006, had also been his first coach around the same time. I shared a little bit about how the coaching course was impacting me more than anything else I had ever done. He seemed intrigued, and I shared that I'd be happy to do a coaching session with him.

However, I didn't follow up with him after that. I did this a lot in my early months as a coach because I didn't want to seem pushy or salesy, and I was afraid of what people might think of me. This overly timid approach was holding me back from giving more people an experience of coaching with me, but despite this unwitting self-sabotage, once in a while I still managed to get into conversations.

Around two months after the wedding, Bruce reached out to me on Facebook and asked me if I was still up for a coaching conversation. He was going to be off work for ten days and so could easily make the time for it to happen. I didn't hesitate: I suggested we speak that very evening and he agreed. As it turned out, we couldn't find a mutually convenient time, but I remained undeterred. I told him I would send him an audio recording that Jamie had produced as a companion to his book, *Clarity*. This recording was something I had Jamie's permission to share with my clients, and it was a great overview of the Three Principles and how our mind's natural state is a clear one. I asked him to listen to it without distractions, to give it his full attention, and then to give me his feedback. I knew that how he listened was as important as what he was listening to.

He messaged me the next day saying that what he got from the audio was that worrying was taking away from his ability to tap into his natural clarity. He felt that worrying had been getting in the way of taking actions he needed to take. He had a lot of negative thinking and was struggling to deal with it. I messaged back pointing out that trying to 'deal' with his negative thinking was *speeding up* his thinking, which in turn obscured his natural clarity. Slowing down, I suggested, was the direction to look in, and this would more likely happen if he stopped trying to fix his negative thinking.

This was enough to have him agree to a conversation, and I blocked off a couple of hours for a call soon after. I did the best I could in this first session, and afterwards we agreed to speak again two weeks later.

Before this second call he messaged me wanting to know what I would charge him. We started to go back and forth on Facebook around the price and I quickly realised I needed to do what I had been pointing out to him. My racing thoughts were causing me to go into 'convincing mode' over my prices. I was overthinking things, and I needed to slow down, which is exactly what happened automatically when I realised what I was doing.

I suggested we have a conversation about pricing rather than discussing it on Facebook messenger. I had messaged him before the call that I had charged another client the equivalent of around £80 - £100 a session, and that I wanted him to be happy with the price and also be committed to the coaching. He was happy to speak about this, and the instinct to have an actual conversation rather than messaging turned out to be a good one. Bruce simply wanted to know that he was being charged a fair price. No negotiations or complex strategies were required to convince him of the value of my coaching; he'd already experienced what it was like talking with me. We soon agreed upon a price we were both happy with—a fee equivalent to £80 a session.

With that, I had signed up my second package client, and it was someone I would never have expected to pay me for coaching. However, slowing down and simply sharing what I knew, and offering as much value as I could, resulted in a friend realising that coaching with me was worth paying for.

I didn't fully realise it at the time, but what had occurred with Bruce that resulted in him becoming a paying client would later become an ingrained process for me and the coaches I help in my school and private practice. Rather than trying to persuade prospective clients why my fee is worth it (or, worse, arguing with them about it), I always want to spend enough time in conversation with a person to allow them to realise the value of my coaching *through their own experience*. They then don't have to guess what might occur if they hire me—they'll have already had an experience of it.

16

Expectation Versus Agreement

I had read online that before starting a coaching engagement with a new client, one should have a clear agreement with them—not just around price, of course, but around how the relationship will ideally support the client. But I had no idea what should be in such a coaching agreement, or how to set one up.

I felt I needed some kind of template, so when a coach in a Facebook group posted that she'd heard coach Steve Chandler's audio 'Expectations versus Agreements' was a great tool for setting up a coaching agreement, I followed the discussion. This woman had just signed up her first client and was wondering how to use the audio in this way.

Another coach commented that he had sent the recording to a client prior to their first session and asked them to listen to it. Then he spent the first thirty minutes of their first session talking through his coaching agreement with his new client. Another coach in the group suggested I get a copy of this audio by signing up for Steve's newsletter.

I signed up immediately, then downloaded and listened to the recording. Now, as you know, at this point I had been around personal development for a long time. One of my former mentors had even taught me about managing my own and other people's expectations around having more success in life. However, I hadn't ever heard anyone talk about expectations or agreements like Steve did, and as I listened, I found myself wishing I'd heard the distinction many years earlier.

Steve suggested that expectations between two parties can go only two ways. Either you meet an expectation—which leads to nothing, because it was expected—or you don't meet it, which leads to disappointment. In this sense, you can only be disappointed if you first have an expectation.

He offered a solution: instead of having expectations, create agreements with the people you're working with. Rather than living in a world of expectations and setting yourself up for disappointment, you can instead create clear agreements with people (and yourself) to avoid disappointments and be more effective in the world.

What sets an agreement apart from an expectation is that both parties have to agree for something to become an agreement. For example, I might expect a client to turn up to sessions on time, and I might even tell them about my expectation and have them sign a document where this is clearly spelled out. However, it only becomes an agreement if both the client and I understand and agree that the client will always show up on time and be clear about what that means—that is, for example, a minute late is late. What is also important to note, is that in creating an agreement, I have to give the other person an opportunity to say no, or to offer an alternative. Their agreement is their buy-in, and it thus becomes a co-creation between us.

Wow! Why had no-one explained this to me years earlier? It would have saved me so many disappointments in relationships, at work and with myself.

For example, in my day job as a procurement manager, I lived in a world of expectations. My stakeholders had expectations of me and my department which were often unrealistic and which made meeting my targets more challenging. Similarly, my boss and the company had expectations of me and my colleagues which we often disagreed with. One year, for example, we were given targets to meet which mainly depended on another team and which we had very little influence over. When we tried to question these expectations, we were told 'the target is the target.' This attitude generally doesn't lead to a committed workforce; it certainly didn't in my case.

I also immediately saw why a coach would want to share this distinction with a client prior to starting a coaching engagement. It would be really effective to put any expectations from both the client and the coach on the table and talk through them to reach an agreement ahead of time. For example, I might set an agreement with a client around coaching 'homework.' Rather than simply giving a client a set of exercises to practise and expecting them to complete them before we next meet, I can take a different approach. We can discuss the exercises to make sure the client feels good about them. Then we can see how much time they can comfortably devote to them between sessions. We then create an agreement around that, instead of me just expecting them to do something. This kind of agreement takes my client's needs and schedule into account. It can even help a client bring a higher level of personal investment to the exercises because they've helped create the agreement.

This approach made so much sense that I implemented it immediately. I asked Bruce to subscribe to Steve's newsletter and to listen to the audio of 'Expectations versus Agreements' before our first session. In a way, him doing this as preparation for our work together was even more important than it might have been with a different client, because Bruce was a friend and would no doubt have certain expectations as to how we would work together. If we addressed these immediately and created agreements for our coaching relationship, we could sidestep any potential unspoken expectations.

Another coach in the Facebook group, Jane Harris, kindly offered to share her coaching agreement template with whoever asked for it, including me. It was a straightforward, two-page document, and after a few tweaks to make it sound more like me, I had created my first coaching agreement. I talked this through with Bruce at our first session and the whole process was much easier and cleaner than I had imagined; in fact, it set the tone for our entire coaching engagement.

While this agreement has certainly evolved, I still use elements of it with clients today. Over the years I've found that many issues with clients can be avoided by not only having a strong coaching agreement with them but also by spending time talking it through with the client before our first coaching session. I typically take over an hour to talk this through with a client; the feedback for this process has been overwhelming positive. It changes the tone of our work together and often brings in a higher level of commitment from the client. I don't limit this to private coaching either. I also create strong agreements with my group clients and in my coaching school.

I was learning in leaps and bounds, because signing up clients was encouraging me to ask for help with whatever I needed to learn in the moment. I had previously thought I needed all the information before I started, but this simply wasn't true—nor was it possible.

Learning on the job was clearly an effective way to advance in the coaching profession.

17

Clients Don't Always Want a Discount

I was speaking with Hank, a digital animator who was feeling like he had lost his mojo. After a couple of conversations, I felt like I could really help him drop his overthinking habit through pointing out where he was believing his feelings were an indication of his circumstances, so I decided to make a proposal. Hank was open to exploring how we might work together longer term, and based on the experience of our calls I felt like he could become my next package client.

On the phone with him I spent a few minutes re-iterating my understanding of what he wanted and how coaching could help him with that.

So far so good.

I talked him through what the package would look like: eight coaching sessions taken two each month for four months. Along the way I would send him relevant resources.

I was putting off the final piece: the cost. Finally I blurted out that this would be £800 total. I was thinking he would probably say yes, and so I was surprised when he said the cost was too high for him.

I had a whole rush of feelings as my mind chatter started up, but I centred myself and stayed in the conversation as best as I could. I wasn't quite ready to put the phone down and I had a feeling that Hank wanted to work with me:

'You came into this conversation expecting a proposal, right?' I asked him.

'Yes.'

'If I may ask, how far away was my price from your expectation?'

'Look,' he said, 'I don't want a discount. I respect this is your work, and you're very good at what you do. I just can't afford £800 right now.'

I felt uncomfortable when he said this. I didn't want to be a pushy salesman because I wouldn't have wanted someone to be that way with me. However, I tried not to engage with my negative thinking and pushed through by continuing with my questions.

'That's okay, I understand. And, to be clear, I'm not offering you a discount. I'm just curious as to what you were expecting. It would be helpful for me, as a new coach, to know that. As in, were you expecting this package to be £100 or—?'

'Oh, no,' he said, shaking his head as if to say he didn't expect it to be that low. 'It's just that my maximum budget is £640.'

I couldn't believe it. My heart was racing and I saw a way I could salvage this. I was also very surprised. Our conversations, I thought, had been really impactful so far, and I was surprised to hear that this prospective client was willing to forego coaching when it was only £20 a session more than he expected it to be.

On the other hand, I knew that having another client would support me in my journey *and* it would really be helpful for Hank to work with me. I also knew that if I offered him a discount, he wouldn't take it, because this wouldn't feel right to him.

I had to think on my feet, and I did so. ‘Hank,’ I said, ‘if I offered you this package at £640—’

He interrupted, ‘I don’t want a discount.’

‘I get that,’ I said, ‘but *if* I were to reduce the price to £640, would you be willing to give me a strong testimonial at the end of our work together—assuming you really felt that way—which I could use on my website?

He visibly relaxed and a smile lifted the corners of his mouth. ‘Sure, I could do that. I’d be glad to. Thank you so much.’

The truth was, I didn’t really need his testimonial. I simply wanted to give him an excuse to feel good about paying the reduced price. I knew this was the best way to really serve him in that moment, and it made sense for my fledgling coaching practice to have another client under my belt.

~

Things were progressing, and I was thankful once again for allowing my gut instincts to guide me. I knew deep down that my early priorities were to get experience as a working coach and not make it all about the money. The money would come later as I gained more experience and, as a result, became more impactful and gained a reputation for my work. I’m glad I didn’t fall into the trap of getting focused on having a ‘high-paying client’—which I have since heard so many marketers tell coaches is *the* way to create a prosperous coaching practice. Trying to create clients who are paying high fees (and that definition is different from coach to coach) can get in the way of the growth of a coaching practice. This is especially true when a coach is starting out, as I was. By staying flexible and open I gained valuable experience that helped me create more income later. This is something I reiterate over and over again in my coaching school: prioritise filling your practice before raising your fees. I think any coach would do well to be flexible early on in their career, until they are consistently at a place where their practice is full.

18

Launching My Website

Back in 2011 a good friend of mine, Sonal, had gifted me a website domain name (www.ankushjain.co.uk) for my birthday. She was encouraging me to start sharing my amateur photography, but at the time I did nothing with it. However, as part of my continued journey towards becoming more visible as a coach, I decided to turn it into a website for my coaching business.

I had a bunch of stories about why I had not used this website earlier: *It will be too difficult*, *I don't know about websites*, *it will take too long* and *I'll just do it later*. But things were different now. I had a desire to really make my coaching business work, so I simply found the information I needed and very quickly put up a basic blog site. I even wrote my first blog, in which I simply introduced myself so that I had some content to share with people.

All the procrastination I had been doing for the previous two years had been unnecessary, but I hadn't known that because I had believed the feelings of doubt, fear and insecurity that were telling me not to take action. Now that excuse had fallen away; I understood more clearly that those feelings were a reflection of my thinking in the moment and not an indicator of whether or not I should move forward.

My doubts didn't subside after I'd written my first blog. I now had to share the site with people, and my fears of being judged were still coming up.

I posted meekly about my new site and first blog post on Facebook: 'I've finally written my first blog post. It's kinda short and a bit shit but I hope you guys like it, and the most important thing is that I took action anyway.'

Not exactly the words of a confident and powerful coach.

Another coach reached out and asked if I was up for feedback. I said, sure—while dreading what he had to say. He told me that even from these two sentences he could see I was trying to lower people's expectations while looking for their validation. This was exactly what I was afraid of—someone seeing through my façade—but here's the interesting thing: I didn't feel terrible about his feedback. He was *right*, and he was constructive in giving me some pointers about how I could have written the same two sentences differently.

However, it was still the case that there was wisdom in what I wrote. The most important thing was that I took the action regardless of how I felt. And even after receiving the negative (actually constructive) feedback, it was still a positive experience. I learned from it and took this feedback forward into my future efforts at online communication. The real lesson for me here wasn't about launching a website or communicating more confidently online but rather about staying in action and putting one foot in front of the other.

I saw that if I continued to do this, I would grow as a coach in leaps and bounds. Now while there are some coaches who focus on having a flashy website and having strategies around posting on social media to establish yourself as an expert, a thought leader or an authority in your field, there are others, including many of those I was drawn to, who suggested websites and social media weren't necessary. I have found that I sit in the middle of these two camps. Rather than using my website or my social media presence to establish why someone should listen to or hire me, my focus has been on connection.

This short post about my blog allowed those connected to me on social media to see what I was up to, to see that I was coaching and to meet me as a human. I would later come to realise that connection and building relationships online were the key to my own financial success, and I've often encouraged other coaches to share more about what they are learning, right now. This could be posting about a book they are reading, an online course they are part of or a lesson or insight they gained from their most recent coaching session. I've found that the coaches attending my school who are the most open about the lessons they're learning are often the same ones who experience the most business growth.

I would come to learn that a coaching practice is built on relationships, and we can use our online presence to build these connections authentically if we are willing to simply show up—without trying to impress anyone.

19

You Can Only Give Away What You Have

I've heard it said many times over the years that you can only give away what you have. This was a challenging lesson to take to heart. Although I had learned a lot of theory about coaching and knew tips and tricks about body language, projecting my voice, becoming more confident and how to be happier, deep down I hadn't really progressed far beyond faking it. Along the same lines, I had of course heard the phrase 'fake it till you make it'—and the problem with that was I felt I'd already been faking it for a long time. When would I make it?

But gradually I realised something was changing within me. For example, as I learned more and more about how my experience of life was a reflection of my thinking moment to moment—and as I took this to heart—I realised that I didn't need to look for approval from my parents anymore. I had been doing so for as long as I could remember, especially with my father, and I had resented them for not giving me the feelings of approval I craved. I hadn't yet realised that they *couldn't* give me these feelings. Ironically, I was upset with them for withholding something from me that they didn't even have.

This resentment hadn't always been visible on the surface, and in many ways it seemed we had a great connection, which got better as I got older—but my seeking their approval was a thorn in our relationship. It was the one thing that was getting in the way of our relationship really blossoming. Now, given my new understanding about the nature of thought, it no longer made sense to look for a feeling of approval from anyone, including my parents, and I finally saw they couldn't give it to me. Feelings of approval came from *my* thinking, not from their actions—no matter how much it looked the other way around.

I could see that dropping this approval-seeking would be a good thing for me. What I did not expect was that it would actually lead to them saying the things I had always craved to hear. One night, I was texting my Dad good night and I spontaneously wrote:

'Love you, pops'

And he replied:

'Love you, too. Though I may not always say it, I do. I am so proud of you that you cannot imagine.'

If this had happened in late December and not in May, I may have called it a Christmas miracle. For years I would have given anything to hear those words from my father. I could not have imagined how quickly this change would come—and only after dropping my thoughts about needing acknowledgement, approval and dare I say, love. Since that text was sent by my father, our relationship has deepened and grown. Do we always see eye to eye? Of course not. Yet, there is a level of mutual respect and love that wasn't there before.

I share this story because it shows that not only was I learning new information, I was also changing as a person. *I was no longer faking it.* And I had more to give—to my parents, my siblings, my work, my friends and my clients. I didn't need to rely simply on 'book-learning' and information; I could talk with some authority as to the power of transformation from experience, and from understanding where our experience comes from. I finally had something really worthwhile to share.

In our profession of coaching, personal growth *is* business growth, and vice versa. Each year when I'm choosing who to invite as external faculty at my coaching school, I ensure that these people are running very successful coaching practices—some of our faculty make over $1,000,000 a year—and also that they are living a quality of life we would want to emulate regardless of how much money we make. This is reflected in my business too—I know that as I continue to be a better husband, father, friend, sibling and son, the more my business grows.

20

You Can Impact People Even When You Don't Know What You're Doing

I had a few clients under my belt but I still felt like I had little idea what I was doing. As I've said, I felt I was basically winging it. This felt exhilarating, bewildering and scary all rolled into one. What I *did* know was that what I was learning from Jamie Smart and his colleagues (like Dr Keith Blevens) about the Three Principles was some of the most impactful material I had ever discovered. In fact, I felt like there was 'Ankush pre-learning' about the Three Principles and 'Ankush post-learning' about them.

Now, I knew a guy named Henry from some online personal development communities I was part of. I'd even crashed at his place when visiting Norway the previous year. We would sometimes message each other on Facebook, and he often asked me for advice, which I was happy to share. One day he messaged me saying things weren't going so well. He said, 'Think I just recently hit the bottom, so I just have to climb a little to regain clarity.' When I asked him what he meant he said he had 'a lot of mental clutter that has been a bit stressful to process.' When I said it sounded like things were weighing on him a lot, he agreed, adding that he was looking at attending a meditation course to help him.

It sounded to me like he could really be helped by what I had been learning, so I suggested he read Jamie's book *Clarity*. He replied that he was taking a break from reading because it was 'just more chaos in the mix.' From knowing Henry a little bit I had the impression that he was someone who had a lot of good ideas of what to do with his life but never seemed to really commit and move forward. The more he thought about the direction he wanted to go, the more confused he got.

I was reluctant to push too hard as I knew that someone has to be open for advice in order to act on any suggestions I might offer. So I offered an easier alternative: I explained I had an audio that could help him . . . but he might not be interested, and it was fine either way.

This softer approach worked, and he asked me to send it to him. This was the same hour-long Jamie Smart audio I'd sent to Bruce. I requested he listen to it with his full attention and no distractions, and I offered to have a conversation with him afterwards.

The next day he messaged saying that not only had he taken my advice and listened to the audio, but had also been inspired to buy Jamie's book and begin reading it. He'd found it all truly helpful, and I reiterated the offer of a conversation. He was enthusiastic, and a few weeks later we jumped on a call.

I hadn't considered this friend a potential client. I knew he didn't have a lot of money. He had been saving up to study in the UK but had been put off by the cost of rent and tuition fees. However, I also knew that talking with him would be great practice for me, and that this was vital for growing my business—not to mention the possibility that I could actually be of service to him.

We got on the video call and he started telling me all the things he had been doing and how he had gotten himself into a mess. For one thing, he was having difficulties with his studying abroad application. He needed a personal recommendation from a teacher and was struggling to find one. He wasn't even 100 percent sure about what he wanted to study. On top of this, he didn't have the money to make the trip to the UK, nor the cost of covering his expenses there. His biggest challenge was lack of finances, and he confessed that he didn't even have enough money to do a proper grocery shop. I listened quietly as he spoke, my mind open to what he was saying. I did not feel the need to say anything, until at some point words came out of my mouth that didn't seem to be coming from me. But they came with a deep knowing.

'You're innocent,' I told him. 'Everything you have done up till now is innocent.'

This was true. Like everyone, he had done the best he could do with the thinking he had. Yet he was judging himself for actions he had taken (and not taken) based on this thinking, and this judgement was a heavy anchor weighing him down—and keeping him from moving forward.

Tears started running down his face as I repeated these words. It was clear I had gotten through to him—and even more importantly, that he saw the truth of these words for himself. He immediately said he wanted to sign up for one more session—this was all he could afford—because he wanted to capitalise on the shift.

I got off the call surprised and having a hard time believing what had just happened. As I say, the words that came to me in the moment—that he was innocent—had seemed to come from someplace else. It was like the 'Ankush' I was normally had gone quiet, and a deeper part of me had taken over and shared the right words at the right time. Was this coaching? I wasn't sure. But regardless, the process had changed this man's world—and that was what I was in this profession for.

A few days later he sent me this sentence to use as a testimonial on my website: 'I recently had my first session with Ankush, and within the first hour we had already had a major breakthrough. Ankush said something that completely bypassed all my defences and hit straight home. It is hard to describe it with words! I was just blown away. Can't wait to see what comes up in our following sessions.'

I have since learned much more about how to coach clients, how to set up sessions, when to talk and to build rapport and so on. But I have never forgotten this moment and what it taught me: that the most impactful conversations come from a place deeper than the intellect and beyond all techniques, strategies and systems.

→ old version of me weighing me down

21

Signing Up for More Training

I had reached the end of my initial training with Jamie Smart, and he was launching a new programme for coaches branded 'Clarity'—after his book of the same name. I was interested. How could I not be after my first programme with him had been so life-changing? But I was also unsure about signing up for more training. I'd had big plans to be making at least £30,000 per year by the end of the training I'd already paid for. Yet I was only making a fraction of that.

All the same, I couldn't deny that things had started to turn around, albeit slowly. I'd realised through reading *The Prosperous Coach* that first and foremost I needed to give people a deep experience of coaching with me. I hadn't been doing that deliberately up till then. Most of the time I was simply (and unsuccessfully) trying to convince people that coaching was great. But until you've had a deep experience of coaching it's hard to understand what it even means to be coached.

Because of this I'd started offering a long session at no charge so people could immediately experience what coaching with me was like. And I think as a result of this approach I signed up a few clients. I had moved them from *imagining* what coaching with me was like to being able to make an informed decision based on their actual *experience* of coaching.

So with things moving in the right direction I eventually decided to take the plunge and sign up for the Clarity Practitioner Programme with Jamie. I hadn't yet made back the money I'd spent on my training to date, but I didn't want to lose the momentum I had been gaining, and I knew the structure of the programme would be good for me. There was also something about putting my money where my mouth was. If I was going to ask people to pay money for me to coach them, wasn't it only fair (and common sense) to put my own money down for ongoing coaching and training?

I'd been saying I wanted to be a coach, and I was focused on it, but by actually paying for my continuous education as a coach I was really showing myself that it was important. I had learned in my twenties that when I paid for anything, I was more likely to make use of it. I knew I had hours of content from Jamie that I still hadn't listened to . . . but that it would most likely just sit unlistened to on my computer unless I was in some kind of structured programme. When I had to show up in person in London, I knew I'd be there.

I also didn't feel particularly confident yet as a coach. As I mentioned earlier, I didn't often feel that I knew what I was doing. This can be seen in my story of coaching Henry, which I shared in the previous chapter. It was great that the right words had come at the right time in our conversation, but this was a new experience for me and I wanted to learn how to incorporate it into my practice. So while my results seemed to be good, I also knew that I could learn a lot more in order to become more impactful and effective—both in enrolment calls and with my existing clients.

Big picture, in terms of creating a business around coaching, I was learning that being a really effective coach can take longer than we originally anticipate—at least I was finding this to be true for myself. It certainly takes longer than most of the marketing for coach training programmes makes out. I was also starting to see that a prosperous professional coaching practice requires an ongoing, significant financial investment in educating oneself. This makes sense when you think of other professionals, such as doctors, lawyers, and psychologists. Consider the learning they undergo before they can take on clients and have successful careers. Even in my job as a procurement manager, I'd had to learn on the job, and this had taken years. During that time I'd undertaken professional training on negotiation, legal regulations and contract writing. If I'd really wanted to progress and become a procurement director it would have made sense to do an MBA. To be a really great procurement professional—in fact, to be great at *anything*—I would never really want to stop learning.

Why should coaching be any different? Often it's the coaches who re-enrol in my school or in private coaching who are the ones who end up making the most money, as well as the biggest impact. I don't believe this is a coincidence, and looking back I don't believe for a second that I would have had the trajectory I've had as a coach had I not kept re-investing in coaching and training programmes.

22

Implementing Systems

One evening my younger brother and I headed into Birmingham City Centre to grab some food after work. As we were walking back to the car, my mobile phone rang. It turned out to be a client calling me on Skype, and I suddenly remembered I had booked a call for that evening. I apologised to my brother and told him I needed to take it.

Furthermore, I couldn't move from where we were standing, because I would have lost the Wi-Fi signal—I was lucky enough that my phone had connected to a free hotspot in the first place—and so he had to wait an hour for me to complete my coaching.

When I was done, we walked back to our car, and my brother, a man of few words, said simply, 'You can't do that again.'

He was absolutely right. I was charging people for conversations with me and it was completely unprofessional to forget when I had calls. I had managed to get away with it this time but I considered this an early warning. I wouldn't fly by the seat of my pants like this in my day job—in fact, I *couldn't* have done so without quickly running into trouble. At that job I used an online calendar, so it dawned on me that I could do the same for my coaching calls. (I later refined this system by ensuring that my coaching calls were on both my work and personal calendars.)

I discovered other ways to support both myself and the client using my calendar. If I put a meeting into my calendar I could also send a reminder to the person I was scheduled to speak with. This obviously made it less likely that the client or prospect would forget about the call (something that had also happened). I felt this gave the arrangement a more professional feel, making it more recognisable as a coaching conversation rather than a casual chat. My language around this shifted a little too. When I started to book in conversations with a potential client I would use phrases like, 'I'll block off ninety minutes in my calendar so we can have a good, long conversation.'

As it turned out, there was more in common with my regular job and coaching than I had first realised. They were both professions that required the use of systems to ensure I was as effective as I could be. I loved the fact that there was so much flexibility in how I worked and ran my projects as a procurement manager (my day job). The same was true for my new profession of coaching. I could learn from others, test things out for myself and use my own common sense to create a structure and a system that worked for me.

Over the years, these early systems have continued to evolve to help me be more effective as a coach, use my time more productively and have a more significant impact on my clients. In essence, I've had to show up as a professional coach just like I did as a professional procurement manager. I've had to invest my time, energy and, on occasion money, to create and maintain these systems. It's been a process of moving from being a 'hobby coach' to a real professional. I've noticed that as I've taken this profession more seriously to create solid systems, it's coincided with my own professional self-esteem rising around the profession.

There were times when I wished someone would just tell me

what to do and give me the complete roadmap for running my coaching practice. In fact, this was one of the reasons I had signed up for my coaching training. Yet I hadn't anticipated that the freedom to create my business however I wanted was something I would come to really cherish. Every coach gets to create their coaching practice in a way that works for them, and this is truly a wonderful thing. Early on, this freedom—aka the lack of a fixed way of doing things—can show up in embarrassing moments, like the one I had with my forgotten call. But when you see that these moments are giving you a wake-up call and an opportunity to create your business your way—a better way—this freedom turns out to be a real blessing and source of satisfaction.

Often coaches come into my school looking for a system for client creation, creating agreements or even what to charge. I love sharing ideas, systems and strategies that have worked for me and my clients, but ultimately I point them to testing everything and then using the system that works for *them*. Because that's what makes this profession so rich: the opportunity to create a business that is deeply personal and aligned with who you are and what you want. For me, systems aren't about rigid rules, but about creating the outcomes we want in the way we want to create them.

23

A Humbling Lesson

After the end of my first training with Jamie, I found out there was a large, three-day conference happening in London featuring a whole host of speakers who were grounded in the Three Principles understanding. Dr Keith Blevens would be there, and so would others whom I had only heard on audios or watched short snippets of on YouTube, like Dr George Pransky.

I signed up and was really looking forward to being deeply impacted. After all, I had learned so much from Jamie, and he had learned from many of the speakers at the upcoming conference. So I felt I was moving closer to the source of these fundamental ideas, and I fully expected to be hit with insight after insight.

On Day One I arrived eager and excited, happy to see so many faces that I had previously only seen online. I settled down and started listening to the speakers. No insights came at first, but I assumed everything was just warming up.

However, it soon occurred to me that each speaker seemed to be saying things I had already heard many times before, like:

We are only feeling our thinking in the moment.

Our circumstances cannot create our feelings

I was underwhelmed and, frankly, disappointed.

In addition to the speakers on stage, there were also a number of breakout sessions—smaller groups—several of which ran at the same time. You chose which ones you wanted to attend. One of the breakout sessions I attended was with a lady called Elsie Spittle. At the time she was the most experienced teacher and facilitator in the world working from the Three Principles understanding. It made sense to hear what she had to say.

As I listened to her speak, I felt my mind go very quiet. On the surface, Elsie seemed to be telling a simple story about her life and friendship with Sydney Banks, the man who first articulated the Three Principles. Yet while what she said was so simple, it deeply impacted me. Her presence and energy took hold of me and kept me rooted to my chair. I felt like I was in a trance or had been drugged because the experience was so mesmerising.

I walked out thinking, *Wow. I don't know what I heard, but I know this lady has seen something* way *beyond what I see.* By contrast the rest of the conference seemed unremarkable.

At the final session, Elsie commented to the whole group about how much she had learned in the previous three days. Now *this* I wasn't expecting. I was convinced that there was nothing new being discussed, and yet this lady, who had been sharing these Principles for longer than anyone (several decades), and who had the most incredible presence, was saying that she had learned something.

There were only two reasons I could think of as to why our experiences had been so different. Either she was a little slow on the uptake and I was smarter than everyone in the room . . . or perhaps I was missing something that was right in front of me.

I guessed it was probably the latter.

Over the years I'd seen this pattern play out again and again with myself. I'd come across something that seemed so simple that I assumed I understood it immediately. Whether it was the Three Principles, an enrolment concept—such as giving people an experience of coaching versus selling it—or a coaching skill like deep listening. No matter how simple a concept seemed on the surface, there was always deeper to go and more to see. Whenever I believed the thought, 'I already know this,' I was closed to hearing what was being said. Closed to hearing something new. This is true to this day, and it's something all of us do innocently. But once we realise we're doing it, we can let it go.

The Three Principles understanding was helping me to see that while I am feeling my thinking moment to moment, I don't need to stay caught up in any one thought or belief. There is always the possibility of dropping my thinking and learning or seeing something new.

If at the conference I had recognised my disappointment in not hearing something new as simply a thought, a belief, I could have dropped it earlier and potentially heard a lot more over those three days.

Perhaps Elsie had learned through the years to listen to each speaker from an openness beyond her moment-to-moment thinking. Consequently, she was always open to what was being said—whereas a newcomer to the Three Principles, like myself at the time, would listen not from openness but instead through a filter of existing beliefs. In my case, this filter was a dense web of circular, negative thinking that was kicked off by believing the thought, 'I already know this stuff.'

Being willing to go beyond what I thought I knew, beyond my beliefs, beyond my moment-to-moment thinking, would take me deeper. It was the path of mastery. In fact, every mentor I had ever worked with was willing to go beyond what they already knew. Years later I would read a quote from the book, *The Way of Mastery*, which summarised this beautifully: 'The only difference between being a master and being a student is that the master has mastered the art of always being a student.'

Is there anywhere in your life or coaching where you think you already know everything there is to know? You might be bringing an element of this 'knowing' to this book and simply be looking for what you don't know. I invite you to leave all that you think you know to one side, and read the rest of this book, and any book, from a place of being a complete beginner. I invite you to treat any learning material in the same way, and I'm positive you will take more from it if you do. What do you have to lose?

This is why I always begin my coaching school by speaking about listening. Because if someone is closed, I could be sharing golden nugget after golden nugget, and they'll miss all of it. But if they're open, even just a little, they're far more likely to hear something that truly serves them and grows their business. The quality of our listening shapes the depth of what we see, and in turn, the impact we're able to have.

24

Impact Your Clients Like No-One Else

I was now five sessions into coaching Hank, the digital animator, and he was getting a lot out of it. He'd felt like he'd lost his mojo with regards to his creativity and had hired me to help him re-discover it. My approach was to help him see that he hadn't ever lost access to his creativity. He was just temporarily unable to see it because he was taking his clouded thinking about it seriously. This is to say that if we have a thought that we've lost our mojo and we *believe* that thought, we give power to it. As we return to it over and over again to explain why things aren't going the way we think they should, we experience a reality of losing our mojo. It's a self-fulfilling prophecy of our own making.

As I challenged his beliefs, doubts and fears, his mind started to settle down. My coaching wasn't about giving him more techniques, strategies or things to do. It was the opposite. It was helping to remove the mental clutter from his mind, which in turn allowed him to access that source of creative energy that was always there.

Out of the blue, I received a hand-drawn image from Hank telling me that I rocked. (There may also have been a swear word involved). It really touched me that my client would spend time sketching something specifically for me. It showed me that I was on the right path, and it meant a lot to me.

I had heard Rich Litvin say words to the effect that as coaches we should impact our clients like no-one else would. I knew I was still a novice coach with a lot to learn but receiving this kind of feedback from my client felt like it represented a huge milestone in my coaching career.

This approach of powerfully impacting clients aligned with my own personal value system. I wanted to *really* deliver for my clients. The same of course was true in my day job; I liked to deliver good results there too. But coaching felt different—way more personal and rewarding. I didn't simply want to learn how to coach and then how to get paid for it. I was in this profession because I wanted to make a profound difference in the lives of others. To me, this was more important and fulfilling than the fee I made.

No-one had taught me this, but I remember giving myself permission, even in these early days, to do whatever made sense to me with my clients. On the one hand I really wanted to learn from Jamie Smart and others the 'how-to-coach' aspect of the business. I was always on the lookout for best practices. And yet at the same time, I also instinctively understood the importance of dropping what I thought I knew and doing and saying whatever made sense in the moment to truly help my client.

I later realised that these early instincts were spot on. Coaching is one of the most creative professions there is. The best paid coaches are those who, while having a firm grasp on how to coach and the various methodologies involved, simply show up empty and are willing to break all the rules in the name of serving the client. I didn't want to hire a coach who had a cookie-cutter approach to his or her clients, and it would later dawn on me that most other people didn't either.

Now you might be wondering, how can I impact and serve like no one else? I can't offer a recipe for how to serve like no one else—that would be a cookie-cutter approach—but I will share some examples of what I did, which I hope will inspire you to create your own.

1. Gifting clients a book to read alongside your coaching sessions. There are so many wonderful books that both Jamie Smart and Steve Chandler gifted to those in their programmes. In addition, Steve Chandler would often assign books to me during our coaching sessions. Reading was profoundly impactful for me and for many clients over the years, and assigning books to clients to read was a simple way to increase my impact.
2. Offering spot-coaching. It was really helpful for me to be able to reach out to my coach outside of a scheduled coaching conversation to ask a question. I remember being able to call up Jamie on an ad hoc basis and Steve Chandler was always encouraging me not to wait for our next formal coaching session if I needed support before then. This was invaluable and something I offer to my own clients. A two-minute voice note reply to a short question can be very helpful for a client.
3. Getting creative with an impactful gift. This isn't something I would do all the time, but on occasion I have seen something that would reinforce a point I made in a coaching session with a client. For example, I once spoke to a client about Rolex watches and how part of their value came from them being limited to buy; some models have wait lists of several years. This client and I talked about him being like a Rolex and not needing to work with everyone who wanted to work

with him. To reinforce the point, I purchased a canvas print of a Rolex Daytona watch to keep on the wall behind his desk.

4. Perhaps the best example I could share here is to keep growing myself. Steve Chandler modelled this beautifully for me. He and I worked together for nearly nine years, and during all that time he would constantly be learning and growing. This influenced his coaching and meant that I was constantly being coached by a better coach. He believed this is part of the reason many clients of his would work with him for many years—in a sense they weren't working with the same person. I have continued to follow his example, and in addition to working with him for many years I also attended his school three times—even as I was being mentored by various Three Principles teachers. And I believe I'll keep doing this kind of growth work for as long as I'm able.

25

Getting an Accountant

As I started to get more clients, I had to make a diligent effort to keep track of billings, expenses and payments. I had essentially been making up my system as I went along. However, I knew that it would make sense to find someone who could advise me professionally, and I asked some of my coaching colleagues if they used an accountant.

Some people advised me not to hire one so early on in my business because of the cost involved. But after thinking about it for only a minute, I realised that to file my accounts myself would take me at least ten to fifteen hours. If I spent that same time creating a coaching client, I could easily cover the cost of an accountant. Also, a good accountant would be able to advise on ways to legally reduce my tax bill and operate more efficiently, which in turn would help pay for the associated costs of hiring one. I'd also far rather spend that time coaching than filling my tax return.

My colleague Malachy Donaghy used an accountant called Sujal and sent over her details. I also checked out a couple of other options using Google, but I found that Sujal was great. She was very professional. Something I really liked about her was that she was happy to offer advice and support before I signed up with her. She was modelling in her own business what I was learning worked for coaches—give prospective clients an experience of what it would be like to work with you in advance. Serve first and foremost, without expectation.

Not only were Sujal's prices competitive, but she also offered to come and meet me for an initial meeting to talk through my accounts.

She had good ethics too, which was important to me. I had heard stories of people hiring accountants and perhaps bending or even breaking the law in order to pay less tax. I wanted someone to advise me to be tax efficient but who also modelled the values I held important in my own business.

I was pleasantly surprised when, in our first meeting together, she essentially earned her fee. She advised me that I could legally expense an amount for working from home as well as 50% of my mobile phone bill and other things I hadn't thought of. I was sold and promptly signed up as a client.

I have been one ever since, and I've also recommended numerous UK-based coaches to her because of the great service she provides me. I have come to see how great a decision it was to hire a good accountant early on. I know of other coaches who operate very inefficiently from a taxation point of view, and it costs them thousands of pounds a year. Some of these have accountants who leave something to be desired, and others are doing it themselves.

I didn't outsource much in my first few years of coaching, but finding a good accountant was definitely worth looking for. The bigger-picture question here for coaches is this: where do you want to invest your time? To get more specific, how can you best serve yourself and your clients? Will taking the time to learn the ins and outs of tax law for independent business owners be the most efficient and cost-effective use of your time? Or would investing in, say, more training or time spent in enrolment conversations, better serve you and your clients better?

These are questions that every new business owner can usefully ask. Certainly there are times when it might make sense from a pure cost perspective to wait, but there is another element too. Even when you only have a few clients and it may be harder to make up the financial cost, hiring an accountant is a powerful statement of intent. It's telling yourself that you are a professional and you are in this profession for the long-haul. I've often suggested to coaches to consider hiring an accountant earlier than they might have done for this very reason. This mindshift is a powerful one and worthwhile taking into account alongside the time and efficiency savings.

26

I Was in a Rush

At fourteen months into my coaching journey I had coached seven paying clients and received just under four thousand pounds in coaching fees. However, it felt like my progress was too slow, and I wanted to go faster. I had assumed that once I committed to training as a coach it would only be a few months before I replaced my corporate salary. However, it wasn't working out that way, and I was starting to feel frustrated.

It didn't seem like many coaches around me were faring much better. The whole client creation part of building a coaching practice seemed a lot more challenging than I initially thought it would be. While I had signed up seven paying clients, it didn't seem like I really understood what I had done that worked, and this made it challenging to replicate it. Perhaps these seven were a fluke? Or maybe I had exhausted my network of potential clients and I would not, or could not, sign up any more?

I didn't understand then that creating a coaching practice doesn't always happen fast. It can for some coaches, but for the vast majority of us it seems to take a bit of time. Looking back, I realise I wasn't doing too badly, especially considering that I still had a full-time job and had been coaching for just over a year. But without that perspective, I was feeling at a loss as to what to do.

I met Jamie for an in-person coaching session and asked him for some advice on how to speed up my progress. He asked me a number of questions, including,

'How much do you want to earn from coaching?'

I truthfully didn't know, but I came up with a number: '£50,000' I said. I don't know why I picked that exact number; it just seemed about right, probably because it represented a figure that was a little lower than what I was making at my day job. 'If I made £50,000 then I would quit my job and coach full-time.'

Jamie then asked, 'How many clients do you want, ideally?'

Again, I had no idea. However, I had heard that the well-known and successful coach Rich Litvin only coached five high-paying clients a year. I thought that sounded cool, so I told Jamie I only wanted five clients.

'Great, so you can charge £10,000 a year each to five separate clients, and that will give you your £50,000.'

He went on to explain that as I was building to get paid £10,000 for a year, I could also charge £5,000 for six months of coaching or £2,500 for three months of coaching. This was very logical given the answers I had given him.

If I hadn't been in so much of a rush to 'make it' as a coach, I would have dropped my sped-up, urgent thinking. I would have slowed down and got in touch with my own inner wisdom. Perhaps I would have told Jamie that I didn't need to make £50,000; rather, I simply wanted to be making more than what I was paying for my training, and I wanted to see an upward trajectory in my income. Perhaps I wouldn't have asked anything at all, because I might have slowed down enough to see that things were actually moving in the right direction.

I'm also sure I would have told Jamie that I love coaching

people and that I'd really enjoy having as many as ten clients while still working my day job. I got such a thrill from coaching that it really didn't feel like work. If I had recognised my urgent thinking, I would not have been in so much of a rush. I would have seen that this sped-up, somewhat desperate feeling was not an indication that I needed to push myself to charge higher fees.

In other words, and as I would later come to see, the very same slowing down that I encouraged and helped my clients with could and should have been applied by me to how I was building a coaching practice.

After my conversation with Jamie, my fees suddenly jumped from £1,000 for 10 sessions to £2,500 for 6 sessions over 3 months. Of course, while I could increase my fee, that did not mean my practice would grow accordingly. I could have kept it at the same place and developed my enrolment skills further. The missing piece for growing my business wasn't that my fees were too low, but that I was simply not skilled enough in enrolling clients into my practice. I couldn't see this as long as I was buying into my sped-up thinking. I was too focused on the immediate desire for financial returns.

The Three Principles understanding that I had been introduced to by Jamie and which I was now sharing with clients was the key to slowing down. It wasn't a 'technique' I needed to learn; but rather it was important to simply recognise that the feeling of urgency was just a thought or a belief. It wasn't forcing me to speed up, and I didn't need to respond to it as if it were. When I saw this, I naturally slowed down. I de-identified from my urgent feelings.

This was a good thing to do, because sped-up thinking never seems to create an ideal context for good decision-making. Rather, good decisions always seem to occur when we're not feeling rushed or anxious to get anywhere.

Perhaps you can recognise the same truth in your own life and coaching practice? I've met many coaches over the years who thought that their sped-up thinking and associated feelings of anxiety were telling them that they weren't progressing fast enough in building their coaching practice. Perhaps this is based on seeing courses that advertise systems purporting to help you create a six-figure practice in six weeks. This sped-up thinking has often led them to purchase these same programmes and try to implement systems which rarely work. Sometimes they do this over and over again, not realising that the answer is not in a system which promises fast results overnight but rather in simply moving forward one step at a time (and this can lead to results they want far quicker than they realise).

This is something I see regularly in my coaching school. Many coaches join because they want to grow their business and increase their income—which is a beautiful goal. But often, they believe the key is to raise their fees and that the school will teach them how to get paid more for doing the same work.

Instead, I invite them to do something far more counterintuitive but ultimately more powerful: get full at their current fee (whatever 'full' means to them) before they consider increasing it. Again and again I've seen that those who take this path not only grow more sustainably but actually go on to make more money than those who raise their fees prematurely. Why? Because it's usually easier to enrol clients at their current rate, and once they're full, they tend to feel less urgency about signing the next client. From that place of ease, confidence, and service, their business grows far more naturally.

27

Attending Dicken Bettinger's Event with Chantal Burns

In June 2013, a fellow coach and colleague, Chantal Burns, invited me to a small, intimate group programme with herself and Dr Dicken Bettinger to deepen our understanding of the Principles in a business context. The focus was increasing your impact as a coach through the quality of your presence, and uncovering resilience in the face of ego and insecurity.

As I had delivered some training within my organisation, Chantal thought it might be a good fit for me, and I immediately signed up. The one-and-a-half-day programme took place in July at Chantal's home in St Albans, just north of London. There were only nine of us there, including Dicken. The calibre of the group was very high. Not only was Chantal a successful coach and trainer working with organisations, but other attendees included Jamie Smart and Ian Watson, who delivered Three Principles training courses similar to the coach training I was doing with Jamie.

Dicken had been delivering Three Principles-based programmes within organisations for many years. And because our group was small, there was plenty of opportunity to ask questions and dive deeper.

A couple of things really stood out to me. Firstly, Dicken's wife Coizie was there, but she didn't sit in on the training. We met her during the breaks and at lunch, and it was clear that they had a fantastic, loving relationship, even after many decades of marriage. Here was someone talking about how to help organisations be more effective. He spoke the 'corporate language' I was used to. However, he also embodied this incredible love for his life partner, which I wasn't used to seeing or even hearing about in the workplace.

Over time I would come to notice that Dicken and Coizie weren't unique amongst the Three Principles community. In fact, the most respected teachers and mentors of the Three Principles always seemed to have the most long-term, loving relationships with their life partners.

This really intrigued me, as I hadn't seen it in any other spiritual or personal development community. The more understanding I gained, the more I was able to see why this wasn't just a coincidence. An understanding of the Principles leads to more love and understanding for yourself and others (especially those closest to you).

In my own case, it helped me to drop many false beliefs about myself, allowing me to fall into the innately loving feelings I was born with. From this place I could share those feelings with the people closest to me—versus trying to find them in another person. I would say it is almost inevitable that a deep exploration of the Three Principles leads to more loving relationships in your life.

I also started to see what was different about the Three Principles compared to other types of coaching and training I'd experienced. Imagine a funnel where the Three Principles are at the bottom. At the top are approaches that simply focus on the goal or outcome that a client wants to achieve. Below this are approaches that focus on behavioural change. If behaviour changes, then the client's goal or outcome is more likely to be achieved.

Further down the funnel are approaches focusing on our emotional state. If people feel good, they can undertake the right behaviours and achieve the goal they want.

Next come approaches focused on changing a person's thinking, such as NLP or hypnosis, because once thinking changes, people feel different, and as a result, their behaviour changes and they achieve the outcome they want.

What Dicken shared during our event was that the Three Principles are deeper and more upstream than all of these other approaches because they point to how the mind actually works—as opposed to trying to change our thoughts, feelings or behaviour. It's about understanding the system itself, because once we understand the system, everything else corrects itself. (Or everything else flows from that)

For example, once people understood that germs caused disease, this changed the way doctors (and patients) behaved, which led to a huge reduction in death during surgery. Previously, when it was thought diseases were caused by miasmas (foul smells), for example, doctors wouldn't bother to wash their hands or sterilise their instruments.

In the same way, once people understand that their feelings are a reflection of their thinking and not their circumstances, other people, their past or anything else, their behaviour begins to change accordingly, often automatically.

For example, when I saw that my own anger wasn't a reflection of the 'stupidity' of the person I was angry at, the angry feelings started to dissipate quickly, and I became calmer and more present.

I began to see just how powerful this work called the Three Principles was, and why those who taught, consulted and coached from this understanding were so effective—and very often quite happy in their own personal lives.

28

Increasing My Fee

My client, Bruce, mentioned earlier, completed his package of eight sessions and was interested in renewing with me. Through our work together, and with the various resources I had sent him between sessions, he had learned to slow down a lot. His understanding of the Three Principles was deepening. I also knew the sessions were valuable because he was letting other people know about my coaching and telling them how helpful it had been for him.

His initial agreement had cost £640, a figure I had allowed him to split into two payments. He wanted to renew our agreement and he knew my price had increased, but I hadn't told him by how much. So, when I told him my new package rates—the lowest-priced option of which was now £2500 for six sessions over three months—he was very surprised. I was asking him for a fee which was quadruple what he had initially paid, and for fewer sessions. Unsurprisingly, he said he was out. He explained that he wanted to renew with me, but he simply couldn't afford that sum of money.

I'll admit: I felt uncomfortable and my mind started to race. Thoughts popped up like, *Why did you ask him for such a large increase?* and *You're an idiot for being greedy.* Thankfully, I recognised these charged thoughts for exactly what they were: simply thoughts.

I allowed my mind to settle, and even though I had heard you should never ask this question, I asked, 'What can you afford?' I wanted to get some more information on where he was at and what numbers he had in mind.

He said, 'I could afford to pay you a thousand pounds. But I'm not expecting you to reduce your fee. I respect your work.'

He was obviously sincere, and not simply looking to negotiate down the price. What I didn't want was for him be less committed to the coaching because the fee was so comfortable. So I asked, 'What could you afford that would make you uncomfortable?' He looked at me, curious, so I explained, 'I think it's important you have some skin in the game. Think about it this way: it's not about me making more money, it's about you being more committed.' And then I added something I truly felt: 'I'll trust whatever number you come up with.'

He took this in quietly, then said, 'Can I take a look at my finances and think about that?'

'Of course. Take some time.'

This line of thinking was influenced by reading *The Prosperous Coach* by Steve Chandler and Rich Litvin, reading Steve's newsletters and listening to some audios they had both created for coaches. I had started to see how important it was to have a committed client and that higher fees helped clients to be more committed.

A few days later we had another conversation, during which he said, 'I've looked at my accounts, and I could afford £1500. It wouldn't be easy, but I could do it.'

'Okay,' I said, 'let's do it.' I really respected him for his honesty and sincerity. I saw clearly that it was less important he pay my full fee, and more important that the stretch of paying £1,500 gave him a new sense of commitment to our work together. I felt the energy of our relationship change for the better at that point. He was bringing a different degree of focus to our sessions, to any work we agreed he would do in between sessions and to the entire coaching process.

I could only have found this solution to the issue of my fees seeming too high for a client through my understanding of the Three Principles, which kept pointing me back to the role of my thinking in my experience of life. The more I allowed this understanding to play out in my life, the better my decisions seemed to be, and the less I rushed into things.

After years of running headfirst into situations and making them worse, I was finally starting to tap into my own common sense and wisdom. This slower approach felt good. For years, I had been thinking that other people's wisdom was better than my own.

I know coaches often struggle with raising fees because of a whole host of thoughts that come with that process. *What if the clients says no, or worse, they are offended? What if you lose a potential client because you are being greedy?*

On the other hand, I've seen many coaches drastically raise their fees because they listened to the advice of an expert, and it resulted in a huge drop in clients signing up. I encourage you to slow down and let your thinking settle so you can see more clearly about a way forward that works for you.

29

I Couldn't Coach Everyone

I used to believe I could coach anyone. That confidence had been fuelled by a series of great early client experiences, so for a while it seemed true. But towards the end of 2013, I met someone who quietly dismantled that belief. I took on a coaching client named John, who reached out to me on Facebook after reading a post I had written around the topic of being masculine that caught his eye, and we set up a call.

John was struggling with being more authentically himself, and as I often did with prospective clients, I sent him the hour-long audio by Jamie Smart called 'The Clarity Activator,' which was a great introduction to the Three Principles. I'd seen it help many people gain insight and settle down their thinking. I felt that if John could get a glimpse into how his thinking was creating his experience of life, his mind would also settle, and he would simply be himself more.

However, John had a different response. After listening to Jamie's audio, John said that on the one hand he agreed with what Jamie was saying, but he also felt that the recording was messing with his head. He also said that Jamie was talking about things that were similar to what he was exploring himself.

At this point, it would have really made sense to slow down, ask more questions and explore what was going on for him. However, I missed that opportunity to explore John's experience and bring my best listening, which would have helped guide me in my coaching of him.

Nonetheless, at the time I was riding high after having great results with everyone I had worked with so far. Consequently, I had a lot of confidence that I could help anyone, regardless of what problems or challenges they were facing. So after John and I spoke that one time, I emailed him a proposal for us to work together at the rate of ten sessions for £1,000. (He was my last client at this rate before I dramatically increased my fees.) He was hesitant, in part because of the cost, and perhaps because of some uncertainty around what the coaching process would be like.

What I see now is that it wasn't the time to sell. It was the time to serve, to help him experience more of my coaching before asking for a commitment. This could in turn have supported him in making a more informed decision about whether coaching with me would be a good investment for him. It would also have helped me see whether he would be a client I could really help.

Instead, we had a conversation after I sent my proposal and I confidently suggested that working together would be great for him, based on the misguided confidence I had at the time.

This became clear because of what occurred *after* he signed up—namely, more of what occurred *before* he signed up. I found it difficult to help him have an impact on his challenges. Whatever I had done that worked with other clients didn't seem to work for him, including the resources that had really helped others. I was learning that effective coaching wasn't a one-size-fits-all process. A book that I assign to one client might have a huge impact and lead to insights and breakthroughs, but with another client it might not make any noticeable impression.

I was also learning that the best clients for me were those who were enthusiastic about working together. It would take some time for this to fully land but my experience with John started to show me that it wasn't a good idea to rush into a coaching agreement with a new client.

I also didn't realise at the time that I was so focused on the need for me to have a big impact on John, and how this need was getting in the way of my really listening to and helping him. Perhaps it should have been by this point, but it still wasn't clear to me just how much the Three Principles understanding could have helped me realise I was putting pressure on myself through my own misguided thinking. This pressure had the opposite effect from what I wanted—that is, it made me less impactful as a coach and less likely to be able to help John. It would be years before I finally realised it wasn't my job to help any individual who seemed to be open to coaching. Coaching is an intimate relationship between two parties, and it requires that both the coach and coachee be open to the process. No coach is perfect for every client.

A few months later, I ended up refunding John for our last three sessions, as we weren't making any progress and we were both feeling frustrated. I'll admit I felt pretty awful about it, but it was also an incredibly valuable lesson for me that I really needed to take my time with a potential client before they sign up.

At the time that lesson seemed to be about slowing down so that I could avoid having to refund a client because I didn't want to feel awful again. Yet what I *wasn't* seeing was that my feeling awful was down to my *thinking* about refunding a client, not about the actual act of refunding him. I could of course instead have felt relieved about ending the relationship.

Practically speaking, too, it simply makes sense for coaches to slow down before signing up a client—not just to avoid the discomfort of a potential refund, but because it's not good business to have clients unhappy with your service.

30

I Started to Be More Direct

I was really drawn to content from Rich Litvin and Steve Chandler after reading *The Prosperous Coach*, and I wanted more. I had now moved from struggling to create clients to having five regular paid clients, in part from applying what I was learning from them. I reached out to Rich and purchased the audios for an intensive weekend that he and Steve had run for coaches in May 2013. It was not something that had been advertised as for sale, but another coach in my network had purchased them and let me know how great they were. Rich agreed to let me have a copy of the recordings for $297.

As I listened to the audios I realised something. I could be more in service to people if I was more direct with them. There was still a part of me that was using the idea of service to try to *get* something (namely a client), and therefore I was still trying to avoid offending people.

There was a young man I had been having conversations with via Facebook. He'd been to many coaches, done seminars and read books, and yet he was still in a pretty low place. He felt the whole world had let him down. I'd recommended he speak to Dr Keith Blevins, as I rated him so highly, and I thought if I offered to coach him myself, he was just going to think I was after his money like the other coaches he had met. My mindset was, *I want to help this guy and not take his money.*

After listening to some of the audios from the intensive, I decided to test out being more direct with him. He hadn't hired Keith, as he said he had no money, so I offered to coach him pro-bono on the agreement he didn't tell anyone (I wasn't coaching anyone for free anymore). However, and I admit this was a bit out there for me, I told him it was also with an agreement that he stop whining and complaining. He'd been thinking he was a victim the whole time, and I knew he could see his life differently. Bitching and complaining about everything wasn't getting him very far.

I ended up sending him a few Three Principles audios by the theosopher Sydney Banks which had been profoundly impactful for me. Every time I listened to these audios I heard something new about the nature of life and my thinking that was completely relevant and transformative for whatever was happening at that moment. They were unlike any other spiritual or personal development content I had ever experienced.

I never spoke with this young man in person or on a call, but we did have one chat online via Facebook Messenger. My direct approach seemed to work, as he sent me this:

> Ankush, I just finished the audios and I don't know what to do first. Tell you how great and free I feel? Or tell you that I definitely want more of the audios (not that I need them anymore—yeah, I get it for real)? In fact I'd like to have anything you can share of his cause it resonated with me like nothing else and will only deepen what I already understand NOW. Or should I thank you and tell you that you just helped me get free?

Later he wrote:

> I am sitting here people-watching with a smile on my face. And

> on spotting someone attractive I think to myself that, 'I don't need you—I need me & my love.'

And then later still:

> . . . and I lost it. Until I listened to the audios you shared. Listening to the audios was very intense for me & half of the audio I had tears in my eyes & half a smile. A big, free smile.

I made no money from him, but I did truly serve him, and I felt so good about it. He wrote a testimonial for my website, and I was open to coaching him in the future, but in the moment I simply didn't care about any of that. The important thing was that my mindset had started to really shift from serving in order to make money to having powerful conversations that served people regardless of the outcome. This small but powerful shift would serve me for many years to come.

This mindset later became a foundational principle in my coaching school. Coaches often arrive wanting to serve, but also hoping that serving will quickly lead to income. And while that's understandable, I keep pointing them back to a deeper truth: serving powerfully, without attachment, is not just noble—it's effective. When we drop the agenda and truly serve, the right clients often show up. I've come to see that we cannot outgive the universe. When we serve with an open heart, it will come back to us—though not always from the person we served or in the way we expect. It's as if the universe keeps a spreadsheet, and over time it always balances. The more we trust that, the freer and more generous we become. That shift—from trying to get something, to simply giving something—was one of the most important transformations in my journey. And it's one I now help others make every day.

31

I Started Working with a New Mentor

I had heard from some of my colleagues that Dr Keith Blevens would work with clients in a private capacity. I was enrolled in Jamie's Clarity Practitioner Programme, but I thought that it would be really beneficial to work more deeply with someone like Keith, who had been such a powerful influence on Jamie. It made sense to me that if I wanted to be a successful coach, I should model other successful coaches—all of whom seemed to invest in their own one-to-one coaching and mentoring.

I reached out to Dr Blevens on email and shared a little about my journey and how I was hoping to undertake some sessions with him. One thing that stood out was that he said he would only work with me if I committed to ten sessions. I was a little surprised at this, as I had already invested a significant amount of time and energy on my training with Jamie, so I had assumed I would be an 'advanced' student. However, Keith was adamant that ten sessions would allow us enough time to really dive in deep and help me get clear on what the Three Principles were—and where I wasn't seeing them in action in my life. As this formed the foundation of my coaching approach, it made sense to get a deeper understanding of them.

This turned out to be the best decision, even though I don't remember many of the specifics of our conversations. My mind would often go very quiet. At times it would feel like Keith was sharing a lot of what I already knew, and the thought would creep into my mind that I was wasting my money. Then—BAM!—I would be hit so profoundly by something he said that I would sit stunned for the rest of the conversation.

This had an impact in two main ways on my life.

Firstly, as I kept seeing more deeply that there were no exceptions to my reality being created by my thinking, I dropped more and more of the erroneous thoughts and beliefs that were clouding my mind. This resulted in my being happier and more present than I had ever been, despite whatever was occurring in my world.

Before being introduced to the Three Principles understanding, I used to believe, like most people, that my feelings were caused by whatever was occurring in the world. At least, I felt like outside circumstances had a large degree of influence over my feelings. I would therefore use self-development techniques and strategies to try to cope with these situations and process the feelings I interpreted as coming from them. This was of limited help in living a happier and more present life.

Through my work with Keith, I dealt much more easily with events that might once have seemed far more problematic. For example, at the time I was having a disagreement with my landlord, who had let out the pub below my flat to two gentleman who were running it as a nightclub. They played music so loud late at night that my room would shake. My flatmate eventually got so upset that she would shake with anger. While understandable, I realised the anger wasn't coming from the actions of our neighbours downstairs but from our thinking about their actions. I was able to have cordial conversations with them about turning the music down to a level that was acceptable to both of us. This was only possible for me because I wasn't getting caught up in a whirlwind of angry thinking. It also allowed me to have enough clarity to move out and find a new apartment that was much better suited.

My sessions with Keith also changed my professional life. My clients were now getting coached by someone who had many more examples of how an understanding of the Three Principles was truly transformative. I could share these examples in my coaching sessions where appropriate, and they seemed to land very well with my clients. I was also more coherent in my expression of ideas and insights when there was a 'teaching moment' in a coaching session—rather than fumbling over my words, which I used to do.

I hadn't realised when I started coaching that one programme or course wouldn't be enough to help me be a prosperous and truly impactful coach. I was embarking on a lifelong journey of growth and learning which would never end. The more I kept an open mind to learning, the more impactful and prosperous I would be as a coach.

32

Not Holding Back

At the start of my coaching journey, I would often hold back certain ideas and insights from whomever I was talking to before we entered into a coaching contract. I believed that if I gave them everything I had, they wouldn't want to pay me for coaching. If I found out a new idea, metaphor or resource that would help someone, I wanted to keep it in my metaphorical toolbox or coaching bag so that I could bring it out at some point later (preferably after they had paid me).

After diving deeper and deeper into resources from Steve Chandler and Rich Litvin, I started to implement the idea of serving the person in front of me without holding back. I realised this didn't just mean being more direct with them; it also meant giving them absolutely anything at my disposal that I thought could help them.

It was only when I started to do this wholeheartedly that I realised how much value I had been holding back from potential clients. No wonder my coaching practice wasn't growing as quickly as I wanted it to! I would also often hold back anything of value from other coaches, because I was still very competitive—driven by my own insecurities and feelings of lack around my professional self-worth.

I even went so far as to tell clients not to share with others what I had shared with them because I had a fear that then other people wouldn't want my services. It seems so odd now, looking back, but I was placing a lot of emphasis on the information I was sharing with my clients as the basis for why they were paying me. My mindset was one of limitation and lack, and I hadn't yet seen that this wasn't based on reality. It simply reflected my beliefs around creating clients and income from coaching. I thought it was challenging to find people who were open and willing to pay for coaching, that I didn't really know what I was doing, and I needed every edge I could have over other coaches.

One morning in early 2014, while in the shower—where insights often occur—I realised that Rich Litvin and Steve Chandler model a spirit of holding nothing back. I had heard them talk about what they'd learned from other coaches. While I was also open about training with Jamie Smart, I wasn't as open as Rich and Steve seemed to be about everything they had learned from their own coaches and mentors over the years.

I've often thought about what advice I might give my younger self at the start of my coaching journey. One answer that always pops up in my mind is to share more about the journey. I can see there would probably have been a huge benefit to my coaching practice if I had been more open about signing up for coach training and sharing the books I was reading, the conferences I attended and insights I was having from all these places.

Steve and Rich also didn't seem to hold back any super-secret ideas until people paid them. It hit me that this was part of what made them so powerful and prosperous as coaches. Their mindset seemed to be one of abundance; the opposite of mine at the time. It seems so obvious now that the more helpful I would be *before* someone paid me, the more likely they would want to be coached by me. This concept wasn't clear to me back then, and my logic was clouded by my insecure thinking about my own abilities as a coach to help others.

Despite this insight, it still felt edgy for me to be willing to give more and more value to potential clients. At the same time, I knew the best way to learn was to simply test the idea. So I started to do this on my Facebook page, in Facebook groups and in my coaching sessions.

As you may have guessed, it didn't have any of the detrimental effects I was worried about. Instead, I saw I was gradually becoming more visible to potential clients. Not only this, but I could see that my perceived value was rising in their eyes. It's similar to giving people an experience of coaching before taking them on as a client. I started to realise that the more I gave, the more people would want to work with me.

Years later, I found myself applying this same principle when creating materials for my coaching school, my men's immersion or a one-off programme. Now I compete with myself to give more away than ever before, whether it's resources for coaches, posts on social media or even this book.

I can do this because I've learned that no matter how much I give away up front, the magic—and what people actually pay for—happens in the experience itself.

33

Becoming More Impactful

In early 2014, Jamie Smart and I met up for dinner in West London. We had developed a friendship, and I felt like I could talk to him openly. I always learned something from our conversations, and I also felt that having taken his course I could give him helpful feedback from my viewpoint as a client.

I confided in him that while I was learning a lot from his practitioner programme, I still didn't feel confident in my coaching ability. Yes, my clients were getting good results. Some had even renewed their coaching agreements. But I didn't feel I had the rock solid confidence that he did in delivering great coaching to my clients. I still felt like I was completely winging it.

Jamie suggested that I listen to an audio of a three-day programme he had hosted with Dr Mark Howard back in 2012. I'd actually been given access to these recordings when I first started working with Jamie, but had never listened to them. Now I dove in.

There were hours of helpful content from Dr Howard, but two points in particular really helped me.

Rapport

The first point was about rapport. It already made sense to me to have a positive connection with a client or prospective client, but Mark took this to another level. To Mark it was an absolute *prerequisite* to have a real, deep level of rapport in order to help clients have any kind of insight or transformation.

When I thought back to my coaching calls, the ones that didn't go as well as they might have were also the ones where the client and I didn't have a strong sense of connection. Mark pointed out this wasn't a one-off event with a client. It is important to build rapport over the course of a conversation or series of conversations. It's something to maintain and deepen. Why is this so important? If there is a good feeling between us, a client will be more open to hearing me.

Mark also spoke about how this ties in with the Three Principles understanding. If I see that my felt experience of life—that is to say, my feeling state in the moment—is simply a reflection of my thinking and not of who I am at my core, *then who I am is not my thinking*. The same is true for my client. In the recording, Mark was talking about a level of rapport that went beyond our thinking, our beliefs or our personality. It was about tapping into our own essence and seeing the essence of our client. I believe Jamie calls it 'soul-level' rapport.

This was a game changer for me in both my client calls and my conversations with prospective clients. It moved me away from trying to be impressive or having some kind of fake connection based on what I said. I started to see the perfect human I was talking to, beyond their moment-to-moment thinking. They felt that.

I now call rapport the currency of transformational conversations. I see that the deeper a connection I have with the client, the deeper we can go in our coaching. Coaching can be limited by how open a client is willing to be. I've often found, both in myself and in clients of mine, that people don't fully open up immediately for fear of being judged. Falling into this feeling of 'soul-level' rapport creates an incredibly safe space for clients to truly open up.

Sharing What You Know

Secondly, Mark talked about only sharing what you know. Now, I knew that coaching was about asking questions and helping clients come up with their own answers, but I also talked a lot in my coaching sessions. I struggled with talking too much and sometimes would mute my microphone to stop me from jumping in while the client was mid-sentence. Not only this, but I was often clumsy with my words or metaphors. I tried to be like Keith Blevens or Jamie Smart by attempting to emulate their coaching style as a way to learn, because I saw them as being so effective with clients. Needless to say, this often didn't land particularly well. I was slowly learning that every coach and mentor I looked up to had their own style and that I would need to find my own; it would also evolve over time.

Mark pointed out that once we have deep rapport with clients, we will see an appropriate teaching moment if it arises. However, rather than regurgitating what we have heard from our own coaches, teachers and mentors, it's more powerful to simply share what we know for certain from our own experience.

This was another game changer for me. I realised that while I had trouble articulating the Three Principles understanding to my clients or prospective clients, I would have no trouble sharing my own experiences around anger, productivity and relationships.

I'd had insights around certain topics where I could share with absolute certainty. For example, I had struggled with productivity for years in my corporate job. I had tried all manner of systems and techniques to help me, but none seemed to make a significant difference. Once I started to learn about my feelings being a reflection of my thinking in the moment, I started to not pay so much attention to the feeling that arose when I had a task to do that I thought was boring or difficult. I simply let the feeling pass. In the meantime, I got on with the task at hand. My productivity skyrocketed. This was also helped by my not getting sucked into distractions when my anger arose at work. For example, if a seemingly unhelpful email came in from a colleague, I stopped getting sucked into a vortex of anger. I also stopped talking about it and sharing my upset with others. I simply took a breath, let the anger pass and got on with my day.

All of a sudden I had taken a leap forward in my confidence as a coach, and I became more effective in my sessions. My existing clients noticed this.

Perhaps if I had listened to those audios earlier I would have taken a shortcut on my learning journey, but perhaps I listened to them when I was finally ready to hear them.

Years later I would create an online programme for coaches with Dr Howard, which we took over a year to create.[3] It was an honour to create something with someone I truly admired and I had learned so much from. We connected everything I had learned about coaching, enrolment and client creation with his experience as a psychologist and Three Principles practitioner. And the two main topics shared in this chapter—rapport and sharing what you know—were central to the online programme.

[3] https://ankushkumarjain.podia.com/building-the-impactful-and-sustainable-3p-coaching-practice

34

Speaking with Steve Chandler

One thing I had read in *The Prosperous Coach* and heard from Rich Litvin and Steve Chandler was that every coach should *have* a coach. I had convinced myself that doing my coach training with Jamie was enough, but it was starting to dawn on me that I needed more support, especially for the business side of my coaching practice. I was subscribed to Steve Chandler's email newsletter, and he had mentioned a few months earlier that he was willing to work with clients who couldn't afford his higher fees. I thought it would be worth reaching out to him.

He requested that I send him an email if I wanted to speak with him about coaching, and here is part of what I wrote:

> I'm exceptionally passionate about coaching, which to me means changing people's lives. I'm currently on my second year's training with Jamie Smart, and he asked me in December what I'd like to achieve in 2014. I told him I'd like to be a full-time coach. He asked what else, and I said nothing else mattered. It's like I don't even have a choice. I told him that if I did nothing else in my life except coach and shift clients,

> affect them and ultimately help them be happier, then what greater thing could I ever achieve except that? I have an inkling that you feel the same way about coaching. I have really been helped by yourself and Rich Litvin to start creating clients and I have a deep respect for you both because of that.

When Steve wrote back he mentioned that he was a longtime student of Dr George Pransky's work and that he had received a great deal of coaching from Dr Dicken Bettinger, with whom he was still working. He invited me into a conversation, and we set up our first call for early February 2014.

It didn't turn out to be quite as I expected. I was used to speaking with coaches and Three Principles-based teachers where we would just talk about anything, and our gently meandering conversation would lead to insights. Steve, however, was more direct. He didn't waste time with small talk. I had told him I wanted a coach to help me create more clients and grow my business. He suggested the best use of our time would be if I shared a couple of examples of potential clients, and he could coach me around creating them as *actual* clients.

He was really direct, sharing practical and eminently useful approaches and understandings. I asked him if we could work together and, if so, what that would look like. He suggested that the only thing he would commit to was a package of six sessions at $4,000. This was unusual in my experience. Most coaches seemed to want to sign up clients to as big a coaching package as possible, and yet Steve said he would review how we did after six sessions before deciding whether to continue. I told him I was very interested and I would be in touch. I was still nervous about spending the money on a coach and wanted to be really sure. I had $4,000 but I assumed I would need significantly more than six sessions to shift into becoming a full-time coach. I had heard and read stories of people coaching with the same coach for years. This wasn't the only reason that I was nervous. I hesitated because the investments I had made up to this point had been great for helping me learn and grow as a coach, but I still hadn't made back the money I had invested. While I was drawn to coaching in a way that I had never been drawn to anything else before, I didn't have an unlimited pot of money to keep investing and hoping it would work out.

I obviously didn't realise then that Steve was going to have a bigger impact on my coaching and my income than I ever imagined. Spoiler alert: We would go on to work together for eight-and-a-half years without a break in our coaching agreement, and I would attend his school three times in a row and eventually return as a guest speaker. So much of what I now teach in my own coaching school—especially around sustainable client creation, fees and integrity—has been shaped by what I learned from Steve. His generosity and relentless service mindset laid a foundation that still supports me today, and now it also supports every coach who walks through the doors of my school.

The next day, I got an email from Steve's colleague and publisher, Maurice Bassett. He informed me that Steve had gifted me access to his Wealth Warrior Movement programme, which had an annual cost of around $300. He also wanted my address so he could send me some things in the post.

I was surprised, but not as surprised as when the packages turned up. Steve had not sent one but four or five books, all written by him. I was not used to this kind of generosity, and my sceptical thinking popped up: *Oh, he probably just had these lying around. They wouldn't have cost him much.*

Then I looked at the postage costs—around $70 just to post the books! I thought, *Who does this?*

At this point, I had no idea that this wasn't a sales trick; it's just who Steve is. I messaged him on Facebook and told him I would be in touch.

35

Attending a Retreat with Elsie Spittle

I found out in early 2014 that Elsie Spittle was flying over to London from Canada to do a five-day retreat in May. Elsie would attend for three days, and the group would have both an introductory and a wrap-up day without her.

Elsie was the speaker who'd had the biggest impact on me at the Three Principles conference in 2013. I'd felt unable to move when she spoke then, as if I were held in place by an invisible forcefield. I was excited to attend this latest experience and continue to deepen my own understanding of the Three Principles, which was already making me a better coach and giving me a richer experience of life.

The retreat was hosted by Rudi Kennard and his then-wife Jenny. It took place in Colchester, England, at a hotel which had beautiful luxury cabins for rent on site. I didn't know anyone else attending the retreat, so it was going to be a step into the unknown.

I was amazed by the location when I arrived. I'd seen photographs but they didn't do it justice. I was sharing a room with another coach called Jonathan Wilkinson, and our communal area was big enough to comfortably host at least twelve people. Jonathan was massively into his physical health, and he shared with me a lot of his research into the subject, such as why eating butter from grass-fed cows was more healthy; I was fascinated by it all, because he glowed with vitality.

It was on the second day that we all got to meet Elsie. What really stood out to me was that she arrived early and spent time with every single person in the room. There must have been around thirty people there, and she took her time, mingling individually and having one-on-one conversations before the day even started. And it wasn't just small talk for the sake of it. She had a beautiful and calm presence that immediately put me at ease. It was as if I had known her for years, although in truth this was the first time we had spoken.

Over the next few days, Elsie told us stories about how she knew Sydney Banks, the world-renowned teacher, philosopher and author who first articulated the Three Principles. She'd known him as a friend *before* his enlightenment experience in the seventies, and at first she was reluctant to acknowledge that her friend—a simple welder—could have really had a profound insight into the workings of human psychology.

However, it was clear to everyone in the room that not only had Sydney Banks touched on something really true, but also that that *something* had deeply impacted Elsie as well—not on an intellectual level, but at her very essence. She embodied everything she spoke about. I remember very little of the content of what she spoke about during that 2014 retreat, but I *do* remember the positive and loving feeling in the room. It was infectious. I met so many wonderful people that weekend. These included the poet and comedienne Sarah Wood (also known as Mrs. Housecoat and author of *Softest Blue*), and Kim Bailey, a counsellor, coach and healer who's worked with many disadvantaged groups, including those suffering from domestic abuse. I also enjoyed great laughs with Lian Brook-Tyler, who went on to form a successful business partnership and top ranked podcast with Jonathan Wilkinson. Marita Lund even offered to help me with my neck and back issues via an acupuncture session given to me at no charge.

All my life I had struggled to feel like I fit in anywhere, and now amongst complete strangers I felt I'd known these people for years. There was power in the feeling that Elsie embodied and pointed us to, and I knew that if I could give an experience of that to my prospects, I would never need to worry about having enough clients, money or business.

There was something in the feeling Elsie brought that changed everything. I didn't realise it then, but this would later become one of the most important things I aim to cultivate in my own group programmes. Whether it's in my men's immersion or my coaching school, I do everything I can to create that same atmosphere of love, safety and genuine connection. It's something that many participants mention—they feel seen, welcomed, and part of something extraordinary. Coaches can often overlook the power of a great community, but time and time again I've found that this loving feeling is what helps people open up, go deeper, and experience real transformation.

36

Being More Visible While Being Scared

I thought I needed to increase my online presence in order to create clients and grow my practice. I reasoned that if no one knew I was a coach, no one would consider hiring me. If, on the other hand, I was being interviewed, creating content on social media and sharing things that helped people, potential clients would reach out. Working with me would feel like the next logical step.

I started creating a variety of online content. This began with writing social media posts I thought would be helpful for people, as well as looking for opportunities to interview and be interviewed by others. It was time for me to stop hiding, to stop being so timid about coaching. I had been reluctant to be more visible online earlier for fear of what people might think or say. I knew now, deep down, that those insecure thoughts weren't telling me to be cautious and hide; understanding this didn't mean that those thoughts disappeared, but it did mean I could take action and move forward even while they were still there.

In February 2014 I recorded a conversation with a friend and colleague who had been a coach for a decade. He was one of the mentors for a men's community of which I was part. He had seen a shift in me and had also started exploring the Three Principles understanding—which led to him seeing something in it for himself as well.

We jumped on Skype and recorded a conversation. Some people watching may have assumed that I was confident and had a lot of self-belief, but inside I felt like I really didn't have a clue what I was doing. I was part of this community and I wanted them to think highly of me, so I was feeling self-conscious.

Jamie Smart once told me that he had gotten better at public speaking by finding as many opportunities as he could to practise it. That made a lot of sense, so I tried doing it myself. I took every opportunity to share what I knew. It was (sometimes painfully) clear to me that I wasn't as articulate as my mentors Jamie, Keith Blevens or Mark Howard, but I also knew that the only way to improve was to practise. I later learned that Steve Chandler used the same approach to master public speaking. All of my mentors, teachers and coaches had put in the hours to get to a stage of competency where they seemed naturally gifted at their craft.

I found that I tended to be nervous for the first few minutes of an interview or recording but that I soon settled into what was really just a conversation with someone else. I wouldn't consciously realise this in order for my thinking to settle down. It would simply settle down as I spoke more. Occasionally a judgemental thought would pop up, but I knew better than to try and engage with or analyse it. And when I didn't pick it up, it simply disappeared.

When an interview ended, my negative thoughts returned: *I bet that was horrible. What did I say? Why did I say that? Perhaps we should record it a second time so I'll be better.*

And yet the feedback that came in was almost wholly positive. Any criticism was something small that I could take as a lesson for next time.

Once again, I was seeing that my thinking wasn't a reflection of reality. Yet for most of my life I would have listened to this negative thinking and simply not tried, or given up after the first attempt.

Nonetheless, I still felt fear and discomfort when creating content. That is to say, my fearful thinking didn't completely fall away. As I've mentioned, thoughts would still pop up around being judged. I knew I was becoming more visible to people who knew me outside of coaching or personal development; friends, colleagues and family (I have a large extended family. My father has over fifty first cousins). However, now that I understood that these thoughts didn't need to stop me from moving forward and improving my skillset, I simply kept taking the next steps, regardless of what I felt in the moment.

37

Bringing Jamie into Work

In February 2014, a leader at work—Peter[4]—was delivering a short presentation to the entire team about his vision and priorities for the next twelve months. He had five or six points to make, with the last one being titled 'Wellbeing.'

My ears suddenly pricked up. This was an area I could really help the department with. I knew that the training I'd received over the previous eighteen months—with both coaching and the Three Principles—was incredibly effective at helping organisations ensure the wellbeing of their people.

I was nervous, but I didn't let my thoughts get in the way. I approached Peter after his presentation and asked if he would be available for a conversation about his wellbeing priority, as I had been undertaking some training outside of work and I felt that I had some things to share that could be helpful. He agreed, suggesting I put thirty minutes in his calendar via his secretary.

Wow, I thought, *that wasn't so hard* . . . But now I had to deliver on my suggestion in a short space of time. Of course, I felt a little insecure about convincing this senior colleague about the value of what I'd been learning in my training. After all, this was one of

[4] Not his real name.

the largest companies in the world. It had won awards for looking after their employees.

I allowed these thoughts to dampen my enthusiasm and what I knew to be true—namely that what I had learned through the Three Principles was having a greater effect in companies than any other traditional approaches currently being used in business.

Because of this I decided to hold back (something I had done throughout my life). It felt safer to tell Peter that I had been learning about this wonderful new paradigm in psychology (the Three Principles), and that I could set up a meeting with my mentor and colleague Jamie Smart, who was more of an expert in this field. I thought Jamie's credibility through writing a best-selling book would speak to Peter, whom I believed valued these things.

Peter agreed, and I excitedly contacted Jamie. I was already envisioning Jamie bringing the Three Principles into the department, it having a huge impact and thus creating an opportunity for me to be Jamie's sidekick and help deliver the training. Jamie was open to the opportunity, but more level-headed and grounded about it.

At the first meeting with Peter, I witnessed a masterclass in coaching and enrolment by Jamie. While I was excitedly in my future thinking about what this could mean, Jamie really slowed down and asked Peter a bunch of questions about the company, the department, what the team was like and, importantly, where Peter envisioned the team moving. This opened up the conversation much wider than the initial topic of wellbeing for employees. Peter told us that he would love the wider business to see his employees as trusted advisors rather than back-office workers whom they could rely on as and when needed. Jamie asked Peter what was in the way of that happening and guided him to see how the work he did could help facilitate this vision. This potentially opened up a much bigger opportunity than I had initially envisioned.

I learned more in that one hour than I had in countless hours of training and studying coaching. While my nervousness and insecurity had held me back from talking with Peter directly about what I could offer, I was learning so much watching Jamie in action. His slowing down, asking questions and probing beyond the surface level issue had transformed the entire conversation.

However, it wasn't all smooth sailing. Peter told me afterwards that while he liked what Jamie was saying, he wasn't convinced he would use him for a large transformation project that would take the department on a journey to become trusted advisors. I had been feeling a little nervous about Jamie pitching such a potentially large project. I didn't want us to lose the opportunity by going for a more ambitious offering. However, it wasn't all bad news. The company had been looking for coach training for their executive team—people like Peter and his equivalents—and Peter saw that Jamie had extensive experience in this area as well.

When Jamie and I spoke about this I expressed the idea that what Peter really needed was more of an experience of what Jamie offered. That is, he needed to see the impact of the Three Principles approach before he could truly be open to a vision that both Jamie and I saw as possible. Jamie agreed he would put forward a proposal to coach the executive team and give Peter and his colleagues this experience. Peter accepted the proposal, and it seemed like a formality that things would go ahead. I was incredibly excited for this opportunity and continued to daydream possible outcomes for both the company, Jamie and, of course, myself.

And then market conditions changed. The price of a key commodity tanked, which meant the company abruptly fell under huge cost pressures. Just as Peter was getting sign-off for Jamie's proposal, the CFO issued an edict: all training programmes were to be stopped, and no new ones could begin. I admit this was challenging for me. I'd felt like I was so close to really getting my coaching career to take off and had pinned my hopes on this project—only for my bubble to burst. Even though I was seeing more and more clearly that my feelings were always a reflection of my thinking in the moment and not a reflection of my circumstances, I felt deeply disappointed. We'd had several meetings with and without Peter to get to this point. I had hoped that this could have led to a huge opportunity for Jamie and myself and create a stepping stone for me to move into coaching full-time. I also knew it would have had an extremely positive impact on everyone in the department.

As a side note, it seems that training and coaching support are some of the first things to be pulled when a company is in financial trouble. Of course, this can be counterproductive, because support is withdrawn when it's needed most. I've seen coaches do this as well as companies. There is often a temptation to reduce expenditure on coaching or training if your income drops but I have found this often leads to the opposite of what a coach hopes for. Rather than save money and have more profit, their income tends to drop further. I treat coaching and training as a non-negotiable cost in my coaching practice. In fact, it's better to call it an investment, because great coaching always returns more to me in so many ways, including financially, than I invest.

Jamie was once again more pragmatic and saw the situation for what it was: a great opportunity, and something we both learned a lot from. This helped me stay somewhat grounded about it. Looking back, that's exactly what it was, and once again the circumstances were not dictating my feelings no matter how much it looked like it. I took a breath, learned some valuable lessons and kept moving forward. The Three Principles understanding was so helpful during these early years of coaching because there were so many seeming highs and lows. Had I not had training in how the mind works, it would have been more of a challenge to deal with things when they didn't go well. This didn't mean I didn't have low moments, but I was able to take them in my stride far more easily because I knew the feeling was temporary.

38

Not Everyone Will Support You

One of my biggest fears around becoming more visible was getting negative reactions online. Intellectually, I could understand this fear was based on a collection of thoughts I had held onto. The thought of needing love and approval . . . The thought that I would be harmed without them . . . The thought that exaggerated the potential outcomes of misspeaking.

I hadn't really embodied the understanding that my fear would simply pass if I didn't hold onto it. However, I was going to get an opportunity to see this in action.

In early June 2014, I wrote a simple post on Facebook:

> We are only ever feeling our thinking (not our circumstances) moment to moment.
>
> Right now I'm listening to some instrumental music and feeling love, happiness, peace and enormous gratitude . . . and it's a really deep feeling.
>
> It's got nothing to do with the music, the weather, the day or anything outside of me.

A bunch of my Facebook friends really liked this, but one

person decided to challenge it. We went back and forth in the comments section around whether what I was expressing was true or not. It appeared to me like he was being very dismissive of what I wrote, and I feared looking foolish on social media. I still partly operated on the misunderstanding that in order to be a successful coach I needed to look impressive—or even like an expert.

Eventually I asked Jamie to comment on the post to 'back me up,' which he did, and that seemed to end the debate. However, when the metaphorical dust had settled, I saw that it had simply been a storm in a teacup. Something I had blown out of proportion. The person who disagreed simply had a different point of view. *This was only a problem because I wanted the whole world to be cheering me on.*

'Thank you for your wisdom, Ankush! You're so wonderful. How can we pay you?'

Thankfully, I had learned enough to know that I could keep moving forward despite people not agreeing with or supporting me. That realisation didn't make it any less comfortable at the time, but I didn't die. I wasn't even injured. It was only my ego which may have been dented a little (and that isn't the real me).

Looking back now, I can see that the person I went back and forth with in the comments section was asking some valid questions. At the time I could have used the exchange to improve my writing and my own understanding of my work. He had even reached out to me in 2012 at the start of my coaching journey to ask for advice to help someone he knew with an addiction.

I hadn't yet seen deeply enough to realise that this had been a chance to deepen a relationship rather than defend an opinion. It would also be many years before I realised that part of being more visible meant that there was nothing I could do to avoid *some* criticism. It came with the territory, and that was okay. If someone was harsh in their criticism, this often had more to do with them than it did with me. Isn't that the same offline as it is online?

39

Heading to Norway

In November 2014, Jamie Smart was going to deliver a weekend workshop in Norway alongside a successful relationship and dating coach called Morten Hake. I had met Morten briefly in 2012 at an annual summit he organised in Oslo, which he generously invited me to as a guest. We were Facebook friends through an online men's personal development community.

I knew the workshop itself would be a great experience. The trip would also offer a tremendous learning opportunity in that I could watch Jamie deliver a workshop to a group that was unfamiliar with his work.

I contacted Morten Hake and mentioned that I knew Jamie was coming over. Morten invited me to join and I jumped at the opportunity. This is what I had been hoping for. I asked Jamie if I could give him some company and take the same flight as him. He said yes, and suddenly I became his unofficial assistant. I had hours with him at the airport, on the flight and in Norway, not to mention seeing him in action in the workshop.

As mentioned, Jamie had shared the Three Principles understanding with Morten several months earlier. Morten had been so excited about the implications of this understanding that he threw or gave away all his other personal development books and created a podcast dedicated to sharing it with his significant following. He called it The New Paradigm Podcast.

Having Jamie on the podcast while they were together in Norway seemed too good an opportunity to miss. And as I was there too, Morten asked me if I would also like to be a guest, independent of Jamie. I was delighted and a little nervous. It was the first time I would be interviewed as a coach, and about the Three Principles.

I kept Mark Howard's advice in my mind: simply talk about what I knew. I may not have been an expert in coaching or in the Three Principles, but I was an expert in my own experience.

We didn't fix an exact time to record the podcast, but I followed up with Morten and made sure we recorded it before we left. I was persistent as I didn't want to miss this opportunity. When we did sit down, the recording time flew by, and the final podcast was over an hour long! Morten's enthusiasm helped: he was clearly excited to learn about the Three Principles and the implications for his work. He had been coaching for seven years, and in our conversation he spoke about how he'd never seen people change as fast as he had since being introduced to the Three Principles understanding. I talked about how much this work had changed me personally (especially my relationship with my family) and how life felt much easier to navigate than it had before.

Morten asked me what people usually came to me for, and I told him that there were actually two things. Firstly there was what they *thought* they were coming to me for; for example, help with a career change, connecting more deeply with their partner or perhaps to grow their business. Secondly, there was what they were *actually* looking for—aka to be happier, to know that they are okay and that they are enough.

Morten had given me a great introduction, saying he felt I had a very deep understanding of how life works, as well as a calm vibe, very open and non-judgemental. However, I still had judgemental thoughts about myself. I wasn't sure how I had performed on the podcast. My thinking would tend to revert to the old story of *I could do better*. Perhaps this was an artifact from my school reports where I was constantly told I was bright but lazy. But Morten assured me it had been a great conversation, once again showing me that my thinking wasn't a true reflection of reality.

This was one more step on my journey to becoming a professional coach. I had to face a fear that looked very real—recording an interview—and show myself that this fear didn't mean I couldn't take action. If only I had realised this earlier in my life, I would have been a lot more successful in my previous career.

Better late than never!

~

If you want to listen to my interview with Morten, you can find it here: https://creators.spotify.com/pod/show/morten-haugum-hake/episodes/NPP-001--How-Thought-Creates-Our-Reality-with-Ankush-Jain-e45j41/a-ag5kqi

40

A Referral that Never Went Anywhere

In June 2014 I received a message on Facebook out of the blue from a young man looking for a coach:

> Hi Ankush,
>
> I hope you don't mind me getting in touch. A friend of mine named Kayla King[5] suggested I reach out to you.
>
> I'm interested in speaking with a coach as I've hit a bit of a crossroads in my life and I'm not sure what kind of direction to take. I feel like I need to pursue a career change, but the thought of it is quite scary.
>
> I'd like someone to talk to so that I can be more effective in future plans.
>
> It would be great to hear how you might be able to help.
>
> Thanks,
>
> Kevin

This was wonderful. Kayla was a friend of mine whom I had

[5] Not her real name.

known for several years. She'd seen my posts on social media about coaching. Perhaps, I thought, my efforts at being more visible on social media were finally working. Kayla hadn't told me anything about Kevin but had suggested he reach out to me for coaching. Maybe this was the start of a whole stream of referrals coming my way and having my coaching business really take off. At this stage I had only created ten clients in total, and typically I was only working with one or two at any given time.

Kevin seemed very keen to discuss his situation further when I offered him a conversation. I was certain he was going to turn into my next paying client.

As usual, I sent him the hour-long audio by Jamie Smart that I sent all my potential clients to listen to before we spoke. This was now part of my system in having prospective clients turn into paying clients. I figured that the more value I gave up front, and the more a prospective client understood what my coaching was about, the more likely they were to hire me.

In our messages on Facebook, Kevin said he was looking for career coaching or guidance. I explained that my speciality was all-around state of mind and how that affects our decision making, performance and ability to connect with others. I particularly enjoyed helping clients get in touch with what they really want to do, which can bring up anxiety for them. It's a strange phenomenon but a common one that you might relate to. People often feel more comfortable in a career which feels safe (even if you might be made redundant at any point), but the thought of switching careers to something that truly lights them up can bring up fears and self-doubt. In response, Kevin seemed even more keen to speak.

During our first conversation, which we set up straight after I got back from Norway, we explored what Kevin was struggling with, his challenges at work and his experiences to date. He'd already had one career change, and he was still only in his twenties. I started to see that Kevin's issue wasn't about finding his purpose or finding the career that lit him up. He was, in fact, operating under the misunderstanding that the right job or career would make him feel fulfilled and happy. This was the same misunderstanding he'd had years before, which had led to his first career change. After that switch, he'd enjoyed his new career for a while, but eventually the same feelings of discontent returned.

I could relate to this. I had spent much of my own life chasing a good feeling or running away from uncomfortable or unpleasant feelings. At work I would avoid stepping too far out of my comfort zone into another role which could have advanced my career—out of fear of performing badly in the new role. In my personal life I was always searching for the right woman to make myself feel fulfilled and happy. At home I constantly felt my parents were the cause of my stress and anxiety. It took many years to realise that all of my feelings were a reflection of my thinking and not my job, partner or parent.

I knew it sometimes took a bit of time for this realisation to hit, so I set up another call with Kevin for a week after the first and sent him another couple of Jamie Smart's audios. I figured this would help him see what I was pointing him to; if he saw this, I knew it would turn his challenge on its head.

However, by the time of our second meeting he hadn't yet listened to either audio. This was a red flag, but I was so keen to create him as a client that I didn't ask him about it. I thought that if I challenged him, I would upset him, he wouldn't like me, and he wouldn't sign up as my client.

I hadn't realised that clients didn't sign up to *like me*—they wanted me to *help them*. Looking back, it would have been far more helpful to Kevin if I had enquired about why he hadn't yet listened to either audio, and explore that.

Kevin asked what I charged and as soon as I said £2,500 for 3 months, I saw his face drop in shock. He told me that the fee was far more than he had expected and that he would struggle to pay me that kind of money.

Because I'd heard coaches talk about how money is never the real reason for why a prospective client won't sign up, I offered Kevin a third conversation, and I asked him to make sure to listen to the audios I'd sent him. A couple of days before our call he asked—without offering a reason—if he could reschedule. I agreed, but this was another red flag, and I was too insecure to raise it with him. I felt like things were tenuous, and I was thinking that if I were ever going to convert him into a paying client, I had to have him like me. I didn't want to rock the boat!

I had learned from listening to Dr Mark Howard, how important having rapport with a client was, but that didn't mean that I had to be passive and avoid contentious questions. I could have real, deep connection and rapport with someone and create strong agreements with them. I could challenge a client or prospective client in a loving way in order to help them. Holding back wasn't helping them or me. Rapport is important in a coaching relationship because it allows coaches to be direct, to address blind spots the client may not realise they have and to challenge a clients' thinking—but have it be heard as being in support of the client. Part of the skill and art of coaching is having a conversation about a topic that may seem difficult or uncomfortable but without the client feeling judged. In this case, I could have explored where else in his life Kevin agreed to things and then didn't do them. Was this a pattern that was playing out elsewhere, and, if so, what was the implication that he might not be seeing?

On our third call Kevin still hadn't listened to the two audios (third red flag) but he seemed more than happy to keep speaking to me. My gut told me that even if I kept our conversations going it was still unlikely to lead to him becoming a paying client. So at the end of our call I told him that I was here if he needed me, and that he knew where to find me. A month later, I sent him message on Facebook with a link to a resource that I felt could be beneficial for him to watch, and he never even read the message.

I was seeing yet again that not everyone would become a client of mine. It was also becoming more clear that I didn't need to be liked by everyone, and this shouldn't be my goal anyway. While I was improving my system for speaking to prospective clients, it was still evolving. I had assumed I could either be liked or be obnoxious but I had yet to see that there was a whole ocean in between the two, and there were many other ways to be present with and support clients.

I've had many clients tell me over the years that something I said annoyed them (or sometimes stronger words) but that I was right and they were thankful I'd said what I said. I never veer towards obnoxious or unkind, but from love I can ask pointed questions like, 'What if your spouse is right?' or 'What is the gold in this situation?'

In summary, being a professional coach means putting helping the client as a higher priority than the consideration of what they might think of me.

41

Starting My Podcast

My experience with Morten Hake inspired me to create my own show. I felt that I could also interview various people about the Three Principles, with resultant benefits for myself and others.

Firstly, I wanted more resources to share with potential clients of mine, and some of the content that was available at the time would not have resonated with me. Not because it was wrong, but because the language often used in Three Principles-based content was more spiritual, and I thought this might turn some people off before they even started exploring it.

I believed I could create content aimed at people brand new to the Three Principles, and which would open them up to the power of this work. In some existing Three Principles content, the practical applications of the understanding weren't as obvious. This is part of why I later wrote my first book, *Sweet Sharing: Rediscovering the REAL You*, as I noticed that sometimes people exploring the Three Principles would overlook the practical implications they pointed to (as I had when I began my exploration). I decided I wouldn't even use the words 'Three Principles' without explaining them first. I would instead assume that anyone listening to the interview had no prior knowledge of this understanding.

Secondly, I realised I was more drawn to content on particular topics rather than listening to people speaking more generally about the Three Principles or coaching. I asked myself: What topic would *I* want to know more about?

The answer was easy: relationships. One thing I had noticed about all the wonderful Three Principles teachers I'd met so far was that they all seemed to have really loving marriages. In fact, those words don't really do their relationships justice. They seemed to have marriages where they were still in the honeymoon phase even after thirty or forty years. This was unusual and I, perhaps a little selfishly, wanted to know what they knew about creating successful relationships. I had just started dating a young lady and I didn't have the best track record in this area.

I also realised that the majority of Three Principles teachers and mentors were in their sixties and seventies. They had incredible knowledge and wisdom to share, but who knew how much longer they would be around for? I wanted to play my part in capturing their wisdom for posterity as much as anything else. This was something I felt I could do.

Finally, I believed that if I created content for others, it would get my name out into the world and help me create coaching clients for myself. I didn't know exactly how that would work, but again, I didn't want to overthink it. I just wanted to take the next step.

I decided to keep the title of the podcast simple and call it *The Relationship Series*. I reached out to a couple of colleagues who were doing the Clarity Practitioner Programme with me. I asked if they would be open to being interviewed, and they said yes.

It turned out to be so simple. I had no idea about how to interview people well, so I consulted the tool that always has the answer: Google. Within minutes I was listening to a short clip with veteran English broadcaster, Jeremy Paxman, who was seen as an excellent interviewer known for giving politicians a hard time on his show. He perhaps wasn't the *exact* role model I was looking for, but I learned something very important from him: always ask the question that the audience would ask. That really stuck with me. Rather than asking questions to my guests as Ankush Jain the coach, I imagined asking questions as someone who had no idea about me, coaching or the Three Principles.

I wasn't familiar with the technology to create a podcast but I had help. Two of my former clients were incredibly supportive of my work; Henk Kok and Cory Stephen. We had already created a few pieces of content for a men's group we were all in. They made it easy for me to get started because they took care of the recording and took the raw audio and turned it into a podcast. All I really needed was an internet connection. They not only turned the audio into a final podcast—they also supported me in getting it online. I would later hire Krystian Matusik to handle all of this for me. I knew it would take me a while to figure it out if I did it all on my own and I likely wouldn't be as good at it as someone else who did it for a living.

I realised pretty quickly that I had been playing it safe with regard to my guests. I wasn't asking Three Principles teachers who I felt were a 'big deal'. So I challenged myself to do this, reasoning that the worst they could say was no. I started with those with whom I already had a relationship: Jamie Smart, Dr Keith Blevens, Dr Dicken Bettinger, Rudy Kennard and Elsie Spittle. They all said yes! From then on I let invitees to the show know that these 'big names' had already been interviewed by me, which I felt would make it easier for them to say yes.

I hadn't yet seen that the show was *not* going to suddenly create a lot of clients for me. But I did learn a lot about interviewing, creating content and simply taking the next step in building my practice. Also, importantly, being in conversation with so many veteran Three Principles teachers deepened my understanding immensely. I often asked the questions that *I* wanted to know the answer to, and which I felt would also serve anyone listening. In this way, I became more impactful in my own work. In the longer term, this contributed significantly to helping me create more clients.

There was also a wonderful and unexpected side effect of this project. My father became the most avid listener of the podcast. In a way that was the most important outcome for me because—if he liked it and it was in some way deepening my relationship with him—I felt like it meant I was on the right path.

42

Signing Up for the London Intensive with Rich and Steve

I still hadn't signed up for coaching with Steve Chandler. I kept going back and forth in my mind about hiring him. It felt like a big decision, because it seemed I was hanging my hopes of building a successful coaching practice on hiring the right coach. While I'd had some successes, the possibility of actually being able to quit my job and go full-time into coaching felt quite distant.

I had told Steve both at the end of our call and in messages afterwards, that I wanted to hire him. My fear, however, was that I would pay him thousands of dollars and not end up much further along in my coaching career. I told myself that he was very different from my Three Principles-based mentors, and this made me question whether or not he was the right coach for me.

At the same time, I wasn't *looking* for someone like my Three Principles mentors. In hindsight, it would have been better to simply be honest and direct with Steve about my concerns. At the time, however, I tried to save face by simply telling him I was going to sign up soon. That is, I avoided having a direct conversation for fear of upsetting 'an authority figure'—a pattern I'd engaged in for most of my life.

I then got an opportunity that helped me with my decision. In early April 2014, Rich Litvin sent an email to his list announcing that he was delivering a weekend intensive for coaches with Steve Chandler. Normally these were held in U.S. cities, but this one was in London. I jumped at the opportunity. Now I could meet Rich and Steve in person for the first time. I'd get a deeper experience of Steve before making a decision to hire him—without even catching a flight.

One thing that stood out to me almost immediately was that while the intensive wasn't taking place until July, I started receiving email content and resources from Rich and Steve's team designed to help me grow as a coach as soon as I signed up in April. Many were resources that they were selling separately to others or which were unavailable to the public. They weren't playing around when it came to service and going above and beyond expectations. I made a commitment to myself to go through all the resources before the intensive because I wanted to maximise my investment.

By the time, the dates rolled round I felt like I had already received my money's worth. The 'bonus' resources were really that good, and I had seen the topic of service in a deeper way, which I was already implementing in my own practice.

As far as I was concerned, I'd already received a return on my investment in the intensive, but then Rich and Steve shared that the legendary coach Steve Hardison had been convinced to attend. Steve Hardison had coached Steve Chandler for well over a decade (and Rich Litvin for a year).

He was the guy behind the guy!

Steve Hardison charged $150,000 for a year of coaching with him at that point in time. That just boggled my mind. I would have paid for the intensive just to meet him. Needless to say I was looking forward to the weekend.

One of the great things about Facebook is that before the intensive I was able to connect with other coaches who were also attending. Many of them were flying in from the States or Europe to attend. A few of us arranged to meet at the Satay House Malaysian restaurant in the Paddington area for dinner—another opportunity I immediately seized upon. I wanted to extract every single morsel of value from this experience. If successful coaches were meeting up, I wanted to be there.

I ended up sitting next to a coach called Billie Allen, with whom I'd connected a few months earlier on Facebook. The group were talking about travelling and languages, and at one point I blurted out that I was no good at learning languages. It was the sort of self-deprecating remark I would occasionally make in social situations so that people might like me more—because it made me look humble. It was part of a pattern of playing small which I had done my whole life.

In truth, not being good at languages was a negative belief about myself that I had held onto since my school days, despite eventually getting an 'A' in my French GCSE exam (a standardised test you take at age sixteen).

At first I didn't think much about this comment, which would have gone unnoticed in a typical social setting. But I wasn't in a typical social setting; I was in the company of great professional coaches, and the topic of conversation was *coaching*. Billie immediately pulled me up on the remark.

Ankush: 'I'm no good at languages.'

Billie: 'Is that true?'

'What do you mean?'

'Not being good at languages is a belief, not a fact. When you say you are no good at languages you are hypnotising yourself to believe that you are no good at languages.'

I stared at her, dumbfounded.

She rightly saw my statement as transparently untrue and unnecessarily limiting. I was a little taken aback at her directness, but immediately saw she was spot on. She helped me see that if I kept telling myself I was no good at learning languages, then that's exactly what I would experience.

I hadn't seen the irony of speaking this thought out loud and thinking it was truth—and not just a thought or a belief, but a permanent part of who I was. Billie calling me out on it helped me see that it was a complete misunderstanding of that part of myself. This was ironic for a coach like me whose work was to help clients shine a light on their beliefs and thoughts and help them disconnect that thinking from who they are. It was *especially* ironic in the context of my company at dinner.

I never forgot Billie's comment; in fact, it's stayed with me as a profound recognition of how even innocent remarks often highlight our blind spots. This wasn't just about learning languages but how we can misuse language and thought to create limiting realities for ourselves.

Here I was, not even having begun the intensive yet, and I was experiencing wonderful insights. I was in the company of coaches of a different calibre from many of whom I'd interacted with up to that point. If the attendees were this good, I reasoned, the next two days with Rich and Steve would be incredible.

I wasn't mistaken.

That experience changed how I listen, especially with my clients, but also with myself. I've developed a sharp ear for throwaway sentences because I've learned they often contain the doorway to a breakthrough. When I catch myself or others using limiting language disguised as casual conversation, I remember Billie's gentle but direct challenge. This is something my clients can attest to.

The intensive also taught me something deeper about service. Rich and Steve's approach of serving from the moment someone signs up, rather than waiting for an official start date, became a lens through which I viewed all my interactions. I started asking myself: How can I serve this person right now, regardless of whether they've paid me anything? Or how can I have a coach make their money back from their investment in my school before we formally begin?

These weren't just business lessons but life lessons that transformed how I showed up in the world. And they started before the actual intensive had even begun.

43

The London Intensive, Day 1

I woke up on Saturday 19th July feeling excited. This was not a normal weekend but one that would have a huge impact on my coaching career and life. After weeks of emails with bonuses and logistical details, and after the wonderful dinner with some attendees the night before, it was finally time to meet some of my coaching heroes in person and experience what Steve Chandler called 'the LIVE version of the Prosperous Coach' book he had written with Rich Litvin.

I felt a buzz of energy as I walked into the venue in Paddington, London for the Independence Intensive. As I received my badge, I looked around, a little intimidated by the number of coaches, most of whom in my mind looked confident and secure in themselves. I had liked to think I was doing well and was a good coach, but deep down I was finding coaching a much more challenging profession than I had originally anticipated.

I recognised several of the coaches in the room. Some I'd met the night before, some I recognised from their Facebook profiles and others I knew from my training with Jamie Smart. However, I wasn't here to simply make more friends or just chat with existing ones; I wanted to maximise my learning, so I found a seat in the front row.

This approach was echoed by Rich Litvin right at the start. As he opened the day, he asked us to reflect on why were we there. What was the *real* reason? Many people had flown to London to attend this weekend, and he was encouraging us to get the most out of our investment of time and money. I knew straightaway why I was in the room. I had been on this coaching journey for twenty-two months, and while I had made progress, I wasn't creating clients at the rate I needed to turn coaching into a full-time career. And it wasn't really about money. I was drawn to coach in a way I had never been drawn to anything else in my life.

I was comforted by some words from Steve Chandler as he introduced Rich Litvin on Saturday. As well as acknowledging Rich as a wonderful former client of his, an amazing learner and someone he enjoyed writing with and learning from, he spoke about the inevitability of turning coaching into a career.

He said: 'If you stay on the path, no matter how slow you go, you will get there. It's only the distractions that stop people from succeeding. It's only the side roads.'

That was music to my ears and exactly what I needed to hear in that moment. All I needed to do was to stay on the path. That was it. No heroic leap out of my comfort zone was required. I could do this.

It became obvious over the course of the day that more than a few of the coaches in the room were doing very well financially. Many worked with business owners, entrepreneurs and other coaches. One coach had a billionaire client. My feelings of intimidation ramped up, but I also realised I could learn a lot from these people, so I spoke less and listened a whole lot more.

A few things really stood out from that first day. As well as having the opportunity to meet Steve Chandler—who was very funny—for the first time, I was surprised by one of his sessions. While he talked about how coaching had affected him personally, including his own journey with drugs, alcohol and addiction, the one session that grabbed me most was where he shared something he called 'The Ladder of Consciousness.' He used this in his coaching; it was an idea he had adapted from the philosopher Colin Wilson.

Steve drew a picture of a ladder and wrote 'spirit' at the top and 'death' at the bottom. In between on the rungs, moving up, were things like 'depression', 'fear' and 'anger', moving up to 'enthusiasm', 'inspiration', 'joy' and 'peace'. All of us, he said, operate less effectively when we're lower down the ladder, and more effectively the higher up we go—that is, towards a higher level of consciousness. What he was pointing to was that the inner worlds of both coach and client are as important as the outer worlds of strategies, technique and tools.

While this is not the exact same idea as the Three Principles, the concept is more aligned to them than I had first realised. An understanding like this was important to me in hiring a coach. One of the reasons I'd been hesitant to hire Steve was that the Three Principles had become such an important part of my understanding and approach as a coach that I wanted to continue integrating it into my work moving forward. Now I understood even more of where Steve was coming from, and it resonated with me. At some point during Steve's session, I realised I was ready to hire him. In fact, at the end of the weekend I followed him out of the venue to let him know this as he jumped into a taxi.

At one point Rich Litvin said he had been tempted to save a particular exercise for the second day because he felt it was so good, and he wanted to end the weekend on a high note. However, he realised this would be holding back, so he delivered it on the first day.

(Unfortunately, even after reviewing my notes, I can't recall what the exercise was.) This really hit me, because it made me see I'd often hold back what I considered my 'best' coaching or my best resources from my clients or prospective clients so that I had something in my back pocket for them. I reasoned that if I gave them everything up front, I might not have 'the goods' later down the line. Rich's gesture helped me realise that this was not based on sound logic but instead a reflection of my fearful thinking—and something I didn't need to listen to.

I had acted the same way in my corporate job for as long as I could remember. I worked in a very target-driven field and I would never share how well I was doing with my boss, because I wanted to have a little wiggle room in case anything went wrong. I was even given feedback from my manager that I wasn't as forthcoming as another of my counterparts, but I had convinced myself I was simply acting prudently. This was yet another time where I saw that the insights that served my coaching business had far more universal application in my life than I had realised at first. In this case, holding back was not just unnecessary; in some respects it had been doing more harm than good.

Rich wasn't just forthcoming in sharing his 'best' throughout the day, he was really forthcoming about himself. He shared stories that were vulnerable. He shared how he struggled to make small talk with people, how his father had an incurable disease and how he can take things far too seriously (and how his wife reminds him what is important). This depth of sharing really impressed me, and through it I felt more connected to him.

Rich's vulnerability reminded me how tempting it is—especially as a coach—to want to put our best foot forward, to look like we've got everything figured out. After all, who wants to hire a coach whose life is falling apart? And yet, over the years I've seen how powerful it can be to let clients see the truth. I've learned to consciously share when things aren't going well, and what I'm learning through it. In my men's immersion, I'll often talk about facing the very same challenges my clients are bringing. In my school, some coaches assume I never struggle, that business is always easy for me. I make sure they leave knowing otherwise. Because yes, people do come to me to learn what I've figured out—but that doesn't mean I have it all handled all the time. That humanness, that realness, is part of what makes clients want to hire us. In a profession where we're so often taught to position ourselves as experts, I've come to see that the real power lies in being human.

44

The London Intensive, Day 2

The other highlight of the weekend happened on Day 2. I met The Ultimate Coach, Steve Hardison, for the first time. This was something special. We were all told to be on time—the doors would be locked once he started his session. This guy meant business!

The first thing I noticed was how tall he was, and how perfect his teeth were. I have to admit, I judged him in part based on this! My mind put him in the category of brash American coaches who charge a lot of money and have people buy into their cult of personality. However, I was so impressed by Steve Chandler and Rich, and they spoke so highly of Steve Hardison, that I was willing to believe I was missing something. I am so glad I did.

I didn't realise it at the time, but my judgement of Hardison was a reflection of my own self-judgement. I didn't like the way I looked, and so I would often judge others for the way *they* looked. I had struggled to make money as an entrepreneur (both as a coach and at a previous business running networking events), so I judged others who were making what I considered a lot of money. I struggled to speak about love because I had never loved myself, and while I had felt love for others, it had always been conditional. It would be years later before I finally saw these judgements for what they really were: a mirror reflecting my self-image.

Hardison spoke about how much he loved his clients, including Steve, Rich and another coach in the room: JP Morgan. He didn't just give this lip service; he really spent his time on it—something I wasn't expecting. He powerfully acknowledged them in a way that I had never heard anyone acknowledge another human being. Here was someone who coached the best in the world, including politicians, CEOs, sports stars and other world-class coaches . . . and he was talking about love—not new techniques, strategies for client acquisition or how to make more money. Here again I'll admit I had some judgemental thinking come up, but the more I listened to him, the more it seemed he meant what he said. Not only that, but I reasoned that if he really loved his clients in this way, and this much, I could see why they paid him. I reflected how I had never met anyone in my life who loved me and was as committed to me as Hardison was to his clients. While my teachers, parents and managers had supported and guided me, I always felt like it was not enough. I craved praise and approval from them, because ultimately I didn't feel that for myself.

Hardison was both speaking about and demonstrating a way of being beyond simple client satisfaction or delivering great service. It was clear that he was 100 percent committed to his clients, like a mother is to her newborn child.

While in my mind I was judging Hardison for talking about love, *he* wasn't holding back at all. He wasn't worried about what any of us were thinking about him. This again was something I could learn from—not only in my coaching but my life as well. I had received feedback in my corporate job after completing my graduate training that while I was professional and good at what I did, they wanted to see more of 'me' and not just my professional image. And yet here I was doing the same thing in my coaching career.

Presenting myself in a certain way to appeal to people, versus sharing whole-heartedly, without concern. This was another area in which the coaching profession was continuing to challenge me in ways I had not expected.

Looking back, I can see how much of what I witnessed in Steve Hardison that day has become a part of how I now show up for my own clients. I never forgot the way he spoke about love. He opened the door to me not just appreciating my clients but truly loving them. Today, whether I'm leading my coaching school, working one-on-one, or running my men's immersion, I aim to bring that same depth of presence and love. I used to think I had to prove my value through tools, techniques, and strategies. But now I know: it's who I *am* with my clients that matters most. That, more than anything else, is what transforms lives.

45

Not Taking No for an Answer

The morning after the intensive I sent Steve Chandler the following message on Facebook.

> Hi Steve,
>
> Let me know when you are back in the US and available for a call. Some things have changed since we spoke a few months ago. At the time I was really up in my head, trying to go at a hundred miles an hour. You were right. You hinted that I didn't need a coach. I slowed down and didn't hire anyone.
>
> I really enjoyed the London intensive. I got a lot from it. I'm now clearer on what I want. I'm passionate about coaching. I genuinely love it. I've never enjoyed something (in terms of career) as much as I enjoy coaching. Nothing even comes close. It's so rewarding when I know I can change a person's life. It could be small or it could literally alter the direction of their life.
>
> I was really impacted by how Steve Hardison takes this to such a deep level.

Where I am right now is that I have two paying clients. I'm having conversations weekly with potential clients—reaching out to people I can serve. I am networking with other coaches, and opportunities come up. I have created a small community of powerful men on Facebook whom I serve, and I'm looking to create some content to share by interviewing other coaches.

Where I could use support is on improving my conversion ratio, as I have so few hours to devote to new conversations (because I still work full-time). I'd like to maximise the impact of my introductory sessions, or more often have them with people who are likely to turn into clients. At the moment it is a scattergun approach.

Secondly, I'd love some support and to hear your opinion on all the activities I'm doing and the time I'm spending on them. At the moment I can see that conversations get clients. So I could stop all other activity and just get into conversations. On the other hand I enjoy networking and building community, and I've seen it raise my profile as a coach, even amongst family and friends, some of whom now ask for advice. It has also increased my confidence and pushed me out of my comfort zone.

I'm being very open, because if we work together I'd really want it to be a good fit for us both. I know your time is valuable and you are one of the most experienced and top-rated coaches out there, and from my view I am so committed to coaching. I have never been so committed to anything in my life.

I look forward to hearing back from you.

Ankush

I was excited and nervous as I waited for Steve's response but I didn't hear back from him. I knew he was flying back to the U.S. from London, and that he was a busy guy, so a couple of weeks later I followed up with him via email to see if he had received my Facebook message

I was gutted that evening to receive the following email:

Dear Ankush,

So SORRY I have been away from my email . . . My coaching calendar is over-booked at the moment and I am fully focused on developing the upcoming Advanced Client Systems course. If you register for that it will move you forward faster (financially) than coaching with me personally would.

If you're open to that, I'll add in a few personal coaching sessions too, but I'm not taking any coaching clients until that course is over.

Love and light,

Steve

I had missed my chance to work with Steve on a one-to-one basis. I looked at the link for the course he mentioned and I realised I would not be able to do it because of the amount of time off I would need to attend the in-person portions. I had already taken off a significant amount of time for the live training on Jamie Smart's Trainer Training programme and simply didn't have the holidays left. Feeling glum, I emailed Steve back while walking through

Waterloo train station, telling him why I couldn't do his programme and ended it with:

> Thank you for getting back to me and I wish you every success with your programme. If there is an opportunity to coach with you again in the future, let me know, or please let me know when I should reach out to you again (sounds like after May next year).

I took two steps forward and felt a surge of energy inside of me. I had finally worked out who I wanted to coach me and I wasn't going to just let one email get in the way. I immediately emailed Steve again:

> I just sent the last email, and if I have learned anything from you and Rich it is: if you don't ask, you don't get. You will probably say no but I'll ask anyway. Is there anything that would make you reconsider taking me on as a client? If the answer is still no, could you offer me any advice as to where I could go to improve the monetisation of my coaching over the coming months?

I had no idea what he would say, and I didn't want to offend Steve but I knew I had to ask. Half an hour later, Steve emailed me back and agreed to take me on as a private client for six months as long as I attended the final weekend of his Advanced Clients Systems school. I didn't have all the money in my business account to pay him immediately, but I was in, and I told him so, and that I would find the money. To say I was excited was an understatement. I had no idea at the time what a great decision I had just made.

46

My First Event Didn't Go as Planned

In December 2013 I met up with a fellow Three Principles coach who lived close by called Janet Lindsay (now called Janet Rhynie). We were catching up and talking about the impact the Three Principles had had on our lives. I mentioned to her that this understanding had completely changed my dating life. For years I had believed my thoughts that I could never truly be happy until I found the one woman who would 'complete me'. Perhaps this was a side effect of watching romantic Bollywood movies every weekend with my parents while growing up.

While I may have appeared confident, I was incredibly insecure when I met a woman I liked. My mind would race as I analysed whether she could be the right one for me. If I thought she was, my mind would then tie itself in knots trying to figure out how *not* to mess it up. It's no surprise that I wasn't that successful with women.

However, as I started to explore the Three Principles I understood more and more that I was only and always feeling my thinking, including when I was with a woman I was attracted to. The pretty girl opposite me on a date wasn't responsible for my anxiety. And so things started to change. I was much calmer when speaking with women. I took myself less seriously and started to enjoy being single much more.

I also noticed that the women I spoke with were often doing a version of what I had been doing. They were up in their heads, analysing whether we would be a good fit, and not simply present and in the moment. As a single guy, I realised it would be a lot more interesting to be on a date with a woman who was present rather than in her head.

I shared this with Janet, who mentioned she had a friend who got stuck in her thoughts with men the way I had been doing with women. As we continued talking we came up with the idea of doing an in-person event for women in Birmingham on the topic.

After some deliberation we decided to call it 'Finding Mr Right', and we aimed it at women from the South Asian community. I knew there was a lot of cultural thinking there around getting married, settling down and finding the right partner, and that a Three Principles approach could offer new insights and support in this area. It seemed like a brilliant idea, and I even enrolled another coach, Naila Darr, to join us.

I knew I needed to let people know I was doing this, and I was petrified about what they might think. Nonetheless, I didn't give into my fearful thinking; I moved forward and posted the following on my Facebook wall in June 2014:

> After five months of planning and what started as a conversation over coffee, I'm happy to say that tickets are now on sale for the 'Finding Mr Right' event I'm facilitating with Janet R Lindsay and Naila Darr in Birmingham on the 5th of July. This is for Asian women who are still looking for love. We are really excited to share our insights with women, which will be different from any other advice out there.

Now I just needed to wait for the signups.

And then my worst fear came true. My female cousin left a comment almost immediately:

> Is this a ploy to find a woman for yourself!!?

This was quickly followed by a comment from a female friend from university:

> Ha! Was about to say the same—lots of single Asian (and dare I say desperate!) women in a room with you, Ankush?!

I wanted the ground to swallow me up. What would people think of me when I was getting these comments on my post? I was tempted to delete them and pretend they had never been posted but I gathered myself and realised this was actually an opportunity to explain what I was really up to.

I replied to my cousin:

> Haha. I thought I'd get some responses like that. I had the idea for this event last year as I saw the pressure that single people in our community get to settle down. I know for me it felt like a lot of pressure, and I put this pressure into every interaction/relationship I got into. Underneath it all was a belief that I would never really be happy, or that I wouldn't be complete in some way if I didn't find someone to settle down with.
>
> I've spent the last two years training and getting certified as a coach. I have many clients with whom I

> work one to one, but this was something I was really drawn to put on as it was close to my heart. Partly because I can see what happens when people end up getting married believing the other person will make them happy. Instead I now see that happy people have happy relationships and happy marriages.
>
> I couldn't do this on my own, so I found two great (and very experienced) facilitators to help pull it together. Janet and Naila have over twenty years of experience each. Together we are looking to put on a great event. If you know anyone who could benefit, please pass along the details.

As it turned out, I hadn't needed the ground to swallow me up, I had simply needed to be truthful. Janet and Naila chipped in, and my cousin even suggested that she would pass on the details to some friends of hers who were single.

Great! I had handled my worst fear and now we could get on with delivering a transformational experience for the attendees. Except no-one signed up. I paid for online advertising, reached out to radio stations and spent many hours getting the copy perfect for the web page. However, there were crickets. Eventually we had one young lady sign up; she was a friend of my sister's, recently divorced, and I had previously passed on some audios from Jamie Smart to her which I thought would be helpful.

Janet and I decided to go ahead and run the event even though we only had one paying client, and we lost money on it. Naila understandably bowed out as she didn't live close by. However, I knew I would learn something from the experience. The young lady who showed up told us she would have cancelled if she'd known she was the only person attending the event, but by the end of the day she was really glad she had come.

One big takeaway for me was that that having a great idea isn't enough to have people pay for an event. I spoke to Jamie about it afterwards and he hit the nail on the head. He told me that my clients were signing up with me for one-to-one coaching because they often had a relationship with me, or I was part of online communities where I was well-regarded. This event, while being a good idea, was aimed at an audience where I didn't have a community of people who knew me as a coach and valued what I said. This was an invaluable but hard lesson which helped me sell out many events in the future. I now create events for people who are already in my network and community and with whom I have a good reputation. I encourage other coaches to do the same and not try to market coaching or programmes to people who have no knowledge of the coaches themselves.

Side note: Years later the only attendee of the 'Finding Mr Right' event would become a client on my women's immersion, which further highlights that this really is a relationship business. People tend to hire coaches with whom they have an existing connection. This doesn't mean they've had to have been a good friend, but they need some experience of you to trust that you will deliver what you are saying you will.

47

The Importance of Commitment and My Calendar

On the evening of 29th of August 2014, I had my first paid coaching call with Steve Chandler. I was nervous, scared and excited all rolled into one. I sat at my desk in the bedroom of my flat near London Waterloo station with my notebook and pen at the ready. I didn't quite know what to expect when I called him on Skype, but I was ready. Steve started off by asking me if there were any questions I had around some existing clients. We were straight to business, and I liked this.

I told him about a client who had been a no-show on a recent call, and when I brought up the importance of keeping agreements with him, he told me I was being rigid. I hadn't known how to respond to this.

Steve told me he wouldn't work with a client who didn't keep their agreements. I immediately lodged this in my brain, because the truth was that I wasn't always 100 percent my word, and I had been known to break agreements on occasion. This was especially true with being on time to places. I used to hate being early to a meeting and just waiting around for someone else.

I had just convinced Steve to take me on as a client, and the last thing I wanted was for him to end our agreement, so I made a mental note to always be my word with Steve, especially being on time for our calls.

Steve coached me around how to help my client transform his relationship with commitment. As he did so, I took everything in as if it applied to myself as well. He explained that if my client's word didn't mean anything to him, then his self-esteem was low. He didn't trust his own words.

This hit home for me. Back then I really didn't put a lot of value on my own word. There were more times than I would care to admit when I had committed to something and then not followed through with it. So Steve's perspective on this was an incredible gift, and it would go on to change my life. From this interaction on, I determined that my word would take on greater importance and increase my effectiveness in the world.

This wouldn't be the last time this happened. I soon realised that I could always learn from my clients' problems and challenges. There is a synergy in many conversations between coach and client that can help both grow. I find the best coaches apply everything they share with a client to themselves too.

Steve asked me how I typically spent my week with regards to coaching time. No one had ever asked this of me before. I looked at my online calendar and talked him through what I was typically up to. That week I had one client call, a call with a colleague and a recording slot for my podcast. I was also attending a training and had a call with a prospective client. The previous week I'd had a recording slot for a podcast, a call with a colleague and one call with a prospective client. This was pretty typical for me.

He introduced me to a new idea, first explaining that there was nothing inherently wrong with what I was doing (which was a relief). But he said we could break down my activities in relation to how quickly they would lead to income for me. Some of what I was doing was quite likely to lead to someone paying me. Other activities *might* lead to that in the medium term. And of course some might never generate money—or might only do so in the long-term.

For example, speaking with my colleagues in the coaching world wasn't likely to bring in more income in the short-term. It might eventually lead to clients, or to creating joint programmes with them that generated money, but since many of my colleagues were in a similar boat to my own, this wasn't likely at that time. Similarly, while I was enjoying creating my podcast on relationships, it wasn't creating any queries for coaching with me. Yes, I was building my skills as an interviewer and gaining visibility amongst people who could become clients in the future, but it wasn't likely that someone would listen to me interviewing another person on the topic of relationships and then want to hire me. If anything, it was more likely to lead to a client for the person I was interviewing.

Then Steve pointed out the obvious point that I had been missing until then: *If I focused on activities that were likely to bring in income in the short-term, I would make more money.*

This seemed almost too obvious. I'll admit it might even have felt a little 'too' ordinary and commonsensical. I don't remember if I was impressed or underwhelmed, but I couldn't deny the simple and inescapable logic. How had I missed this?

Steve explained that in the coaching profession, one of the best ways for me or any coach to create income was to have a conversation with someone who could turn into a client. So, if instead of one call a week with a prospective client, I could increase it to two and thereby double my opportunities to create paying clients. Simple.

Now, if I was limited on time, which was true because I was still working full-time at my day job, I could reduce the amount of time spent on activities that were unlikely to lead to income in the short-term. These included creating audio content and my podcast, as well as networking with colleagues. That time would then be freed up for prospective client conversations.

I could even look at how much personal development I was doing—meaning trainings, readings, seminar, etc.—which again wasn't 'bad.' But could I replace an hour of reading with an hour of conversation with a prospective client? This was certainly something to test out.

Could making more money as a coach really be this simple? I soon found out that this advice—on our very first coaching call—wouldn't only be true for me in 2014, but would stay with me for years to come. It would also apply to my life beyond coaching. If I wanted to achieve any goal in life, the more time I spent on activities that contributed directly to the goal, the more likely I would be to achieve it, and in a shorter space of time.

Years later, when I work with coaches who want to increase their income, I often walk them through the same exercise Steve did with me that day. It's striking how often they come to the same realisation I did—that they're spending most of their time on activities that feel productive but don't actually create clients.

The shift from low-impact tasks, like posting generic content, to having real conversations with potential clients can be transformative. It certainly was for me, and I've seen it change the game for countless others.

48

An Insight to Quit My Job

In my second conversation with Steve he coached me around several things, including the approach of simply serving one person at a time until I filled my calendar and ways to follow up with prospective clients.

However, the biggest thing on my mind was that I was considering quitting my job, and I wasn't sure whether I should do it immediately or wait. Steve told me to let the understanding of when I should quit show up as a 'knowing' inside me. That is, I didn't need to figure it out; I would simply know when it was time.

Intuitively, this made a lot of sense to me. One of the Three Principles is called 'Mind'. My understanding of that Principle is that it is the energy of all things. You could call it a higher intelligence, a wisdom, that exists beyond thought, something that will always guide you. I believe this is what Steve meant by 'knowing': an understanding arising from a place of wisdom inside me. I may have called it 'innate inner wisdom'; others might call it 'intuition.' But I knew what he was pointing to.

A few nights later, I met up with my friend Leo Tran for dinner in London at a wonderful Lebanese restaurant near my apartment. Leo and I were both members of a men's personal development community focused on excellence in relationships and life. We had met a few years earlier and developed a great friendship and even attended a workshop together in Las Vegas in January 2013. I hadn't expected this dinner would lead to a life-changing insight. While eating some delicious 'mezze' (a selection of small, flavourful dishes) he started telling me that the leader of the men's community we were both part of had offered him a job in Bucharest, Romania, where he was based. The pay wasn't great, but accommodation would be provided, and he would receive a small sum of the equivalent of £100 per week.

A few things suddenly dawned on me. Firstly, this could have been me. That is to say, I could have been as valuable to this leader as Leo was, perhaps even more so in the sense that I had been a member of the same community for longer, attended more of his trainings and had the benefit of being trained as a coach. If I had wanted to, I could have created this same opportunity for myself. In fact, this leader and I had already loosely discussed the possibility of my helping him, but I had always been afraid to lose my corporate income.

Secondly, while the salary was low, it was more than enough to live in Bucharest, which was far more affordable than London. In fact, you'd be hard pressed to spend *more* than £100 a week in Bucharest after your accommodation was paid for, because everything was so cheap in Romania. I hadn't realised that the income I thought I needed was based on living in London. I could quit my job sooner if I moved somewhere cheaper.

Thirdly, I had enough savings to not need the salary. Accommodation could be found for around £300 per month, including utilities, and even if I needed an extra £100 a week to live, that meant I would only need around £8,500 a year to live there. I could live off my savings comfortably for a very long time in Bucharest while building my coaching practice.

It suddenly became very clear. I had been holding back on quitting my job because I didn't feel comfortable that I was earning enough to sustain my living costs in London. However, I didn't *need* to live in London. I also didn't even need to live in Bucharest. I could quit my job and focus completely on coaching without going broke!

The knowing that Steve had mentioned suddenly appeared. All the same, this felt like a big step, so I didn't want to make any rash decisions. I sat with this knowing and decided to speak to a few people whom I trusted to see if it made sense. I spoke to my girlfriend; I didn't think she would be supportive of my quitting a safe corporate job, and yet she was. She could see how passionate I was about coaching. I spoke to some colleagues at work whom I admired and looked up to, and they also said I could stay or leave, but if I ultimately wanted to leave and I had done my sums correctly, why wait? Most importantly, this 'feeling' didn't change, so ten days after first having the realisation that it was time to quit, I handed in my notice. I was surprised at how little anxiety, nervousness or fear I felt during those ten days, which really helped me make my decision.

My line manager, Eric, was surprised—to say the least. He asked me if I was sure, and whether I really knew what I was doing. I told him I did, and that I appreciated his concern and had not come to my decision lightly. I felt like he didn't quite understand why I would leave such a well-regarded company with great benefits, but he could sense my mind was made up. I then spoke to *his* manager, Laura, and relayed my desire to leave, and why. She was in charge of our team and had been the one who originally recruited me. She was also surprised. She had known I wanted to eventually pursue coaching as a career, but she hadn't expected me to leave so soon. I told her that I had reached a point where I couldn't do justice to both my career *and* my coaching practice, and I had given a lot of thought to which one I wanted to focus on.

Peter, the Director of our department, then spoke to me a few days later about taking a career break, but I realised I didn't want to play it safe. 'Safe' was just a thought, too. I could have stayed in my corporate job and been made redundant, despite my betting that it was the 'safe' option. It almost felt as if the universe was giving me plenty of options to change my mind, testing me to see whether I was really going to go through with it. However, the knowing that Steve had spoken about—or the 'innate wisdom', in Three Principles terminology—was guiding me.

I handed in my notice and agreed to leave at the end of 2014. I now had three months to ramp up my coaching practice and hit the ground running in January 2015. I was more energised than ever, and once again my whole world had changed after a single new thought: that I could quit my corporate job much sooner and focus on coaching full-time because I didn't need to live and stay in London.

49

The Birth of My Men's Work

After the difficulties I encountered filling my first event for women, I thought back to the feedback I had received from Jamie. He said the group had been a struggle to fill because the target clients (young Asian women) were not part of any community I had created or in which I was well-regarded. Most of my private clients—my community—were similar to me. They were typically men in their twenties or thirties who were into personal development. They often spent money on coaches, courses and seminars. If I were to run an event again, I saw it made sense to do it for the same kind of audience.

The following month, something seemingly unrelated happened. Rich Litvin announced on Facebook that he was hosting something called the Ninety-Day Money Game. The idea was that you pick a number—an amount of money you would like to create during the ninety days—and then you triple it. This then becomes the amount of money you make in proposals to clients—that is, when you have a conversation with someone and tell them what it costs to work with you for a given coaching package.

This felt super-edgy to me, but I was up for it. I joined the private Facebook group that Rich had set up. Each day, he would offer a new challenge. Early on, one such challenge was to make two proposals that we knew someone would say no to. The idea was to get over the fear of getting a no and not having that hold you back from making a proposal.

I sat down and thought of a wonderful opportunity for two of my former, and earliest, clients: Henk Kok and Cory Chiasson. They were helping me create online content and were also hugely supportive of my journey. I thought: *What could I could propose to them that would be really valuable?*

Cory lived in Canada and Henk lived in Holland. All of our coaching had been done online. The idea came to me to invite them both to the UK to spend the weekend with me, with the parks in London being our seminar room—and I also imagined they would love the idea but say no.

On a call that evening, I spoke to them both about my vision and told them what it would cost.

Ankush: 'Hey, guys. I had a great idea that I wanted to run by you both. You've both worked with me and seen some incredible results from our work. I was thinking, what would be a great way to take this to the next level? Well, I thought that you both could fly to London and spend a weekend here. We would walk through some of the parks in London and talk about where you're at, the challenges you're having in your life and where your thinking might be getting in the way. I would charge you £1,500 each. What do you think?'

There was silence for a few moments, which felt like a lot longer. Eventually Cory spoke:

'While that sounds great Ankush, I can't commit to the programme, I don't have the funds right now.

Henk: 'Me too. It does sound great, and I'm not in a position to make that kind of financial commitment.'

I sensed some palpable tension in the air.

I paused, and thanked them both. I told them they had helped me to achieve my goal of the day to get two no's. They both sighed with relief and it felt like the connection was restored between us. And then out of nowhere, a new thought popped up in my head. I suddenly suggested that we create a group programme for men in London, to take place over a weekend. Cory and Henk could help me fill it and then spend the weekend in London with me to help deliver it. In essence we could have a weekend together, without them paying a fee for the coaching.

They loved the idea, and we started to pull together what I called the 'Powerful Men's Intensive'. I decided to host it in my apartment in London, keep it capped at six participants and charge £600 per person. This would mean I wouldn't have any costs around hosting it, so it would be a very low-risk venture. I would host it over a weekend so there wouldn't be any need to take time off work.

The more I thought about this, the more it made sense. I could work with people at a lower price point than my private coaching, and this would make it available to folks who were unable or unwilling to pay those fees. However, I could still make the same money by having several people in a room at the same time.

In terms of content, I thought about what I wanted to share, and I realised there were two key things. I know that if you've read this far in the book, some of this will be familiar to you, but I feel a little repetition is excusable for at least two reasons. Firstly, the Three Principles understanding takes time to settle in, and secondly, in sharing these ideas again here I hope to show how my own understanding had deepened up to this point in my journey (and, of course, it continues to deepen).

The first thing I wanted to share was the fact that our feelings are a reflection of our thinking moment to moment. This had been a huge realisation for me, leading to dozens of powerful insights. I knew that if the participants got a glimpse of this, they too would have shifts in their own lives. In my mind this would have them show up more powerfully in the world. There were some exercises I had learned during my training with Jamie Smart which would really help me make this point.

This was important, because almost all humans in our society are conditioned to believe that our feelings are caused by something other than our thinking—for example, by how other people treat us and by situations, circumstances and life events. The consequence of believing this is a life of insecurity, fear, social paranoia, and anxiety about circumstances beyond our control. This results in a sped-up mind and poor relationships with others, hurt feelings and 'victim' living, where it feels as if life is happening *to* you, and you're powerless to do anything about it.

Neuroscience and advanced Positive Psychology studies have verified what Three Principle's founder Sydney Banks taught after his own spiritual awakening: other people and outside situations cannot 'make you feel' what you feel. This is a major shift in understanding—at the level of the one where people finally understood that the world was not flat. It changes our relationship to ourselves and the world.

The second thing I wanted to speak to the group about was our innate wisdom, or, stated more simply: trusting your gut. The topic was one I'd heard other men's coaches speak about, but I felt I had gained a deeper appreciation for it through the work I'd done with the Three Principles. The more I saw that my feelings were a reflection of my thinking moment to moment, the more my mind quieted down. From this perspective, I was able to tap into my gut in a way that I had never done before. It was as if the static on the radio had been cleaned up and everything came through more clearly.

I was very enthusiastic about this first event and started exuberantly posting on Facebook about it. Alas, this essentially amounted to spamming various groups as I became desperate to fill my own. This was neither well-received nor effective.

I needed to change my approach if I was going to make the event a success.

50

How I Filled My Intensive

I spoke with Steve Chandler about my approach. He advised me to slow down. He pointed out that posting on Facebook wasn't an intimate form of communication, and yet the event I was creating was extremely intimate.

He advised me to put my energy into having conversations as opposed to posting more online. So I asked myself, *Who would I like to be in the room?* Every time I did, a name popped into my head, and I reached out to that person.

Connecting with one person at a time was a *huge* game changer for me. I found, surprise, surprise, that the people I reached out to mindfully were far more open to having a conversation and joining the event than people I was spamming on Facebook.

Steve also shared the importance of selling all the spaces. He opened my eyes to the power of having no more spaces to offer. Limitation creates value, he told me. This wasn't manipulation but a simple fact. If people know that there are always spaces left, then there is less incentive to sign up. And in the case of this group, it served everyone to keep the numbers low in order to create greater intimacy and connection between attendees.

That made a lot of sense, especially when I reflected about my own behaviours when looking to attend an event or a programme. If spaces were genuinely limited and they always sold out, I'd be more likely to make a firm decision about whether I really wanted to attend.

Steve also advised me that once the group sold out, I could let the people who were still hesitating know this. If they would like, I could keep them in mind for the next time I ran the group.

Not only was this approach much more effective, it was also more fun. I love talking to people. I love having coaching conversations. I love helping people. I didn't need to do something else, like post on Facebook, to start helping people. I could start helping people while enrolling. In fact, this was the best enrolment strategy.

I learned that I was much better able to convey what the intensive was about in a conversation than through copy on a website. One on one I could become really enthusiastic about the intensive, but more importantly I could build rapport with the other person and come from a place of connection *first.*

This may sound like a kind of sales technique, but it was actually deeper than that. In conversation, I could see what the other person's challenges were. Then, if appropriate, I could connect those challenges with the transformation I believed would occur at the intensive. You could call it a more personalised sales approach, and it was all about being of the greatest service to the person I was speaking to—whether they signed up or not.

I eventually signed up the six people I wanted. Five men attended in person and one participated virtually from New Zealand. We adjusted the timings slightly to ensure he could attend most of the sessions.

At £600 per client, this intensive was a huge success compared to my previous event for women, for which I struggled to sell at £25 per ticket. At the same time, I wouldn't have successfully created my men's group without having learned the lessons from my previous experience. The key lesson was that I needed to focus on creating an event for a type of client who already existed in my network: men who were already investing in their own development.

I also learned that events can fill one person at a time through heartfelt conversations. I didn't need to use adverts or desperately try to get the message out to as many people as possible. As I would come to understand again and again, coaching is a relationship business.

I didn't know it at the time, but this intensive was going to spawn my signature programme in the future—the Powerful Men's Immersion, which has been going for over a decade. This lesson about filling groups through conversation rather than broad marketing has stayed with me ever since. When coaches in my school want to launch group programmes, their first instinct is often to create a sales page or market broadly online. I slow them down—just as Steve did with me—and invite them to fill their group one person at a time, through honest, connected conversations. It's simple, but deeply effective. For many, it becomes a turning point. They stop trying to 'promote' and start serving—and that's when their groups begin to fill with the right people.

51

Talk to the Highest Voice in the Room

As part of the Clarity Trainer Training programme with Jamie Smart I was being mentored by Chip Chipman. This was an incredible opportunity to get guidance from someone who had a deep grounding in the Three Principles. What's more, Chip personally knew Sydney Banks.

I loved hearing the stories Chip shared about his own journey with the Three Principles and how it led him from being a contractor building homes on the islands off the coast of Vancouver to getting a corporate job as a Director of Human Resources and then eventually to setting up his own consulting group. Meeting Sydney Banks and learning about the Three Principles had clearly changed Chip's life both personally and professionally in incredible ways.

A week before delivering my Powerful Men's Intensive, I was on one of our regular Skype calls, which I would take from my bedroom in my London apartment. I managed to squeeze in a computer desk and angle the webcam so you couldn't see my bed in shot! The time difference meant I could speak with Chip after work, which was still morning or early afternoon for him in Canada. It worked perfectly.

I asked him if he had any advice for me. He had, after all, been teaching the Three Principles and coaching and mentoring for decades, with everyone from corporate executives to couples looking for relationship help. After I asked, he paused, thought about it for a second and told me another story about Sydney Banks. When Chip was first running groups, he had asked Syd (as he was affectionally called by those who knew him) a similar question.

Syd had told him to speak to the highest voice in the room. Chip in turn explained this to me by saying that if you have a room full of people, some of whom understand what you are saying and some who don't, the temptation can be to speak to the person who isn't understanding you. But everyone gets less out of the conversation if you approach it this way. If, on the other hand, you speak to the person who is understanding you the most, the conversation is elevated, and everyone gets more out of it.

This made a lot of intuitive sense to me. I reflected on past moments when I'd spoken to a group and gotten caught up in trying to convince the *one* person who just wasn't getting what I was saying. This never worked, and in practice it meant expecting everyone else in the room to wait for this other person to 'catch up.'

Flash forward to after my Powerful Men's Intensive, and not only had I integrated Chip and Syd's advice, I also saw it in a whole new way. It wasn't only about speaking to the highest voice in the room, but also the highest voice in each *person*. I realised there were people in the room who were sceptical about, or who didn't yet understand, what I was pointing to. But I knew that every person there had access to innate wisdom. There is no one on the planet who is disconnected from it, even when it seems like it. Sydney Banks often spoke about how it might only take one *second* for someone to have an insight that could change their life forever. On my intensive it became clear that I could speak to the part of a person that already knew what I was pointing to. Perhaps they had

had a glimpse of this truth in the past, or during the intensive. Perhaps they were only getting about 1 percent of what I was saying . . . But if I focused on that 1 percent, I was having more impact than I would focusing on the other 99 percent. That was huge for me, and it would guide many conversations I'd have in the future.

I realised, too, that the same insight applied to individual coaching. I didn't need to convince a client of anything. I could talk about the Three Principles understanding and keep in mind that highest part of the person in front of me. Their own wisdom would hear it. This was especially true for conversations with people who were potential clients. Many times, I would speak to someone who could have turned into a client but it seemed to be a roulette wheel as to how well the conversation would go. When I started to keep in mind speaking to the highest voice, or the highest part of someone, these initial conversations started to go much better.

I remember working with a coach in my school—we'll call him Francis—who had spent over $100,000 on various trainings but still felt completely stuck when it came to building a sustainable coaching practice. From our first conversation, I made a conscious choice to speak only to the highest part of him, the part that already knew how to create clients ethically and sustainably. I was relentless in pointing to that place—even when he couldn't see it himself. A few months in, something shifted. His business finally started growing, not because he learned a new technique, but because he connected with his heart and began serving powerfully from that place.

I am not saying that this was a foolproof way to have great enrolment calls with anyone. But knowing that everyone already had everything they ever needed, in spite of their thinking, changed the way I conducted both coaching and enrolment conversations. How could they be the same after that insight?

You might take a few moments now and consider whether everyone you have ever met and everyone you will ever speak to already has access to their innate wisdom—which will be the best coach they could ever want. What if the role of a coach is as much about waking people up to that possibility as anything else?

52

Getting Creative with Clients

One of the men who had signed up for my Powerful Men's Intensive had made a mistake. He was based in Norway and had booked his flight for the wrong weekend. Unfortunately, he couldn't change it, and so he was scheduled to land in London a week after the intensive. (This was Henry, the same young man I had mentioned in Chapter 20.)

He contacted me about his mistake before the intensive. Since he hadn't paid for the weekend yet, he suggested that he just skip it and write off the plane fare as a loss.

I didn't want to lose him as a client, and I knew it would be helpful for him to attend, so I decided to get creative. I suggested he still catch his flight to London and I could give him a private, one-day version of the Men's Intensive. It might even be better than attending the intensive with everyone else, as he would have my full attention. He agreed.

Steve Chandler would call this a School of One.

I had of course kept all the notes I'd made from the previous weekend, and I talked Henry through the thought-feeling connection, sharing how everything we feel is a reflection of our thinking in the moment. This is important, because Henry, like us all, was brought up to believe that our feelings are telling us about something that's happening outside of us, and this played out in his relationships. I explained that if he goes on a date with a woman and feels smitten, it might look as if that feeling is telling him about the woman. But it's not. It's only telling him about his thinking in that moment. If we explore this, we can see how true it is. It's why so many relationships that start off great can end on a sour note—because one or both parties don't feel the same way anymore. The people in the relationship are the same, but their thinking has changed. It would be as accurate to say to someone, 'I don't think the same as I used to about you', rather than the common phrase, 'I don't feel the same way about you anymore.'

If we associate our feelings with objects, people and circumstances, we often try to control or chase things in our lives which have no bearing on our well-being or happiness. Paradoxically this same misunderstanding will push away useful circumstances or some wonderful people. I told Henry that I spoke from experience here, as I used to think my good feelings came from the woman I was dating—which led me to become needy and insecure; these thoughts had me reacting to her every mood and action towards me. This in turn was poison for my relationship. Henry started to see how he had his own misunderstandings around his thinking, and how it had hampered his own relationships.

I also spoke to Henry about wisdom and gut feelings, and how he could trust something that was beyond his own thinking. He didn't need to choose between his heart and his head.

None of us do. When we slow down mentally, we can access our intuition. Conversely, when we speed up, we can't. I shared with Henry how, when I dropping my 'outside-in' beliefs, my mind slowed down, and I could access this knowing more and more often. Doing so had guided me many times over the previous two years—

for example, to undertake my coach training with Jamie, to move to London and to quit my job.

Over the course of our day together, Henry had some powerful insights and started to see how he could trust his own gut. He left London a different man from when he'd arrived. I loved the day and I was excited for the future, because in a few weeks I would be working full-time as a coach, and I would have more opportunities to help people like Henry have powerful shifts.

I learned that if I stay open, flexible and focused on serving the other person, great things can happen with potential clients. If I had stayed rigid about 'How do I get Henry into my Intensive?' instead of coming from a more service-based question like, 'What would serve Henry?' my successful School of One would not have happened. So, the service focus benefited both of us. I of course benefitted financially, because Henry paid for the intensive. But more importantly I also benefitted professionally—both by learning how to be creative and flexible in a situation that didn't go the way Henry and I had planned, and also because it upped my coaching game to deliver the School of One. And Henry benefitted too: his 'unfortunate' travel planning didn't get in the way of a personal transformation. You could call this a real win-win.

53

Getting Prepared for Going Full-Time

After handing in my notice to my employer, I used my next coaching session with Steve to talk about how best to prepare myself and hit the ground running in my coaching practice. I had a three-month-notice period, and I didn't want to wait three months to get going. I was fortunate that at work my manager had already started taking work off me and seemed to only want me to deal with things that were absolutely necessary before I left.

Steve assured me that many now-successful coaches were once in a position similar to mine. They had learned the skills of client creation, and I could too. He had trained many coaches to do just this.

Importantly, he pointed out that there is a distinction between trying to change the world (which I had been trying to do) and making money as a coach. Up until that moment I had just assumed they were one and the same. I had this romantic idea that I could share the Three Principles understanding with the world and the money would take care of itself. Almost everyone who came across this understanding would ask, 'Why do more people not know about this?' So I knew that coaching from the Three Principles understanding was incredibly transformative, to say the least, but I hadn't fully appreciated that I also needed to learn about client creation if I was to make coaching a full-time career.

The truth is, I was avoiding focusing on making money because I still had many hang-ups around it. My mind was awash with thinking about money. On the one hand that thinking was invisible to me. On the other, it was driving many of my decisions and actions; I believed that the client *transformation* part of the profession was somehow good, wholesome and even spiritual, but the client *creation* part—and specifically income creation—was at best a necessary evil. I may not have put it in exactly those words if you'd asked me about it, but that is absolutely how I felt.

Steve suggested I focus on developing relationships with potential clients while working my notice period. He used the analogy of planting seeds now that I could harvest a few months down the line when I was full-time coaching. Perhaps one of the reasons that I had some money hang-ups was because I didn't see client creation as farming but as the equivalent of *hunting* down my prey (the client)—or at best as farming only the fastest-growing crops.

Steve went further and told me it was possible to actually *enjoy* the sales process. There was no one-size-fits-all approach, so I could create one for myself that was both effective and fun. That sounded great; I was used to 'putting up' with sales, but I certainly didn't enjoy it for its own sake. I saw that it could *lead* to the fun part of my job: coaching people. Yet Steve said I didn't need to wait—the fun could start with client creation.

The best way I could help people decide whether they wanted to work with me longer-term was by giving them a powerful coaching experience with me. Although I'd heard and even practiced this concept before, I still spent many calls with prospective clients talking too much about myself, my coaching and the features and benefits of coaching in general—as opposed to just coaching them on a topic that was a challenge for them. I was still practicing integrating what I'd learned with how I created coaching conversations and relationships.

Steve really turned my world upside down when he said that in order for me to help someone get a better feel for my coaching, I could charge them session by session. I hadn't ever done this for a client, at least not for more than a couple of sessions. I had been taught to *only* charge clients higher fees so that they would be invested, and to sign them up for a package of sessions.

Part of me had expected Steve to share some secret formula I could use to convince my prospective clients to sign up for even larger sums of money. But instead, he offered that I could charge larger fees and do longer-term programmes later, once I'd gotten a feel for filling my practice with paying clients.

In other words, there was no *one* way to build a practice. There wasn't even one set of rules I needed to universally apply in my practice. I didn't need to offer a session-by-session payment plan for everyone, but I could offer one if I met someone with whom I wanted to work if it would enable coaching to happen. I also saw I didn't need to do it forever; Steve suggested I just trial this approach for the next six months. He then said something to me that I will never forget.

'Ankush, if you charge high fees but don't have clients, then you are not a professional coach. If you have a full practice of clients, then you are a professional coach. So, if you want to be a coach, remember: your purpose is to create paying clients.'

This sounds really obvious as I look back now, but it wasn't at the time. I had been overcomplicating my business by charging higher fees than I was actually okay with charging—both for myself and my clients and prospects. In truth, I had been busier a year earlier when my fees were a lot lower.

Steve was turning many of the ideas I had around coaching on their head. I now advise coaches to fill their practice first before increasing their fees. Most coaches I speak to think that in order to increase their income, they need to increase their fees. However, they almost always have not filled their coaching practice at their existing fee level. What typically happens when coaches increase their fees too early (that is, before they are full) is that they find it harder to enrol clients at the new fee. After a while they fall into an energy of desperation. On the flipside, the coaches who fill their practice *first* find it much easier not only to increase their fees, but to do so without any energy of desperation—because they don't need lots of new clients. They only need new clients to replace existing ones who don't renew their agreements.

I have found myself repeating this insight years later in my coaching school. I encourage the coaches in my school to focus first on getting full, whatever that looks like for them. Some resist this at first, but time and time again I've seen it work. The ones who commit to getting full first not only grow faster, but do so with less pressure. When their practice is full, they raise their fees from a place of abundance not scarcity. And the results are almost always more sustainable, more enjoyable, and more financially rewarding.

54

People May Be More Open than You Realise

After I handed in my notice at my corporate job, I kept my head down in the office. I assumed that no-one would understand my motivation for leaving to pursue a new venture. They probably thought I was foolish, naïve or likely to fail. At least, those were the thoughts in my head.

However, a strange thing started to happen. Word got around the office that I was leaving, and colleagues started asking me if I wanted a coffee or a quick chat. During those conversations, many of them started telling me how brave I was for leaving and how they had their own hopes, dreams and desires away from corporate life.

This came as a complete surprise. I had assumed they were all living their best lives and *I* was the odd one out, but once again my thinking was being challenged.

The second thing that really surprised me was how open my colleagues were with me. These were people I'd simply said hello to in the office in a friendly, collegiate sort of way. I may have even had a short conversation or two with them, but we'd never really connected deeply. Now they were opening up to me about their fears, desires and honest feelings.

I was seeing that I had a lot of judgement on my own choice to become a life coach. I thought people wouldn't take me or the profession seriously. This was a function of my low professional self-esteem as a coach, which had yet to develop. I felt as if I were somehow pursuing a 'lesser' profession but that it was my calling nonetheless, and I had to follow it.

This may also have been in part because coaching was rapidly growing as a profession. In London, it seemed that everyone I met was either a beginner life coach or knew someone who was a life coach. I came across many coaches who had done free or low-cost short courses to become a coach and who were making little or no money from this profession. The truth was that I judged them. I felt like coaching was a vocation and you needed to invest time and energy over years to become really good at it, and then to make a good income from it—just like any other profession. A decade later and coaching is far more established as a profession and continues to grow; even so, I suspect some of you reading this may still hold some judgement of other coaches.

While I still believe it's true that the best coaches treat this as a vocation and invest time and money in ongoing training, my *judgement* was and is completely optional. It was also a double-edged sword: my judging other coaches reflected my own low self-esteem as a coach. And this is often the case—judgement of others reflects our own judgemental thinking about ourselves.

I hadn't yet seen that I could be proud of coaching as a profession and of my own role as a coach, and that I could own my choice to leave the corporate world. Instead, I was thinking I would quietly leave and take some time to grow my business. Then, once I was successful, I could announce to the world, 'I am a coach!'

I didn't see at the time how back-to-front that thinking was. In truth, if more and more people knew I was coaching, I would likely create more coaching conversations. And the more conversations I had, the more clients I could enrol. This, of course, would lead to greater income and prosperity.

It would take me years before I consistently 'made a stand' for coaching, before I truly owned my career choice and was proud of the impact of my work. In the beginning, my stand was intermittent, because I mixed up my self-worth as a human and a coach with my career choice and my income.

However, even early on I took small steps in this direction by starting my coaching training and offering conversations to people. There were clues that those around me had great respect for coaching, even if they didn't know what it was, because they were very open to conversations where I might be able to help them. It was simpler than I was imagining it to be. Over time, through continued small steps, my stand became complete and unshakable.

This is why I now encourage all the coaches in my school to actively promote the profession and release their judgements about other coaches. In one cohort, I ran a simple but powerful exercise. I asked each coach to write down a judgement they had about someone else in the room—anything they might be thinking but wouldn't normally say out loud. Things came up like, 'This coach is arrogant' or 'They don't have a clue what they're doing.' I then invited everyone to spend fifteen minutes writing about how that very same statement applied to them. How they, too, had been arrogant. How they, too, had felt lost. Many shared afterwards that it was one of the most powerful exercises they had ever done. It cracked something open. And it helped them realise that judgement of others is always a reflection of a judgement of themselves—and that compassion, both for themselves and others, is the antidote.

55

Referrals Come from Service, not from Asking

While I thought I was getting good feedback from my clients, I didn't seem to be getting many referrals. So, on our second coaching call, a couple of weeks after the first, I asked Steve Chandler for help, assuming he could teach me how to have my existing clients want to recommend others to me.

Once again, Steve surprised me with his response. Asking for or talking about referrals and testimonials, he said, can come across as needy. He wasn't wrong about that, in the sense that the reason I wanted a good system for referrals was because I *felt* needy about getting clients. I didn't want to admit this . . . But I'd been coaching for around two years and my income was far lower than I had anticipated it would be by this point. I was still living under the illusion I could or should have basically replaced my corporate salary within months of starting out.

Steve again pointed me to *service*. I could spend an hour with someone whom a client knew, if it would help them. Not as a way to get a referral but as pure service to my client. Steve suggested I could gift a session with me to my clients, and this would be far more effective than asking for a testimonial or referral. As I reflected on this, I thought about my own experience as a coaching client. If I liked a course, coach or even a book, I would tell people about it. However, if someone asked me for a testimonial, it felt a little uncomfortable; I would feel pressure to say only positive things.

Steve was gently moving me away from looking for gimmicks or tricks and instead leading me to focus on actually being a great coach who gets referrals through their work. I'd heard about other coaches building their businesses on referrals without any websites, business cards or traditional marketing. It made sense that if they provided exceptional service they would be getting regular referrals. I thought I knew what exceptional service meant in this profession, but Steve was starting to help me see that there was a higher level of service than I had imagined, and I could aim for it.

This service-based approach was more in line with how I wanted to operate my business. I'd heard that I needed to have testimonials on my website and online to show people that my coaching was good, but I had personally never hired a coach because of a testimonial. In fact, I often didn't believe the testimonials I saw online because they could easily have been faked. (If a client gives me an unsolicited piece of feedback that they're happy for me to share, that's different. That is genuine and authentic, and I think people can intuit the difference.)

What all this points to is that at this time I was seeing something very clearly: while I had been on this coaching journey for two years, in some respects I was just starting out. I needed to focus on impacting my clients even more than I was already doing. I needed to deepen my understanding and practice of service.

This is something we track closely in my coaching school. Every month, we invite participants to share how many referrals and renewals they've had—not as a performance metric, but as a barometer of how much service they're really providing. Referrals and renewals don't lie.

While I might ask clients from time to time who could be a good fit for a programme I am running, what's changed over the years is how often new participants now come unprompted. Clients frequently ask if they can refer others to my men's immersion, to my school, or for one-to-one coaching. At one point, Sundance Robson, who I see as one of the best men's coaches in the world, even told a client he wouldn't coach him until after he'd attended my immersion. And several coaches in my school have approached me asking, 'How can we help enrol others into your school? We're completely aligned with your mission, and we know how much this will benefit others.'

You can't script that kind of enthusiasm—but you can create it, by serving people so powerfully that they can't help but share.

56

Three Steps to Becoming a Great Coach

On my third coaching call with Steve Chandler, at the end of September 2014, I had a different context for the call. While I'd already hired him to help me be successful in his profession of coaching, I now had three months of working my notice period that would take me to the end of the year, so more than ever I wanted to succeed. This was a huge step for me; for the first time, I would be without a regular paycheque. I felt like someone had just yanked away my security blanket.

Steve explained that if I gave my full attention to three aspects of practice building I would be successful. Two of these steps made complete sense to me; one was a surprise.

Firstly, Steve told me that if I focused on MASTERY in my craft, this would help ensure the success of my foray into coaching full-time. Sit down, he said, and ask myself, W*hat am I doing each day that will help me in my field?* As he said this, I reflected that this approach was no different from what I had once done in my corporate job. I'd once read that if I wanted to be successful in my career, I should spend thirty minutes each morning reading or listening to something that would help me be a better procurement professional. I did this for a few weeks . . . and then stopped.

Of course, this wasn't rocket science. If I had dedicated myself to mastery as a procurement professional, I would have had a completely different experience of that career. No doubt I would have performed at a higher level and been promoted more quickly. I even felt it in the few weeks where I had woken early in the morning to read. In coaching it would be no different, except that rather than promotions, I would make more income as I became more impactful. I had a stronger desire to make coaching work than I'd had to be a master procurement professional, so it felt like the stakes were higher. The logical thing to do, then, would be to devote myself to the game, to learning and practicing with a new intensity.

Secondly, Steve suggested I focus on *relationships* rather than marketing, becoming well-known and looking for followers. The question he asked me to contemplate was this: *Whose lives am I contributing to each day?* After all, coaching is a relationship business. I wish I could say that this second point sunk in immediately. It didn't. To a certain extent I understood that if I developed good relationships with people, they would be more likely to hire me. However, I was still thinking of relationships as a *means to an end.*

This, in fact, was how I viewed *all* my relationships. While I enjoyed many strong friendships, I can't say that I didn't have selfish motives. I still had a hangover from my early teenage years where I had been bullied at school. Back then I had thought the popular kids were immune from bullying because everyone liked them. So, to be safe, I needed to be popular. I created this deep-seated desire to be liked as a way to subconsciously protect myself. What people thought of me became of paramount importance. This was coupled with my misunderstanding that I would feel positive if people liked me and experience negative feelings if they didn't.

In coaching, and in all my relationships, I would have to learn to break this desire to be admired, adored and loved and instead put my focus on the other person. This wasn't a fake-it-until-you-make-it scenario. I had to find my way to an authentic feeling and way of being around this, because it was perhaps the most important thing I could do as a coach in service to others and, while I didn't realise it at the time, it would greatly help in all my relationships.

The good news was that my exploration of the Three Principles was helping me see that my feelings weren't coming from what others thought of me. This was helping me slowly drop my misunderstanding that I would feel bad if someone didn't like me. My feelings were a reflection of my thinking, not of what the other person thought of me.

Engaging this understanding in my life would allow me to be of greater service to anyone. If I were hung up on what someone thought of me, I would be hesitant to say something that might offend or upset them. This was key, but it's not like I flicked a switch and suddenly changed; I would need to continue my exploration in this area, as I didn't yet see how timid I was being in many of my conversations.

The third point Steve made was the one that caught me by surprise. He emphasised that I needed to take care of myself in mind, body and spirit. I'd been ignoring my health, specifically the body part of this equation, thinking that if I took the time to eat right and exercise, it would take my focus away from building my coaching practice. It had actually been a conscious choice to not exercise, as I was looking for every spare moment to dedicate to coaching. My diet had also suffered, and I would often grab my dinner from the local chip shop opposite Waterloo train station on my way home from work. My entire meal consisted of deep fried chips (you may call them fries in the States) with a heavy side portion of tomato ketchup. Not very nutritious, but it was quick. Steve pointed out that there were many benefits from my looking after myself, mentally and physically.

Not only would I lose some of the excess weight I'd started to accumulate, but I would feel better too. When I had exercised in the past I'd always felt good after doing it, and I had more energy for the rest of the day.

Steve and I would have this conversation again the following year; it would take me years before I finally got this full on.

In the book, *The Missing Link*, Sydney Banks encourages the reader to ask themselves this question when selecting a spiritual teacher, and I believe it also applies when selecting a coach:

'Does my teacher reflect and demonstrate the quality of life I desire?'

He goes on to write that if the answer is no, then the reader should move on. In neglecting my health and fitness, I wasn't being a great role model for my clients. I really had to BE someone different from whom I had been in my previous career. Building my coaching practice wasn't just about learning new skills; it required a fundamental shift in how I was showing up in the world.

I was nervous, but ready.

57

Give It all Away and Stay Humble

I had heard from many coaches about giving value to their clients and being generous, and I thought I understood the concept. After all, I'd been to university to study business, my family had run small businesses for generations and my first job was in retail. I also had a self-image of someone who delivered incredible customer service.

All that said, early on in our coaching relationship Steve taught me more about generosity and service than anyone else had before. In one of our first calls, he told me two things in particular that showed both his humility and generosity, and which I tried to model forever after.

When I had asked Steve what it would take for us to work together, we had agreed to a package of attending the final weekend of his school and six months of private coaching. His school was delivered over six months, with daily emails, videos, coaching demos and three live weekends.

One of the first examples of his astonishing level of service was that when I signed up for coaching with him and his school he gave me full rights to use any of his audios from the school. I could send these to anyone – not just my clients, but prospective clients as well. These were audios he sold on his website, yet he put no restrictions or stipulations on my use of them. I was used to coaches threatening people for 'stealing' their content—or at least putting caveats on what we could share, and with whom. But here was Steve allowing me to have full access to his audios.

Wow.

This was a man modelling a truly generous spirit. Being honest with myself I knew that I would not have done the same as him at that time in my life. I could be generous, but I would also hold back. I didn't yet live in a reality where I was surrounded by abundance (at least not in my mind). In fact, it was quite the opposite. The truth is that what *I* saw was a lack of clients and a lack of money.

Furthermore, while a lot had shifted inside me by this point, I still didn't see *love* as abundantly available. I'm not speaking about romantic relationships. Rather, I hadn't quite realised that *love is who I am, who anyone is*—and it can't be received from anyone or anything else.

I had already put Steve on a pedestal before we started working together. That pedestal was getting higher and higher. Yet he also told me something that struck me as completely remarkable: I should refer to him as a colleague, mentor and friend. There was no hierarchy between him and me.

What? No hierarchy?

But he was Steve Chandler! He was the 'Godfather of Coaching'! His former client list was a Who's-Who of the coaching world!

And he wanted me to treat him as an equal. When he said this, I nodded and didn't question him—but I didn't see it. My professional self-esteem was still quite low at this point, as you may have guessed. I was barely making £10,000 a year as a coach, and my expenses were way higher than that.

However, Steve saw something in me that I wasn't seeing in myself—namely, that I had a lot to offer. Yes, Steve was way more experienced than me, both as a coach and in life. Yes, I had hired Steve to learn from him. Yes, Steve was more skilled in many aspects of the coaching profession than I was . . . and yet we were colleagues. We were in the same career and in the business of helping people. We were both dedicated to learning, and we were starting a wonderful friendship as well as a professional relationship.

It took me some time, but over the years I started to see that Steve wasn't simply trying to make me feel better. The more I saw that there really was no hierarchy—between me and Steve or anyone else—the more I was able to take the focus off of *me* and place it where it need to be: on the person sitting across from me. After all, that's what this profession is all about.

This spirit of generosity is something I've carried forward into my own coaching school. While there are some things—like our private recordings—that are for participants only, I encourage every coach in the school to share the ideas, distinctions and tools they've learned. I tell them: you don't need my permission to go and serve the world powerfully with what you've gained here.

One of my clients, Angi Scott, ended up writing a beautiful book called *The Coaching Blueprint* based on what she learned during her first two years in the school. I gave her full encouragement to share those insights. We're not here to hoard knowledge—we're here to help people.

And just as Steve once asked me to call him a colleague, I now do the same. In my school, I invite every participant to refer to me, and to each other, as colleagues. It changes the energy completely. It reminds us that we're equals on the same path: serving, learning, growing.

58

Don't Let Social Anxiety Get in the Way

While I was still working my notice period, I was learning so much from Steve about growing my coaching practice. We'd had only a few coaching sessions, and yet I started to see other coaches who could also benefit from what he was sharing with me. For example, there was a woman I'd been introduced to through a colleague on Jamie's course in 2013. I really looked up to her, as she was further along the coaching path than I was. She had been coaching for longer, had done Jamie's course a year before I did, and had done other training in the Three Principles. She seemed to be working full-time and having a deep impact on the people she worked with, yet I could also see how what I was learning from Steve could massively help her business.

At the same time I felt incredibly reluctant to offer her coaching. I had a lot of thinking about how it would be inappropriate or rude or 'above my station.' I still felt like a new coach.

Of course, these thoughts stemmed from my thinking around my self-worth, as well as my old thinking about hierarchies in relationships. I'd often put people on pedestals and hold back from sharing something that might be helpful because of the small chance they might get offended—Who was *I* to share something with *them*?—even though I didn't have any evidence that this is what would happen.

I brought this dilemma to Steve. I said that if I made a proposal for this woman and me to work together, I'd feel like I was trying to grab her money. Once again, Steve helped me see past my own insecure thinking. He pointed out that my social anxiety was stopping me from being a valuable resource for her and suggested I offer her a nine-session coaching package in which she didn't pay for the first two sessions. After those two, she could continue and pay session by session, or simply stop. This seemed to me to be a lot easier to offer than the full package I had been thinking about. There would be less pressure on her to sign up immediately and we could both explore if coaching together was a good fit; then, ongoing there would be less financial pressure on her by only paying for one session at a time. It would also relieve the pressure I felt of having to deliver this amazing service for my package fee (which would have been around £2,800). Given she would be paying session by session, I could see that I would only need to deliver value for that session. If she felt I wasn't, she could simply stop.

Steve also suggested I just be really honest. Tell her, he said, that I had been hesitant to approach her because I looked up to her.

How refreshing! I could be real, honest and genuine! For so long I had thought I needed to present an image of a well-put-together coach with no anxiety, no hang-ups and no insecurities. Surely if potential clients knew I was feeling all that, they would be put off, right?

But on reflection I realised *I* had never hired anyone simply because they were impressive. In fact, I was most drawn to those who seemed human, raw and real. This, in fact, was one of the things that drew me to Steve. Despite his clear credentials and skillset, he had never put himself on a pedestal or tried to come across as impressive. I loved his self-deprecating humour. Perhaps there was a clue in that?

I still felt uncomfortable, but my Three Principles training helped me see that an uncomfortable feeling isn't telling me about reality, and it certainly isn't a reason to stay out of action. So, I approached the woman.

To my surprise, not only was she willing to engage in coaching sessions with me—she actually seemed really thrilled about it.

I wondered how many other people I had not reached out to (and was still not reaching out to) because of the same faulty reasoning.

59

Problems Are Your Friend

By November 2014 I had already spent over two years looking for clients. At first, I had no clue where I would find them, and over time I started looking for them everywhere: social media, personal development events and even at social gatherings. This didn't always go down too well! Understandably, people often didn't want to get into deep coaching conversations about what was going on in their lives at social event. Nor was I adept yet at gently exploring this with them in such settings.

Steve Chandler turned my approach on its head: He suggested I look for *problems* instead of clients.

A clear distinction! And it shifted my focus, moving me away from simply scheduling calls and focusing on logistics to instead getting curious about problems or challenges that people were having. This provided a fantastic context for a coaching conversation and it also had me be a better listener. If I thought I had to impress people I was just looking for an opening to tell them something that would have them want to know more about me or about coaching. If I was looking for problems, it naturally meant asking more questions and listening.

I was working the last few weeks of my notice period when a colleague at my corporate job mentioned he was simply tolerating his work because he had to pay the bills. He didn't really want to be there. If I focused on *trying to get him as a client*, I wouldn't know where to start or how to approach him. This was a man whose position was slightly more senior than mine, who was older than I was, and who had been in the company longer than I had been. I didn't have any context to approach him about coaching. The only thing I could have done was talk about what I was up to in terms of leaving the company to start coaching full-time and hope he might be interested enough to ask me questions. Even when people did this, most of the time it didn't lead to me coaching them.

However, *focusing on his problem* provided a clear path to serve him. He was in a victim mindset. That is, he felt as though he was at the mercy of his circumstances, and from this vantage point his options looked extremely limited. However, I had resources I could share with him. I knew that through conversations together we could open up a different perspective for him. And importantly, *this could all be done regardless of whether he became a client or not.* Steve Chandler had shared an audio called, 'The Owner/Victim Choice' with his email list earlier that year. I had listened to it after a particularly challenging conversation with my line manager a few months earlier (just prior to my hiring Steve) and it completely shifted my mindset. I saw that if my mind could shift completely from listening to it, chances were high that it could help others who were also feeling like the victims of their circumstances.

I started seeing problems (and therefore opportunities) everywhere. People who were struggling with their love lives, having health challenges, feeling stressed or burned out . . . I knew people who wanted to be promoted but who felt stuck. I knew coaches who wanted more clients. I knew men who wanted a deeper connection in their marriages.

Soon this one distinction—seeing problems instead of potential clients—was opening up a whole different perspective around client creation. I also reflected back to my own behaviour when hiring a coach. At that time all I cared about was whether or not this person could help me with a challenge or problem I was having. My hiring them was *always* in the context of creating some change in my life, in my world. It was never simply to get coaching. So if I related to people through their problems rather than trying to get them as clients, I could start serving them *immediately*. Not only were they being helped, they were also having an experience of my coaching.

Hence, this approach felt less needy. I could simply serve people by focusing on their challenges. Then, if they wanted to continue with me, they could—already knowing how I could serve them. And if they didn't want to continue, that was fine too.

The people who *didn't* continue working with me didn't need me to utilise better sales skills or techniques on them. They simply weren't ready to move forward now. Perhaps they would refer someone else to me, or hire me in the future. In the meantime, I had helped them.

What a mindshift!

60

You Don't Need to Rush to 'Close' a Client

There is a seminal scene in the 1992 film *Glengarry Glen Ross* where Alex Baldwin's character Blake is telling salesmen that they are fired and they have one week to get their jobs back. They complain about the leads they have, and he dishes out some hard-hitting sales advice, including the acronym ABC: Always Be Closing. He was encouraging the salesmen to do whatever it took to close the sales they were after. It was a pure numbers game.

I didn't operate like Blake, nor did I have any desire to, but I certainly felt excited when a prospective client signed up. Once they did, I didn't want to do anything to jeopardise the sale. I used to tread on proverbial eggshells until their payment appeared in my account.

I wish I could say that this tentative approach only applied to coaching clients, but to be honest I was quite tentative in *many* areas of my life. My mind often raced to the worst potential outcome. For example, before I started coaching full-time, whenever I got a job offer I would almost immediately imagine them changing their mind and pulling the offer. Or if I got a date with a pretty girl, I would imagine her not turning up and later informing me she'd made a mistake in agreeing to go out with me.

I hadn't yet seen that my concerns about losing a client before they'd paid me were, as always, just thoughts—random and unconnected to reality. They weren't a reflection of what was happening. Nor were they predictors of future events. I didn't need to tread carefully because of fearful thinking about what might never happen. Doing so wouldn't help me anticipate anything, and in fact my anxious thinking could (and did) distract me from more important things in my life.

Steve Chandler told me about his coach, Steve Hardison, who would sometimes hand people's cheque back to them after they'd paid him—even though back then his fee was $150k for a year (it later increased to up to $300k a year). Among other things, Hardison wanted to clarify that there were no refunds once someone signed up. If the client changed their mind, their fee would be donated to a charity of his choice, because Hardison didn't want to give them a financial incentive to quit. He had other requirements, too, such as prioritising the sessions over other activities and not being late, even by a minute.

Steve encouraged me to take a page from Hardison's book and *slow down* when a client was close to signing up with me. This wasn't a moment to follow the 'Always Be Closing' approach. Instead, my job at this point was to ensure that this was something the prospective client really wanted to do—and that they understood what they were signing up for.

This approach felt super-edgy and uncomfortable at first, but I saw just how logical it was. If a client wasn't fully committed to the coaching process, it wouldn't result in the best outcome for them, and it would be more difficult for me. It would always be better for both of us to know up front if someone didn't want to work with me, as opposed to trying to close the sale and then dancing around the client until they paid.

I soon discovered a paradox: As I started to slow down in my enrolment calls—especially in the part of the conversations where clients expressed a desire to sign up—prospective clients often become keener to sign up. Not everyone, of course, but I began to see that the few who didn't sign up when I slowed down probably wouldn't have signed up anyway, or wouldn't have been a great fit for coaching with me because they weren't really fully committed.

Everything became so much simpler around enrolment. No high pressure, no need to always be closing, no need to worry about what might or might not happen when someone signed up with me. I see now that this understanding applies in every area of my life. Whenever I'm *not* panicked about a particular outcome, slowing down is a logical, natural step; it often happens automatically. I'm not trying to control what happens; I'm simply in conversation with and serving the person in front of me.

This is, after all, a relationship game, not a numbers one.

61

Go Beyond What Other Coaches Do

There was still deeper for me to go.

I thought I understood what service meant. I thought I knew how to create clients through creating relationships. Yet by the time of my sixth call with Steve Chandler I realised there was plenty of room for me to continue growing as a coach. It was December 2014, and it would be our last call before I moved out of my London apartment and back in with my parents to start coaching full-time.

I had finally turned a corner in terms of being more visible online and 'putting myself out there.' I was creating Facebook posts about coaching and was no longer 'hiding,' meaning I was identifying myself as a coach. Nonetheless, somewhere inside I held a belief that if I got a big enough online following, or if one of my posts went viral, I would have finally *made it.* I'd be inundated with clients and I wouldn't need to do the 'hard part' of coaching—namely, creating clients. *They* would flock to *me.*

Steve must have teased this out of me somehow, because during that sixth call he asked me to ponder the question, 'How do you create conversations from your online content?'

This was a great question. I had assumed it was a passive process. Once I posted something online, all I would have to do was sit back and wait for people to contact me. This was my thinking, but in fact it wasn't working particularly well. I rarely had people reach out to me based on a post, and even when they did, it didn't usually translate to them becoming a client. I was clearly missing something. There was more to creating clients than I was seeing.

Steve suggested I build relationships with people who resonated with what I wrote. One way I could do this was to send a private message on Facebook to whoever commented on one of my posts. And I wouldn't send a stock message that I'd copy and paste over and over again, but something personal, something that reflected both the content of my post and their specific response to it.

Steve told me about a client of his who researched the profiles of anyone who liked his Facebook posts. He would also check out their websites and LinkedIn profiles if they had these. Then he would send them personal messages based on what he had seen on their profiles and their comments on his post. I assume this wasn't in stalkerish, creepy way but along the lines of, 'Thank you for your comment on my post about having goals for the new year. From your profile, you look like someone who not only sets goals but achieves them. What are you currently working towards?'

My mind immediately went to the thought: 'That would take too long.' When I voiced this to Steve, he pointed out that it only takes a few minutes to do some research. Of course, he was right. My imagination, my thoughts, were blowing reality out of proportion again. It didn't need to take all that long, and I also knew it would be more fun than I initially felt—and not a chore. Writing messages like Steve suggested would also be a valuable exercise for me in learning how to connect more deeply with people, and it would be much more satisfying than copying and pasting the same 'form letter' messages over and over.

Steve shared something that Steve Hardison had done, and I've never forgotten it. Hardison had a potential client coming to see him who happened to be Muslim. In order to prepare for the conversation, Hardison read the central religious book of Islam, the Koran. That blew me away! Who does that? Obviously, Steve Hardison. (I imagine he felt it was important to understand where his prospective client was coming from, and for a particular reason it seemed appropriate to read the Koran.) Needless to say, his prospective client was also blown away and ended up hiring Hardison.

This simple story showed me just how deep I could go with building relationships and serving. It wasn't just about being polite and doing good work with a smile. It was about creating a connection and relationship with real depth, which would lead to meaningful service on a whole other level.

Steve asked me something else: 'What if the person you were speaking to next was the *only person in the world* who could hire you and refer you to new clients?'

Again, this was a brilliant question, and it slowed me down even more. I mean, if that were the case, then reading the Koran as preparation for a meeting didn't seem crazy. Steve told me that from his perspective there was no extreme like this to which he wouldn't go for prospects or existing clients. (In the years that followed, as my relationship with Steve deepened, I saw more and more evidence of this from him. Yet even at this early stage, this conversation expanded my world and what I saw as possible.)

Up until this point, I had done *no* research on prospective clients. In fact, part of me had argued this was a good thing—it meant I would go into a call fresh and without prejudice. Yet deep down I knew that spending time finding more about someone could only be a helpful. Practically speaking, it was a little like researching a company to which you were applying for a job. But I also knew how *I* would feel if someone deeply prepped for a conversation with me. It would show thoughtfulness, intention and commitment. Why wouldn't I do the same?

Another lesson learned.

62

Delivering Amazing Service as a Public Speaker

As I was gearing up to go full-time as a coach, an unexpected opportunity landed in my inbox. Johnny Epstein, a mentor of mine, had seen on Facebook that I was leaving my corporate role to coach full-time and offered to pay for my flights and accommodation if I would speak at his annual success workshop in Las Vegas. I was excited and immediately said yes—before my fearful thinking could talk me out of it. It was an open-ended invitation in that he didn't ask me to speak about a particular topic or give me a title. I had attended his week-long workshop in 2012 as a client and also returned in 2013 as I mentioned in Chapter 8 where I gave a two-hour talk about my journey over the previous twelve months. Johnny would present most of the workshop with his ideas but would invite other coaches and speakers to present to break up his teaching segments. I knew that presenting my thoughts on the Three Principles would help the attendees get a lot out of the training.

I shared this opportunity with Steve and asked him how I could capitalise on it. He offered two very important ideas.

First, he said that anyone who's organising an event loves it when guest speakers offer free stuff to the attendees. It adds additional value to the overall event and generally leads to greater satisfaction for the attendees. Steve suggested I give away CDs, books, or even a digital gift such as an audio or article beforehand. Offering a digital gift before the event would have the added benefit of building my relationship with the attendees ahead of time, and it would prep them for my talk. I knew exactly what to share: the Clarity Activator audio by Jamie Smart. Jamie gave me permission to do so, as he had done for me in the past with my prospective clients.

This settled my nerves a little. I knew if the attendees listened to that audio, it would be easier for my presentation to really land with them. I still had my doubts about my ability to share something useful with this group, even though I'd had many experiences doing this when working one-to-one with people. Giving a talk to a large audience felt quite different, but I hoped this was mainly because I hadn't done it before.

The other gift that Steve suggested I offer the group was a personal coaching session with me. He advised me to offer it after my talk, to frame this offer as a gift, and to make it clear it wasn't a sales call. There were no strings attached. It would only be for those who attended the workshop in person, and it wouldn't be available on my website or for the general public. These stipulations raised the value of the gift for those in the room.

I knew I was going to talk about something Three Principles related, and as the time for the talk drew nearer, I asked Steve for advice on some specific content. He had been a successful public speaker for years; I'd seen him in action in London and elsewhere. He had also previously worked in advertising, and he shared that a very effective strategy in that field involved 'before-and-after' examples. So, one option was to tell my own before-and-after story in the talk. What had my life been like before and after my introduction to the Three Principles and coaching?

I saw that this would be far more interesting for the audience than watching me try to present myself as an expert imparting wisdom; there was just a chance that this latter approach might make me look 'impressive,' but it wouldn't deepen my rapport with the group. In fact, it could make me intimidating to someone looking to connect with me. When I'd attended the workshop in 2012, I had met a couple of coaches there who were really impressive. They would work with men around their confidence and they had great results. However, I was so intimidated by them, I never asked them to help me. I mistakenly thought they would judge me for asking for their help. It was illogical and yet not a unique thought to me.

I knew I could talk about my own experience over the two years since I had first attended the workshop and I was ready to try out Steve's suggestions although I was still incredibly nervous. Thankfully, I knew on some level that the feeling of nervousness wasn't anything I needed to take too seriously and it would eventually pass, even if I wished it would pass quickly.

63

More Tips for My First Speaking Engagement

In preparation for my upcoming talk with Johnny Epstein's group in Las Vegas, I approached Jamie Smart to see if he had any suggestions in addition to the ones Steve Chandler had offered me. I'm glad I did.

The first piece of advice he gave me was to, if possible, split my sessions over two days. Jamie suggested there would be huge value in having space between the sessions. It would allow attendees to not only digest what I was saying but also perhaps have some insights of their own. It would also give room for questions to emerge before the second session. This made a lot of sense to me. In my one-on-one coaching with clients there was often a big shift between our first and second conversations.

This tied in with what I was learning around enrolment: namely to *slow down*. I used to think I had to impact a prospective client in a huge way on our first call. However, being willing to speak two or three times during the enrolment process took that pressure off me, and I became more effective at helping the other person with whatever challenges or goals they brought to the table. I saw this could play out in the same way for a talk to an audience who didn't know me very well.

The second very helpful piece of advice Jamie offered has influenced the way I now do any training or talk. He suggested I start with what many coaches call an 'intake'. That is, at the start of the talk, I could ask the group about themselves and what they wanted—not only from *my* session but from the whole week they were spending in Las Vegas. Jamie advised that this information could then guide the content of my two sessions.

This was an eye-opening suggestion. It would allow me to focus my talk on what the people in the room wanted to hear—rather than what I wanted to share (or what I *thought* they wanted to or 'should' hear). Now, while I had an idea of what the audience *might* want to hear or know, getting the information directly from the horse's mouth, so to speak, would help my talk be more relevant and of greater service. (I still do this today, in different contexts; for example, when creating a group or my school, I also ask well in advance what participants would like to focus on.)

To ensure I got a deep feel for what he was suggesting, Jamie shared a recording of a short talk he'd done where he demonstrated doing a great intake with the audience. He also shared some great questions he used for this, such as 'If there was a miracle by the end of this workshop, how would you know?' or 'What's the number one goal you could achieve or problem you could solve in your life?'

The combination of advice from Steve and Jamie helped me to deliver an excellent two sessions. That said, and perhaps unsurprisingly, I wasn't feeling confident prior to the talk. My mind kept conjuring up scenarios where the talk wouldn't go well. In fact, even a few minutes into it I was still feeling nervous. I was sitting on a stool at the front of the room in a beautiful mansion in Las Vegas. I had around twenty people in the room (mainly men) who had paid thousands of dollars to be there, all listening to what I had to share. Thankfully I knew better than to engage my nervous thoughts, and they gradually abated. I fell into a rhythm that worked for me and my audience. In fact, I was experiencing the Three Principles in action as I spoke about them. My butterflies were simply reflections of my own busy thoughts; I left them alone, and eventually they flew away.

As both Jamie and Steve had suggested to me, I shared my experience of being at the event a couple of years earlier as a participant and just how much my life had changed. One of the reasons was because of what I had learned at the workshop they were now attending, but the other reason was my journey with the Three Principles. I spoke about my insights around my thinking, which had led to being more productive at work because I was no longer avoiding certain tasks. I used to avoid them because it looked like I would feel bored or unhappy doing them. I also became less distracted by my feelings of anger when things didn't go my way (something that happened often in the high pressure, target-driven environment I was working in). I shared my stories of getting closer to my parents because I started to see that my upset feelings weren't coming from what they sometimes said about settling down. I used to interpret this as pressure and a lack of understanding on their part for what I was going through. Now I would see they simply cared about me and wanted the best for me.

I'd had so many insights that I didn't run out of material, and the audience started to engage and ask questions about what I had seen and how they could apply it to their lives.

I was pleased when, at the start of my second session, a participant shared how he had struggled to sleep for years. After hearing my talk the previous day, his mind quieted down. When he went to bed he realised he didn't need to engage with the thoughts he was having—the ones that seemed to be keeping him awake. He had the best night of sleep he'd had in years.

I hadn't mentioned sleep once in that previous session! I'd been sharing how the mind works and how this understanding had impacted my own life. Clearly his own wisdom had taken the ball and run with it.

Needless to say, I was thrilled at how everything had gone. Before I left Las Vegas I had a number of strong candidates to become clients of mine. The next big question for me was, *How do I move them from enthusiasm into action?*

64

The Half-Life of Enthusiasm

I came back from Las Vegas high on having delivered a successful talk, but I didn't know how to move things forward. I knew I could help many of the people who had been in the room, but I didn't want to seem pushy or needy, so I wasn't sure how to reach out to them.

Steve Chandler told me that the longer I waited to do so, the harder it would be to reignite the enthusiasm within the audience. That feeling, he said, typically fades away, and I could be of the greatest service to people who were enthusiastic about my work by reconnecting with them soon afterwards and guiding them towards the next steps of hiring me—if that's what they wanted.

This made a lot of sense. Many times, after I'd heard a talk or read a book or article that I wanted to explore more deeply, I would either soon forget about it in the rush of daily life, or my enthusiasm would dissipate and I wouldn't do anything. This didn't have to be related to coaching; it could be around learning a new language or even taking the next steps on travel to somewhere I had read about that looked interesting.

Steve suggested I offer a conversation to the people who were in the room, and to do this sooner rather than later. We could then explore what insights they'd had since listening to my talk and the talks of the other speakers and together focus on what was next for them.

However, Steve picked up on some reluctance I was feeling because of my concern around appearing 'salesy'. So, he reminded me that I was running a business, and like any business—whether that's a pub, a shop, an oil producer—it was normal to think about what activities would lead to that business making money. He was highlighting that I had perhaps over-corrected; yes, being a pushy salesman wasn't the way to go, but neither was holding back and simply wishing and hoping that people would hire me.

Here is what I wrote to one of the participants on Facebook:

> Hey Andy,
>
> Hope you are well and got back from Vegas okay. How did you find the whole experience? I'm back home now too. Did you want to put some time in the calendar to have that coaching conversation that I offered?

It was a simple and straightforward message and he responded with:

> YES, definitely! I saw there was a missed call from a +44 number. Was that you? Give me some times you are available and I will set it up. I am at work during the day between 7am and 3pm, so it has to be outside that.

I actually hadn't been the person who had tried to call him but now we were back in communication and we arranged a time to speak. He signed up for my men's immersion immediately after that conversation. Eventually, five clients signed up with me from that one talk, but only after I contacted them first to offer a follow-up conversation.

I was learning that I could build a coaching practice without being manipulative or relying on hard sales techniques—but also how this didn't mean not doing *anything*. If I was serious about really helping people, then I needed to have more conversations—lots of them—with people who felt comfortable saying no to me.

This was fine! Not everyone would want to hire me.

And what's more, I was seeing that the idea of enthusiasm having a 'half-life' applied to me as much as it applied to prospective clients. If I hadn't talked with Steve after the group in Las Vegas, it's quite possible that my own energy around the idea of coaching anyone in the audience would have faded. I had needed to take action before my own thinking started to ratchet up and convince me that it was a bad idea. Thankfully I was willing to do that . . . most of the time.

65

Fill Your Calendar with Conversations

As I approached the last few weeks of full-time employment, I was simultaneously excited about the chapter ahead and filled with feelings of nervousness and concern as to how things were going to turn out. After all, there was no guarantee that I would 'make it' as a coach. I was determined, but it still felt like stepping out onto a tightrope without a safety net.

I thought back on all the advice I had read and listened to from Rich Litvin and Steve Chandler. One thing stood out to me: to create clients, you need to have conversations. So I made a decision: I was going to focus exclusively on filling my calendar with conversations.

I posted in a Facebook group filled with Three Principles-based coaches, offering a conversation with anyone who wanted to know more about what I had done to create clients. I spoke to colleagues at work who were considering a career change to something more fulfilling. I looked for opportunities both online and offline to have conversations.

I didn't discriminate. I knew I could overthink things, and that if I did, it would slow me down. I had only one goal: create conversations.

And I did.

By the time my last day in the office arrived—31st December 2014—my January calendar was dotted with conversations. And I continued to fill it, setting myself a target of two conversations every single day, minimum.

I found that if I wasn't approaching people as sales targets, it was quite easy to create conversations. The people I connected with were current and former colleagues, friends who were into personal development, former clients and, eventually, referrals from existing clients (there weren't too many of these at first).

When I simply looked for an excuse to be of service to someone, conversations seemed easy to create. I often started them with the simple phrase:

'Shall we have a conversation about that?'

Some of these conversations would start with a message from me on social media, along the lines of:

'How's it going? It's been a while.'

I was learning I didn't need some special script to create conversations with people. Nor did I need to find a hidden trove of potential client contacts. I was connected to hundreds, potentially thousands, of people in my email inbox, on Facebook, LinkedIn and in real life. It only took a few moments each day to think about people I could help whom I already knew. Luckily, given my training and personal experiences thus far, I knew there were very few people who *couldn't* be helped.

All I needed to do was see if they were open to a conversation.

66

Is Coaching More Fulfilling than a Day Job?

For most of 2014, I hadn't enjoyed my day job. My line manager and I seemed to clash often. While we had found a way to work together and I had dropped many of my judgemental thoughts about him, I still detected an underlying belief in myself that I was less satisfied at work because of him. Running alongside that belief was another one—that working as a coach was more fulfilling than working as a procurement manager.

As I counted down the days till I left the corporate world for good, there was an expectation that when I started coaching, I would wake up excited and smiling, ready for the day ahead. Most of that year I had woken up wanting to pull the covers over my head and go back to sleep. I had a bunch of thoughts running through my head, including: 'Working at such a large organisation is meaningless', 'My work has no purpose', 'My creativity is restricted within an organisation', and so on. No wonder I didn't enjoy my work. I was believing that these thoughts were an accurate representation of reality, pointing me to get out of the corporate rat race as quickly as possible.

5th January 2015: The day finally arrived. I woke up ready to start my day as a full-time coach. I felt exactly as I had imagined I would: uplifted, happy, excited and not quite believing I had made it this far. I had to pinch myself. I was actually doing something I loved for a living. That incredible feeling stayed with me for the whole day. I had a smile on my face until I went to bed that night.

The following morning, my eyes opened. I was lying in bed at my parents' home, staring at the ceiling, exactly as I had done the day before. Soft sunlight filtered into the room past the gaps in the blinds, and I could hear the faint noise of people moving about in the house. In an instant a familiar feeling arose inside of me.

It wasn't excitement and happiness. Rather it was a feeling of unease, of wanting to stay in bed.

In other words, I had awoken with the exact same low feeling I'd had while working in my previous job.

Suddenly a sense of panic arose. *What have I done? I quit my safe, well-paying corporate job because of a misunderstanding! Oh, crap!*

I started to judge myself for making a foolish decision but the next thought that came to mind was: *Well, it's too late now; I have to make it work. There's no going back now.*

However, if I had slowed down in that moment, I would have seen something important. It's true that I was operating under the misunderstanding that I would automatically feel better and more fulfilled simply *because* I was a coach. But it was also true that even *without* that particular belief I would have still *wanted* to be a coach.

Coaching was a calling, not a goal.

I had been drawn into coaching by something deep within my soul. There was nothing superficial about it. I hadn't just picked it as a career after reading an article like, 'The Top 10 Careers that Make You Feel Most Fulfilled.' It was a very personal calling.

If I had been coaching myself before I quit my job, I would have asked myself, ‘If coaching had no impact on your feelings of work satisfaction—that is, if your work satisfaction was at the same level for coaching as it is in your current job—would you still want to coach full-time?’

My answer to that question—a resounding YES—would have told me I was on the right path.

67

Coaching Is About Possibility

While I had been having more and more conversations with potential coaching clients, these often didn't translate into the person becoming a paid coaching client. Perhaps, I wondered, I wasn't seeing something that would help me in this regard, something I could do to improve my ratio of conversations to converted clients without resorting to pushy sales tactics and trying to 'close' a person.

I brought this up with Steve Chandler in a coaching call and he hammered home the point of exploring 'possibility', of having a conversation with someone and looking at what was *possible* for them if we worked together.

This made a lot of sense to me. Given my exploration of coaching and the Three Principles, I had made huge changes in my own life. I knew that other people, even if they had already been walking the personal development path for a while (as I had been), could still have life be quite different for themselves.

However, while I had an idea of what would be possible for someone if they hired me, I was often coy about exploring this with them in our initial conversations for fear of coming off as pushy. No wonder my conversations didn't often lead to paying clients. Why would they? I was trying to sell a plane ticket without my prospective client knowing the destination. This wasn't happening only in enrolment calls; it also would play out in other areas of my life. I had been uncomfortable in job interviews in saying anything which was too bold for fear of 'messing up'. I was told that I should 'blow my own trumpet' and let the interviewer know that I could make a difference to their organisation and how I stood out compared to other candidates, but I found this a challenge. In meeting women I would play it safe and, especially at the start, present a version of me that wasn't too bold, thinking it was the best way to get a second date. This didn't always work either. In so many areas of my life, being coy and timid was costing me. Now, in coaching, I couldn't avoid it anymore.

Steve encouraged me to follow up my conversations with clients with a heartfelt email in which I really spelled out the possibilities I saw for them. Importantly, it didn't matter if the person ended up hiring me or not. If I really cared about helping them, I would simply let them know what was on offer should they hire me or, in fact, someone else who coached from the Three Principles.

For example, I knew that people could deal with stress a lot better, develop inner resilience, improve professional and personal relationships, handle their anger better, and act constructively outside of their 'comfort zone'—among other things—through the work we could do together. I also knew from personal experience that these changes were sustainable. My work with the Three Principles had been more effective in changing my life than anything else I had come across in my exploration of personal development. In this sense, my own transformation was a foundation I could coach from.

I didn't need to rush this process. I could take two or more hours over the course of a few sessions to really explore what was possible for someone. And I could follow up with emails, as Steve suggested. This was an exciting prospect, and I was keen to test it out. In fact, it was what I had been looking for: a method of client creation that went beyond sales tactics and techniques and came from the heart.

68

Crossing the Line to More Unfiltered Service

Early in January 2015, I spoke with a man called David, a thirty-five-year-old oil field worker from Canada. David was passionate about his own personal growth. He'd worked with a coach in the past and had invested in personal development.

We connected through Facebook only a few days before we first spoke. I commented on something he had posted and asked if he wanted to have a conversation via Skype; he accepted my invitation.

On the call he filled me in on the personal development investments he'd made to date, on why he had been doing these courses, groups and coaching, and what he felt was next for him. It was clear that this was a man who wasn't content with living the status quo. There were, in fact, parallels between his journey and my own.

He became curious about the Three Principles (he'd seen posts by Jamie and me) and so we spoke about them in the context of communication. I talked about different levels of communication, with the deepest level being that of the soul.

Soul-level communication is on a different level from exchanges involving personality, behaviours or thoughts. Soul-level communication occurs when our own deepest essence communicates with the deepest essence of another. Our minds quiet down so much that we communicate from a deeper place, soul to soul. This quiet space is the source of our wisdom, gut instincts and intuition. This is very different from many techniques taught about rapport, which include mirroring body language and matching voice tone and pace. Those techniques require a lot of conscious thought and effort, whereas you *fall into* soul-level communication with nothing on your mind. I would share with clients how a small baby can hold the attention of a whole roomful of adults without any conscious techniques and touch people who might seem difficult to connect with. What if we all still had that ability to connect with others that we had when we were babies?

In the past I would have felt quite uncomfortable talking about such a 'woo-woo' topic. I doubt I would ever have brought it up. Now, however, I was learning to speak from a space of deeper understanding, without filtering myself.

I was surprised when David wanted to sign up before we had even finished the call—in this case, for a six-month coaching package. This was the biggest fee I had yet received. Within two hours I had the money in my account.

From that day on the seed was planted. I began to understand on an experiential level that marketing myself and talking about coaching were not only unnecessary—they were *ineffective* compared to the alternative: diving right in and serving someone on the deepest level possible. This understanding took root within me and over time grew until it could no longer be denied.

I was gradually learning two vital lessons: One, the deeper I was willing to go in these initial calls, the more people wanted to work with me. And two, a focus on helping someone and making money went hand in hand.

69

Understanding the Value of My Work

One of the clients who signed up with me after the Vegas group was Roger. Roger and I had spoken in Las Vegas before I left and discussed how he wanted his life to change, specifically around women and dating. He had spent a lot of money on coaches, programmes and courses, but nothing had made a significant difference for him. I explained that I wasn't a dating coach. He replied that he'd met me a few years earlier at a personal development event where we were both students and now saw that something had shifted in me. He was drawn to that. I remembered him and it was great feedback to see that he had noticed such a huge change in me since then.

About a week after my return from Vegas we spoke again. He shared that he'd had some great insights from my talks, from our conversations afterwards, and from reading *Clarity* by Jamie Smart, which I had gifted to him. His mind had slowed down and he felt in the happiest place he'd been in a long time. This had led him to be more open with others and more present in general.

However, he was afraid that he would lose these newfound shifts in perspective. He had some reason to be, based on past events. Many times, after experiencing a kind of 'seminar high' at a course, conference or programme, he found the feeling was only temporary. This time he wanted things to be different.

After listening to him for a while and exploring more about what his feelings were really telling him—such as those around procrastination—I felt it right to make a proposal to continue our work together: six months coaching for £5,000. While I had been quoting this fee for quite some time, no-one had yet paid me this much.

Roger felt nervous. He said he had the money but he didn't want to spend a large sum again for it only to turn out to be yet another temporary fix. He told me he could pay around £3,000 for the coaching package. I was tempted to take it, but it felt more right to honour my fee while being receptive to Roger's concerns. I made a new proposal.

I suggested Roger pay me the £3,000 now as a deposit. At the end of the six months, if he felt that the coaching was worth the full fee, he could pay me the balance. If he didn't, then he wouldn't owe me anything more. Roger agreed. I was elated . . .

. . . but I never made a proposal like this again.

Why?

Because as it turned out, for the whole of the next six months I was always concerned about making a big enough difference to earn the balance of my fee. Some might think this would be a good thing, an incentive for a coach to perform. Yet it became a hindrance. It wasn't good for me to want my client to change more than they wanted to or *did* change, and that kind of unspoken pressure wasn't good for the client either.

The best way to help a client is to give them the best session I know how to give every time we met, rather than worrying about the outcome from the session—which depends on the client as much as the coach.

70

Flourishing Outside of Your Comfort Zone

In early February 2015 I was excited to fly to Scottsdale, Arizona, to attend the second module of Steve Chandler's ACS school. I had missed the first module in 2014 due to not having enough annual leave from work. I was originally unable to make it to the second module either for the same reason but now, as my own boss, I was free to invest my time where I wanted.

My original agreement with Steve was that I would join his school and attend the third and final live weekend in LA. He would then coach me for six months privately to cover the content I would miss in the first two weekends. Now I was able to attend this second module in addition to the private coaching without any additional charge from him—another example of his generosity.

I pre-booked my train which only cost £6 (around $10) and took the slower underground to the airport rather than the express train. It might seem contradictory to pinch pennies on travel while investing thousands in Steve's school, but without an unlimited budget, being frugal on the small expenses helped me to make the crucial investments in my coaching development. I see too many coaches do the opposite—spend freely on everything except the learning and development that would actually transform their practice.

With that mindset, the next morning, I left East London at 6:00 a.m. and took the underground train to London Heathrow Airport for my flight, which departed at 9:30 a.m. The underground journey took over an hour, and my total trip cost was going to be well in excess of £1,000. I was excited to fly to the States; the early start, which normally would have bothered me, felt like no big deal.

The first flight to Atlanta was nine hours, and then I caught my connecting flight to Phoenix, which took another four hours. The trip was long but uneventful, and it felt like I was embarking on an adventure. I hadn't travelled abroad very much in my corporate career, and here I was flying halfway across the world to learn from the best in my new career. I used an Uber for the first time ever when I landed in Phoenix and arrived at the Hotel Valley Ho in Scottsdale around 8:00 p.m. local time. It was a really nice hotel in an upmarket neighbourhood—Steve hadn't chosen something cheap and functional. I didn't know anyone else in the school so had a simple beetroot salad for dinner in the hotel restaurant and got an early night, given the time zone difference of seven hours.

The next morning I wandered down to breakfast and met some of the other coaches. They were such a fun and friendly bunch. Some were surprised that I had flown all the way over from the UK to attend the school and it started to dawn on me that I might be the only transatlantic attendee.

We wandered over to the conference room where the formal teaching would take place. It was there I bumped into Gary Mahler. He had also missed the first weekend of the school and was new to the group. After a few minutes of speaking with him, I realised I had a lot to learn. This man was charging much higher fees than I was.

He was telling me about proposals he had made to clients for $10,000, $20,000 and more. Some of these proposals led to clients saying yes. My highest fee at the time was £10,000 for a year and no-one had taken me up on it yet. I realised that this was a different room than most. In the UK, it seemed as if no coaches were really making a full-time living from coaching. If I attended a training course for coaches in the UK, most of them would be new coaches, or those with some experience who were often making even less money than I was. It was clear the coaches in this school were at a different level in their businesses.

I took my seat and waited for Steve to share his wisdom and help me turn this fledging coaching practice into something I could make a living from. Steve wrote one word on the board to describe the whole weekend: 'Flourish.' He said the weekend was about teaching us to help people flourish *before* they paid us. Most coaches promise clients they will flourish once they hire a coach, but Steve wanted coaches in his school to help potential clients thrive regardless of whether they signed up for coaching or not.

With these words I knew (yet again) that I was in the right place. This was exactly what I had been looking for. No marketing. No gimmicks. Just pure service.

Steve went on to say that if we have someone in our network who hasn't signed up with us and we want them to, we should ask ourselves whether they've really started to flourish yet.

He then launched into exploring the question: Why aren't people flourishing yet? As I considered applying this self-inquiry to my own life, I could see how it would naturally take me into deeper service of everyone in my life.

Flourishing tends to happen *outside* of our comfort zone he continued—but, of course, not so far out of it that we become paralysed and unable to take action. Rather, it involves taking lots of tiny steps outside of that comfort zone. This reflected my own experience. For example, in the case of my own personal development journey so far, there hadn't been any big overnight changes, no Hollywood-style insights, but instead lots of little steps. It was like going to the gym and increasing the weight on the machine a little bit each time—as opposed to trying to make huge leaps in fitness all at once—and ending up injuring myself.

Steve shared about one of his former coaches and mentors, Dr Nathaniel Branden. I'd not heard of him before, but he was apparently a psychotherapist and author particularly well-known for his work on the psychology of self-esteem. Dr Branden used a sentence stem technique to help his clients gain insights into their challenges. The question stems would sometimes begin with something like, 'If you were three percent more . . .' followed by whatever the person was trying to change, such as: 'If you were three percent more active and fit, what would that look like?' or 'If you were three percent kinder to your spouse today, what would that look like?' He would then ask the client to find ten different endings for each sentence.

Creating a three or five percent change is a tiny step, and very doable. Dr Branden saw that if his clients made these three percent changes over and over, they would add up. This would then lead to real transformation—without requiring a superhuman effort.

I, like many people, thought change had to happen *fast*. As a client this was getting in the way of my making long-lasting changes in my own life—and as a coach it was hindering me from really helping my clients.

Neither I nor my clients needed to push ourselves to do things that looked extremely uncomfortable in order to make progress. We could instead take manageable, small steps forward towards the change we wanted. What a relief!

Steve made a distinction that has stayed with me ever since: The difference between being *courageous* and *fearless* is that being fearless implies there is no negative emotion involved. Being courageous implies taking action in the face of fear. This tied in with my own understanding of the Three Principles, which was that all my feelings, including fear, were coming from my thinking in the moment, and nothing else. This didn't mean that I had to wait until the fear subsided before taking action. It actually gave me *less* of an excuse to not take action when I was feeling scared or anxious.

Steve gave an example of his own regarding his experience with public speaking. By his own admission he was *not* a successful speaker at first. In fact, he'd had crippling stage fright. However, he simply took small—yet courageous—steps outside of his comfort zone, and over time he became a well-respected, well-paid public speaker. This was very similar to a story that Jamie Smart told about his own journey with public speaking. Although his stage fright wasn't 'crippling,' it was still quite intense. He related to me that:

> About a minute after I started, all the blood would drain from my face, my throat would close up, my mouth would go dry and my legs would start shaking. I found that if I could just keep going, it would pass after a few minutes, but for much of my life I'd just avoided doing any type of talk or presentation. When I decided I wanted to be a speaker, it was kind of wild, because I was terrified of public speaking. But I just decided I was going to have to get better at it, and the only way to do that was to do as much of it as I could. So I said yes to every public speaking opportunity that came my way.

He hadn't had crippling stage fright, but the steps he took to improve were the same. He kept doing more and more public speaking and didn't allow his fearful thinking to stop him; eventually he became very good at it.

The message was becoming ever clearer: Building my coaching practice was possible without resorting to tactics and techniques that felt 'off' or making giant leaps outside of my comfort zone. I was also seeing how understanding this allowed me to help clients make changes in *their* lives more easily. Furthermore, it busted through the thought that I and many other coaches have, which is: *If I help someone before they pay me, they won't hire me, because they've already gotten what they need.*

However, if real change occurs through tiny steps rather than giant leaps, we can't possibly give them everything in a session or two.

It was starting to click!

71

Coaching Is a Two-Step Process

On my second day in Scottsdale, Steve explained coaching as a two-step process. Once again this was something that landed so powerfully I've never forgotten it.

The first step, he said, is that the potential client has to *see* their future differently. They must understand that if we work together, their default future—what will occur if they keep doing what they're already doing—will change. Otherwise, why hire me?

They also have to see something differently *now*, something they can't unsee. For example, if someone wants to have more confidence and self-esteem, they need to first see that both are a reflection of their thinking, as opposed to a fixed aspect of their personality that can never change. Once they see this, it will forever alter their perception of themselves and their ideas and experiences around confidence. They see that confidence isn't related to certain activities or something that's hard-wired into them. It's related to their thinking. This understanding can transform their relationship with life. An individual can have high self-esteem and confidence no matter what's happened in the past and what comes their way in the future.

However, this is only step one. The second step in the coaching process is that for the coaching to work, the client has to *live* life differently. It isn't always enough for an individual to experience a shift on the level of thinking. If that's all that happens, the change could remain superficial.

Steve suggested that in an ideal enrolment process, the first conversation has the potential client seeing life differently. Then, hopefully between the first and second sessions they begin to *live* a little differently.

What will really have them eager to sign up to work together, for example, is if in our first conversation they start to see self-esteem differently and the possibility of them having higher self-esteem in the future. Then, by the time of our second conversation they've already started to live from a higher level of self-esteem.

This blew my mind. From the minute we first connected, I could actually help people begin to change their lives in they same ways they might later pay for. I didn't need to be stingy about it. This recognition opened up a whole new level of possibility in my mind, and naturally a whole new level of service as well.

I had learned to do step one, and sometimes this was enough. Helping people have a different vision for their future was vital. But reflecting on the second part of Steve's suggestion made me realise I could have gone further into step two with some of my potential clients in the past. At times I'd stopped too soon, jumping too quickly into making a proposal or spending the conversation trying to convince the other person why it would be good to work with me and what could be different in their life. If I had instead actually helped them start to *live* that different life before any money exchanged hands, the decision to hire me would have been much easier.

This lesson altered my conversations with potential clients

forevermore. I didn't change overnight, but I started to get a sense of when I had really helped the person I was talking to have a deep enough shift that they were ready to work with me.

Alternatively, if after a few conversations I wasn't helping them see and live life differently, it showed me that perhaps we weren't a good fit for coaching, and I didn't need to make a proposal.

I now had a new filter for my clients, one that felt good and which was in alignment with my values.

72

Learning from Other Coaches

One of the things that struck me that weekend at Steve's school, was how financially successful many of the other coaches in the room were. I mentioned earlier how one of the first coaches I met was Gary Mahler. I had been used to speaking to coaches in the UK who were earlier on in their coaching journey than me. I felt like a big fish in a small pond. However, a few minutes into speaking with Gary I realised I was no longer the big fish.

It wasn't just Gary. That weekend I met Melissa Ford for the first time. She asked a question about a proposal to a client worth $25,000. Then there was Karen Davis, who shared that she was in the process of enrolling a senior leader into a $100,000 agreement. This was a place for me to keep my ears wide open and listen. I knew there was a lot to learn.

What really struck me that weekend, and the following weekends, was that the coaches who were making the most money were the kindest, most loving, service-oriented people I'd ever met. I had expected them to be pushy and salesy. I'd even half-expected an energy from these people of trying to get me to sign up to their coaching. In fact, it was the opposite. They were really nice, friendly and eager to support me—without any strings attached.

Steve had suggested I could learn as much from the other

coaches in the room as I could from him. I hadn't believed him. *A nice line,* I had thought. *A good piece of marketing.*

Except it was neither. It was true. I would later take this lesson to heart in my own group programmes. Building strong communities in my programmes is very important to me. I love running groups where people are a strong stand for one another and not just there for themselves. I filter for this when enrolling people in my groups, and I cultivate it through speaking about it time and again. I remember Jamie Smart introducing coaches in his programme to the word 'compersion.' Jamie had learned it from a mentor of his, Johnny Epstein. It is widely used in the polyamory community to describe the feeling of joy when you see your romantic partner enjoying themselves with another person. However, it can of course apply in other contexts, and anyone can feel compersion from knowing someone else is having a positive experience—whether it benefits you directly or not. At the time of attending this first weekend with Steve I hadn't adopted this ethos, although I understood the concept. Over time it would become a core value in my work.

In Steve's school, he formally organised peer coaching. Every month we coached someone in the school, and they coached us, twice. No money was exchanged but we were encouraged to act as if we had paid for the coaching. This was an incredible and eye-opening experience. I got a chance to be coached by amazing coaches like Melissa Ford, Karen Davis and David Schwendiman. These weren't just new coaches who didn't know what they were doing. These were individuals with whom I had powerful, insightful conversations that I really valued.

Many of these led to friendships and professional relationships. I am very grateful that I am still in touch with so many coaches who I met that first weekend in Scottsdale. At the time of writing, Melissa

Ford and Karen Davis have both been faculty members of my AJC Coaching Career School, and I was honoured to write the forward to Melissa's book, *Living Service: The Journey of a Prosperous Coach* (she returned the favour by writing the forward to this book). Coaching can be a lonely profession in many ways. That weekend, I found my tribe. This was worth as much as anything else I learned in Steve's school.

73

The Ultimate Coach

It was the afternoon of Day Two at Steve Chandler's Coaching Prosperity School in Scottsdale, Arizona. Lunch had just ended, but the energy in the room felt different. There was a sense of urgency, a quiet anticipation. Steve Chandler had made it clear: the next speaker was not to be missed.

'Be on time,' he had warned us. 'The doors will be locked. If you're late, you're out.'

I wasn't exactly known for my punctuality, so I made an extra effort that day to keep an eye on the clock. I wasn't going to risk missing what was about to happen.

The moment arrived. Steve Chandler introduced the man he credited with changing his life more than anyone else: Steve Hardison. The Ultimate Coach. I had seen Hardison once before, at the London Intensive, but this still felt exciting in a new way.

Chandler spoke about Hardison with a level of reverence I had never heard before. He made it sound as if without Hardison, this school I was in wouldn't exist. His own life would be unrecognizable. It was the greatest acknowledgement I had ever heard from a client about his coach. He told us that Hardison had had such a powerful impact on his life that he and Hardison had created a lifetime agreement—I had never even heard of that before. That introduction set the stage for something extraordinary.

When Hardison walked in, he wasn't alone. His wife, Amy Hardison, was with him, and she sat on a stool next to him. I thought that was strange. No other speaker I'd seen had done this. But then something even stranger happened; Hardison spent a significant amount of time acknowledging her, speaking about who she was, creating her in front of us. I had never seen anyone do this before, and to be honest, I didn't know what to make of it. Was this part of the lesson? Was this his way of demonstrating something? Or was this just the way he lived? I knew I wouldn't do that with my girlfriend. Hardison was demonstrating the power of creation through acknowledgements, and it was a masterclass, but only if I had been really listening.

Then Hardison reached into a bag and started handing out books, CDs, and resources. But there was a condition—he wasn't just giving things away randomly. He only gave them to people who committed, right there in the moment, to using the resource to learn. He wasn't interested in passive receivers. He wanted to give to those who would do something with the gift. That alone said so much about who he was. He was not rushing anything he was doing but creating powerful agreements with people he had only just met.

All the same, when he started speaking, I'll be honest: my mind was noisy. He spoke powerfully, and I had a feeling he was impacting many of the coaches in the room. But I was caught up in judgment. Not of him, but of myself. I was comparing myself to him, wondering how someone could command such presence, thinking about how far I was from being the kind of coach who could charge \$100k-\$150k a year. The irony is, he spoke directly to that—about how every single person in the room was perceiving him differently. That was a key to his work. Before he could coach someone, he had to first understand how they created their world through their thinking.

He also made something else very clear—he never convinces anyone to work with him. He only works with people who *want* to work with him. That hit me hard—the idea of not chasing, not persuading, but being so solid in what you do that the right people come to *you*. I wasn't ready for that back then. It would take me years before I was. In fact, I wouldn't fully grasp that lesson until 2019, when I finally had a paid session with Hardison—one that led to even more coaching with him.

But what stood out the most from that afternoon was a story he shared about a client who had been $900k in debt. The man had reached out to Hardison, and in their first conversation, Hardison told him that if they were to work together, it would cost $150k. I could only imagine what was going through that man's mind. *I'm nearly a million dollars in debt, and you want me to pay you another $150k?!*

But Hardison didn't let the number be the barrier. He showed the client how he could create that money. And by Monday, the man had done it—he had created $150k over the weekend. Not only did his life change, but he went on to refer countless other clients to Hardison.

Hardison shared this story to illustrate a powerful point: it's often less about clients not having the money to pay you and more about the fact that you haven't yet shown them that you're worth it. That hit me. I had spent so much time worrying about whether potential clients could afford to work with me, but Hardison was pointing to something deeper. It wasn't about the money. It was about value.

That was the kind of client and impact I wanted to have. That was the kind of transformation I wanted to be part of.

Looking back, I barely absorbed a fraction of what Hardison shared that day. My mind was too busy. But even in my distraction, something had shifted. I had seen something new—something that would stay with me for years. And when the time came, I would be ready to step into it fully.

74

Filling My First Immersion

After the success of my Powerful Men's Intensive in 2014, I decided to up the ante and create what I called the Powerful Men's Immersion. Without the constraints of a full-time job limiting my days off, I was able to make this a three-day, live experience and really dive in deep with the participants. Again, this would be around the kind of thinking they experienced that was getting in the way of a better life, making more money, deeper relationships and a whole lot more.

I wanted to create something more professional for this three-day Immersion. So rather than holding it in my lounge, I hired a hotel conference room in Birmingham city centre which was surrounded by other hotels. This way attendees would have plenty of options for accommodation, restaurants and great transportation. I used a good four-star hotel at which I had previously attended a work meeting, and they only charged me £200 per day for the room. All I needed to do next was sign people up!

Some of the first enrolees were clients who had come to the two-day intensive. They'd had a great experience and wanted more. I kept the fee a no-brainer for me *and* for them. They'd paid £600 for a two-day intensive, so I set the fee at £800 for three days. Four clients from that initial group signed up to the Immersion. Now I needed to keep going and get at least eight, but I was hoping for twelve total.

Steve told me that the way to fill any group is to simply keep inviting people until it's full. This seemed too simple to be true, but I couldn't fault the logic. If I kept on speaking to people about the Immersion, some would sign up, and eventually I might reach a point at which there were no spaces left.

This turned out to be true: I signed up another four clients from the attendees at the Las Vegas event. I gave them a great experience on a call or two and let them know that if they had found benefit in our time together, they could continue the work by signing up to my Immersion programme. I told them that, in my mind, this was the next logical stage of personal development for them. I would not be sharing the sorts of things they may have frequently heard from other coaches, but rather the best transformational knowledge I had gleaned from my recent training.

One of these clients was from Canada, one from Belgium and another two were from Norway. I would never have expected these people to travel from so far away for my Immersion, yet simply by inviting them I created the possibility for them to attend—and they did.

Eventually, through continued conversations and sending out Three Principles-based audios and videos, I filled all twelve slots of the Immersion.

It had officially sold out.

I'd learned my lesson from the previous year. I hadn't spent lots of time on marketing, emails or gimmicks to fill this group. I simply stayed in conversations with individuals whom I thought would benefit from attending. I didn't try to find people with whom I had no connection to try and sell them the group. I instead focused on people who already had some connection to me, either as existing clients, potential clients I had spoken to before or men who had heard me speak in Las Vegas and valued what I shared.

Through these connections and during my enrolment calls, I was giving people an experience of being with me before they paid anything at all. In this sense, the Immersion wasn't going to focus on a lot of new information. Most of the people who were attending had heard me speak before or had been sent resources after our previous conversations. The Immersion was designed to be purely about transformation—and that would occur in the moment, in the room.

I didn't know it then but this Immersion group was going to become my signature programme, one that I would run for years to come, and which would evolve into one of the best personal development programmes in the world. However, it all started rather humbly in Birmingham, with twelve people in a hotel room, when I didn't have a tonne of confidence or know how to run groups.

Clearly, I'm glad I started despite those reservations.

75

I Didn't Need to Take This Seriously

My first job straight out of university was a marketing role with a heavy building materials company in the UK. I applied and was accepted to their graduate management training scheme, so in addition to the day job I was given significant training and development over the course of a year. One of the best bits of feedback I got on that programme was that I could be more *me*.

I recall a lady who helped facilitate the programme explaining that it was very clear I was professional and driven, and that I wanted to do well. That, however, that didn't mean I had to hide my personality.

This was incredibly insightful of her. I had assumed that in order to succeed in my professional life, I would have to hide who I was outside of work. No wonder I sometimes struggled to connect with my colleagues in the graduate training programme.

That feedback would have been even more helpful had I really taken it to heart. At the time, I struggled to implement her suggestions and it took time to bring my personality in a congruent way into my work life. Years later, as it turned out, I was doing the same thing in this new career called coaching. I was trying to project the image I thought I needed to project as a coach: Professional, clean cut and polished. At the same time, I also dialled down my humour, which was a big part of my personality.

I noticed Steve Chandler didn't do that, and there were other coaches who were successful who seemed to infuse humour and their personality into their professional as well as personal lives. Steve once told me that 'humour is vital to life.' I would later come to realise that it's also a great way to build relationships with people. And coaching, after all, is a relationship business.

This became clear when I delivered my first Powerful Men's Immersion. As I mentioned in a previous chapter, I hired a conference room in a Birmingham city centre four-star hotel. One of the attendees remarked that I could have probably chosen a cheaper venue to host the immersion. I told him I wasn't going for the cheapest venue, but for one that demonstrated this was a professional training. In my mind, I felt good that I had exceeded his expectations on the venue, and I imagined I was delivering a more polished experience than he thought he would get. I was in 'work mode' during the weekend.

During the immersion I decided to have an 'entertainment evening' on the penultimate night, after the formal teaching part was over. This was something I had experienced on other retreats and programmes I had attended, and I thought it could be a light-hearted addition to the weekend. One of my former clients, Cory, who was helping me run the immersion, was also an amateur singer, songwriter and played guitar. The only problem was that he didn't bring his guitar with him from Canada, so I asked my cousin, Aayushi Jain, who was also a singer, if she would come and sing for us and also lend her guitar to Cory. She did a medley of covers of pop songs with him as well as some of her original work. It was great fun. After she left, the attendees were in great spirits and decided to try their hand at karaoke.

I don't have the best singing voice, but I joined in too and enjoyed the moment. The next day I started the immersion as I had the previous day. I asked the attendees what insights they'd had from the previous day and what was showing up fresh for them this morning. I was expecting a question, or for someone to share a story about an insight they'd had. What I didn't expect was one of the attendees saying his biggest 'aha' moment came from the entertainment evening. He said that when he saw me really enjoying myself, being in the moment and having fun, it showed him that I really lived what I was teaching.

That attendee's observation became an aha moment for me too. All this time I'd been approaching my coaching practice like my former career—with too much seriousness. I thought building a successful practice meant mastering enrolment, perfecting my delivery, and maintaining a professional image at all times. But this moment showed me something completely different. The breakthrough wasn't in pushing past comfort zones—it was in infusing my work with genuine playfulness and humour. When I started simply being myself, that's when the real connection happened. My willingness to be spontaneous, to experiment, to join in the karaoke despite my singing limited to the car—these weren't departures from professionalism. They were what made my work credible. Who would have thought that the secret to becoming a better coach and a more prosperous one was learning not to take myself so seriously?

76

The Seed of a Book

It was February 2015, and I was on a coaching call with Steve Chandler. At this point, I had been working with him for a while, soaking in his wisdom, but I had no idea that this particular conversation would plant a seed that would change the trajectory of my life.

The conversation built on something I had shared at his coaching school only a few weeks earlier. I told the group about an insight I'd had around who I really was. For most of my life, I had seen myself as a shy, insecure guy who craved approval. That was my narrative. That was who I believed I was. But through my exploration of the Three Principles, I had recalled a memory from my childhood—one that challenged everything I thought I knew about myself.

I was a young boy, visiting India with my family. My uncle had gifted me a box of sweets, and I had shared them with a girl I had only just met. In that moment, I wasn't shy. I wasn't insecure. I wasn't looking for approval. I was simply *being*—and who I was being was confident, kind, loving, and engaging. The memory had been buried for years, but when it resurfaced, I saw something profound: *That was who I really was.* Not the insecure man I had believed myself to be for so long.

Steve listened, and then he said something that stopped me in my tracks.

'You could write an entire book based on that.'

It was a simple statement, but it landed deep. Several friends had told me that I should write a book, but I had always dismissed it as a nice idea, something flattering to hear, but nothing I seriously considered doing. But when Steve said it, it hit differently because of who he was. Here was Steve Chandler—an incredible author, a man who had sold over a million books, e-books, and audiobooks—telling me that I had something worth writing about. Me—a guy who up to that point had never seriously considered writing a book.

At the time, I didn't act on it. It wouldn't be until 2016 that I actually started writing, but the seed had been planted. And looking back, I see the power of that moment. The power of coaching. One sentence, one belief from someone I deeply respected, shifted what I saw as possible for myself.

Years later, when I looked back at my notes from that coaching session while writing this book, I saw that I had only written those nine words about Steve's suggestion: 'You could write an entire book based on that.' Nine words. And yet, the moment was burned into my memory.

Now, I see the same possibility for so many coaches. They write incredible posts on Facebook. They send out engaging emails. And yet they convince themselves that writing a book is a Herculean task. Or that they don't know what they would write about.

Steve helped me see that what I *already* knew was worth writing about.

As you know, the book you're reading now is based on my journey in those early years of coaching. And, as I've shared, much of it was full of self-doubt and a desire to keep learning. I'm grateful I kept my notebooks from that time, because they've shown me not only what I was learning, but also how much I already knew.

One thing I appreciate about Steve Chandler is that he never instructed me (or any of his other clients, as far as I know) to write a book. He never pushed it as something I should do. But years later, after my first book was published, he shared with me that writing a book is one of the best strategies for client creation. Not because a book is necessary, but because it allows us to share our voice, our insights, and our journey in a way that can reach beyond a single coaching conversation.

I don't believe everyone has to write a book. But if you've ever had the thought, the nudge, the whisper of an idea—I encourage you to follow it. You never know where it might lead.

77

The Website Myth

By early 2015, I knew my website wasn't great.

I hadn't been blind to this fact. It was a basic WordPress site that I had put together in 2013 by hiring a cheap freelancer on O-Desk (now called Upwork). For $125, he had customised a simple WordPress template, and at the time, that suited my budget just fine.

But now I was thinking I needed to up my game. After all, I didn't have physical premises, so my website was the way people would check me out. Or so I thought.

There was no shortage of advice on the topic. Plenty of people insisted that you needed a professional-looking website, that your 'copy' had to be enticing to draw in clients, and that setting this up was one of the first steps in building a business. It all made logical sense.

And then, I brought it up with Steve Chandler. Once again, his advice was the opposite of what I had heard elsewhere.

Steve suggested that I delay revamping my website and instead focus on building my business. He told me that in this profession, a website was more of a reassurance for people who already wanted to hire me, not the place where people would find me in the first place.

He shared how Steve Hardison—the Ultimate Coach—didn't

have a website for many years because he knew that people didn't hire him based on a webpage. They hired him because they spoke to him.

Steve had a point, as always. When I looked at his own website, it was incredibly basic. If you were hiring a coach based purely on web design, you probably wouldn't have hired Steve Chandler. And yet, I had. His website had nothing to do with it. What brought me to him was the impact of his emails, his audios, and his books. I had already been helped by him before I ever paid him.

And how did I first hear about Steve Chandler? Not through Google, not through his website—but through one of his clients, Rich Litvin. The impact of Steve's coaching was so profound that word got around.

That conversation changed the way I thought about websites—and about business in general. So many coaches believe that if they just have the perfect website, clients will magically appear. But Steve was pointing me toward something different: the real work happens in conversations, not in pixels and templates.

It wasn't that having a website was bad. It just wasn't the priority. The priority was getting in front of real people and making a difference. And that was something no website could do for me.

78

A Business, Not a Hobby

At the end of February 2015, I sat down with my accountant to go through my numbers. In preparation for the meeting, I had been working on my accounts spreadsheet, and the reality was sobering. Yes, I had started to sign up clients. Yes, money was coming in. But when I looked at the actual revenue minus costs, the truth was inescapable—I had made a loss for the second year in a row.

It wasn't all bad news, though. My accountant informed me that I could offset the losses against future income. That gave me some relief. My biggest costs to date had been training with Jamie Smart and now my coaching with Steve Chandler—investments that I knew were invaluable. And despite the losses, I could see things were moving in the right direction.

My accountant pointed out that with the recent sales I had made, I would now be able to take a small salary from my business. She suggested a modest one of £833 a month—a far cry from my corporate income, but a significant milestone nonetheless. Clearly my initial expectation of earning a living from coaching within just a few months had been overly optimistic. But now, for the first time, I would be drawing a salary—however small. This said to me that my practice was no longer a hobby but an actual business. And one I intended to grow. There was no turning back.

I had also prepared for operating with fewer incoming funds, at least for a while. I'd spent over a year reducing my spending, building a buffer of savings, and cutting down my living costs by moving back in with my parents. This wasn't a humbling step for me. My training in the Three Principles was showing me that my experience of moving back home was based on whatever I made of it. I chose to see it as an opportunity—a chance to spend more time with them; it was a blessing rather than something to be ashamed of. When I had moved to London in 2013, my parents had probably thought I'd never come back home. But here I was, and I saw it as a gift.

Around this time, I received an unexpected call from my former boss. He had an offer for me—a contracting role for two or three days a week, doing exactly what I used to do for him.

I could do the job with my eyes closed. It would have provided a safety net.

And yet, I said no.

There were two reasons. Firstly, the pay wasn't great. But more importantly, I knew that taking this job would be a step backward. Working two days a week in a corporate role would restrict my ability to speak with potential clients and grow my coaching business. It would keep me tethered to the past when I was so close to building something new.

I didn't want to operate from fear anymore. I had spent too much of my life playing it safe.

This was the time to back *myself.*

That didn't mean being reckless. I had taken the necessary steps to reduce my risks, to lower my expenses. But it *did* mean making a decision from a place of belief rather than fear.

I wasn't married. I didn't have a mortgage or children. If there was ever a time to go all-in on my business, this was it. Because I knew that if I didn't do it now, I never would.

79

Stacking the Cards in My Favour

As I approached my first Powerful Men's Immersion, I wanted to ensure it went really well, and I felt some nervousness. It was going to be twice the size of the men's intensive I had done the previous year. Also, there were several people in the room with whom I had not had much interaction. Furthermore, the programme would take place over three days rather than two. I imagined freezing and running out of things to say, or the attendees having a terrible experience because I was out of my depth.

So I slowed down and asked myself: How could I get closer to *guaranteeing* the programme would be a success? I now liken this to going to a casino and stacking the cards in my favour to make it more likely I'll have a winning hand (only with the men's immersion, it's not cheating).

One of the things I had noticed was that new clients sometimes wanted to debate with me about the Three Principles. We could get into some back and forth about whether we really have an experience of life based on our thinking and not our circumstances. They would throw out scenarios to look for an exception to what I was saying. Often, however, if I sent them an audio by Jamie Smart, or if they read his book, they started to have insights of their own and see the implications of this work. After that, frankly, the conversations I'd have with them became easier.

I learned from Steve Chandler and Rich Litvin's event in 2014 that I could send a lot of resources to attendees beforehand. So I ended up sending four different audios by Jamie, a TEDx talk by Michael Neill called 'Why Aren't We Awesomer?', four videos by Sydney Banks and an article by Dr Keith Blevens, plus a few other resources. If anyone went through all of these resources beforehand, they would likely have mindshifts that would alone be worth the price of attending the immersion.

I remembered something I'd learned when getting my post graduate diploma in management (which I had completed in 2006 with the Chartered Management Institute). One of the modules had been on learning and development, and in it I was taught something I've never forgotten. Our lecturer stated that managers will often send an employee to a course to identify a weak area, such as time management. However, the typical one-day course often doesn't have much impact on the employee, so the company's investment in the course doesn't yield a great return. To maximise any training course, it's what you do *before* and *after* it that's most important.

For example, if an employee is going to attend a training course on time management, they will get much more out of it if they review the content of the programme, perhaps read any books recommended by the programme, and do any appropriate prep work ahead of time. They might also speak to colleagues about time management to understand how other people do it and then test these practices themselves. This could all take place a month before the actual training. This way they'll start their training from a very different place than where they'd be if they hadn't done any of this advance work. Their questions will be different, their understanding of what they're there to learn will be deeper, and ultimately they will get more out of it.

If they don't do the training in advance, they have to learn everything from the ground up: for example, time management schedules and best practices, problems you can encounter, different approaches and so on. This barrage of information on a one or two day training makes it likely that none of the new learning will stick. Applying this to the immersion, it made sense to give the attendees all the above information because I knew they would be starting from a different place—and frankly, this would make my life easier.

And it worked! Several of the attendees got some major insights about their lives from listening to and reading the resources I sent them.

All of the resources were ones that I had been given permission to share by the author, or they were ones I had found publicly on YouTube or via a Google search. So the financial cost of sharing these was zero, but the impact was high. It only took a small amount of time—something I had much more of now that I had left the corporate world.

I spent less time on what happened after they left the immersion. Steve Chandler was a fan of being 'complete' at the end of a programme. It's something he did at the end of each coaching school he ran. Over the years I would play around with having a follow up webinar but I could never find a date that everyone could commit to, and I did wonder what the impact would have been if I'd been able to schedule it.

Around 2017 I received some feedback from a client who had attended many other group programmes. Based in part on this, I started finding it more effective to address during the immersion how people could take their learnings and keep them alive once they went home.

However, even without having this approach down in 2015, the first immersion exceeded all my expectations.

80

The Power of Preparation

The more I reflected on the importance of preparation, the more I realised how this principle had played a quiet but significant role throughout my coaching journey.

When I first started out, I thought the magic of coaching happened entirely in the session itself. I imagined that the value I provided would come from the conversations I had with clients in the moment—the insights sparked by something I said or a powerful question I asked. What I didn't fully appreciate at the time was how much of the transformation could happen before we even spoke—if the client was willing to engage with the work in a deeper way.

I saw this clearly during the lead-up to the Powerful Men's Immersion. By sending out resources ahead of time, I was setting the stage for insight. Those who took the time to engage with the audios, videos, and articles often showed up to the immersion already in a different state of mind. They were more open, more curious, and more willing to explore. The conversations we had with them went further—faster. It wasn't that I was doing better coaching; they were simply more receptive to what I was pointing them towards.

But this wasn't just about them—it was about me, too. I realised that if I wanted to create the best conditions for insight, I needed to prepare myself just as thoroughly as I was preparing my clients.

In the weeks before the immersion, I found myself going back to the very same materials I had sent out. I re-listened to Jamie's audios, watched Sydney Banks' videos again, and re-read articles that had once sparked insights in me. Each time, I saw something new. I was stacking the cards in my own favour—not just by preparing the clients, but by grounding myself more deeply in what I was teaching.

Part of my preparation also involved hiring Dr Keith Blevens for a couple of conversations. While I also reviewed materials from Jamie, my main preparation came from these sessions, and they were invaluable. Keith told me that in his experience, people needed a lot of repetition, because the Three Principles were revolutionary in their implications. He believed that many people would initially miss just how profound and far-reaching they were. Obviously, sending resources ahead of time allowed participants to spend more time with them.

Keith was one of the best guides on the planet when it came to deeply understanding the Principles. He had mentored both Jamie Smart and Michael Neill, and I felt incredibly fortunate to have access to him. He taught the Three Principles using a simple diagram that illustrated this understanding as a fundamental new paradigm in psychology. It was incredibly useful to be reminded of this perspective, and he generously shared his diagram with me, allowing me to use it during my immersion. I had a large copy printed out and laminated.

These two conversations with Keith helped me take my own understanding of the Principles deeper, which in turn allowed me to teach them more effectively to others. One key insight I took away from that time with Keith, and which has stayed with me ever since, is that the Principles are not personal. They are pointing to the implications of a logical system. They are not just a new belief system replacing an old one. Instead, they are a pre-existing truth.

Understanding this helped me to respond to anything people brought up—not only at that particular immersion but in future ones, and in my coaching conversations. No matter what circumstance or situation a client brought up that seemed to be causing them to feel something, our psychological system doesn't work like that. This was true whether the situation was something that happened in the past, was currently happening, or was something that the client imagined would take place at some point in the future.

The fact that the Principles are a pre-existing truth allowed me to cut through to the heart of the issue in the immersion. For example, it might look to a client like they are lacking in confidence but when I explore what they are thinking it becomes clear that they think taking a particular action will cause them to feel fear or anxiety. Consequently, they'll avoid taking that action. They then will take this to mean they are lacking in this feeling of confidence.

Knowing that everyone's experience of life is created by the same psychological system guides me to ask questions to challenge their current thinking. I might ask, 'Have you ever felt confident?' or 'Do you need to feel confident before taking any action?' Through these questions they can realise themselves that they don't need confidence. It only looks like that when it seems that taking an action will create fear.

If the Principles were simply a new belief system, I would not have the confidence in them to coach so directly around people's thinking, because everyone's experience would be created through their own unique psychological system. If that were the case, I would have to try to understand that system first, and I would have no idea in advance if my coaching and questions would help them experience any insights.

I also prepared for the immersion using a couple of exercises I had learned from Jamie Smart. During the immersion itself, I put this preparation into practice. One of these exercises was to ask clients to go out into any shop, take an item to the checkout, and then offer a lower price for it. This is something that isn't the 'done' thing in the UK, and it helps to show clients that whatever happens, it's their *thinking* about the situation that will create their *experience* of it. When I ran this exercise on the first day of the first immersion, some people were met with confused looks from cashiers, some had light-hearted interactions, and others were outright rejected. People had all sorts of reactions and experiences—but one chap in particular refused to do the exercise at all.

When we came back into the room and spoke about it, he had a huge insight. He realised that his refusal had nothing to do with the actual exercise itself, but with the fear and discomfort he had built up in his mind around it. It wasn't the act of negotiating a price that was the problem—it was his thinking about it. That moment of insight hit him deeply. In a flash he saw how this same pattern played out in other areas of his life, and how he allowed it to hold him back. The simple idea that his experience was coming from his thinking—not from the situation itself—changed the way he saw challenges moving forward.

What I came to understand was that preparation wasn't about controlling the outcome—it was about creating the best possible conditions for insight to happen, both for myself and for those I served. I had no idea that a client would refuse to do the exercise and that his very refusal would lead to a huge insight for him. But I *did* know that having some exercises like the one above would likely generate conversation, insights and a discussion wherein we could explore people's experiences. In my own experience as a client, these exercises had helped me have insights in a way that I hadn't had from simply listening to someone at the front of the room.

I began to see that this principle of preparation applied far beyond immersions or coaching sessions. Whether I was preparing for a client conversation, a talk, or even writing a Facebook post—the more time I spent deepening my own understanding beforehand, the more relaxed the delivery became. The fear of freezing or running out of things to say began to fade away because I realised that powerful service doesn't come from having the perfect script—it comes from how deeply you're connected to what you're sharing.

This shift in perspective gave me a new relationship with fear. Instead of trying to avoid nervousness or self-doubt, I started seeing preparation as an act of love—both for myself and for the people I was serving. It was a way of giving the best of myself, not by trying to force an outcome, but by creating fertile ground for something greater to emerge.

81

Unexpected Connections

One day, I received a message from Jane Roberts, a recruiter I knew from my corporate days. I had worked with Jane during my time as a procurement manager. We had kept in touch over the years, and she was aware that I had left my corporate job to pursue coaching full-time.

Jane reached out to ask if I would be interested in any contracting roles in procurement. This wasn't surprising—most people I knew from my old world assumed I would eventually return to it in some way. But I had already turned down a similar offer from my former boss, and I wasn't about to change course now. I politely declined, reaffirming that I was fully committed to coaching.

Jane had recently been promoted within her organisation and now had a team of her own. She was well-connected in the regional procurement community, with relationships spanning a number of organisations. She suggested that she might be able to arrange for me to do a talk for the regional chapter of a professional association, which she was involved with. She saw it as a good networking opportunity for me and I also thought it might lead to additional opportunities. I could combine my knowledge of procurement with the Three Principles and make a meaningful difference to organisations.

I started to feel as if this woman would be the ticket to all my future clients.

I was open to the idea of the free talk, but in a coaching call with Steve Chandler, he slowed me down. He told me not to get ahead of myself and—most importantly—not to forget that Jane was a real human being. If I impacted her deeply, she would be more likely to refer me to clients, and also more likely to hire me herself or bring me into her organisation.

In my enthusiasm, I had focused on the speaking opportunity. Steve reminded me that the relationship with Jane could potentially be far more valuable than the talk itself. This was a lesson I had to be reminded of many times over the years in my work with Steve: don't forget the person right in front of you.

It might seem like a slower process for client creation, but actually the opposite is true. Focusing on one client at a time has created many clients for me over the years and is more likely to lead to referrals. Trying to chase a referral or a group of people through an organisation has rarely worked in my experience, and it can lead to what may look like promising opportunities that never ultimately lead to clients.

I asked Steve whether it was a good idea to do the talk for free, and he said that at this stage of my career, waiving my fee would be a smart move. However, he assured me that in five or ten years, I would be paid well for speaking gigs. He suggested that for the future, I should set a day rate of £1,000 plus expenses for speaking engagements. While I nodded along in agreement, I was petrified at the thought of saying that number out loud.

Steve was a strong advocate for having fees ready in advance. He even suggested having a starter package for Jane (or anyone else who might be interested)—four sessions for £1,000. This way, I wouldn't fall into an endless cycle of free conversations that never went anywhere.

I was still caught up in putting Jane on a pedestal because of her connections and seniority within her organisation. But Steve told me something that completely shifted my perspective. It wasn't about expertise or experience. It didn't matter who was older or younger, who earned more, or who had more corporate experience. All that mattered was whether I could help Jane see something new—something she was blind to—that would make a significant difference in her life.

Steve was helping me to be seen as a professional. Not just by Jane, but by anyone. And this started with *me seeing myself* as a professional first.

Jane and I ended up having a few coaching conversations. They were extremely impactful for her. I gifted her a signed copy of *Clarity*, by Jamie Smart, which she loved, and I shared some additional resources with her. However, when it came to working together formally, she ultimately came up with reasons why she couldn't spare the money.

I was disappointed. But, once again, Steve was incredibly helpful. He told me something I never forgot: When a client doesn't sign up with you, you are spared. I didn't quite understand this at the time but I would come to see that the best clients for me are those who are enthusiastic about working with me. Any client I need to persuade or cajole to hire me will often be less enthusiastic when we do sign up, and less committed to the coaching. It is far more enjoyable for me to work with clients who really want to hire me. I'm also spared from investing time and energy with someone who isn't truly ready, which frees me up to serve the clients who are genuinely committed and therefore more likely to see meaningful results.

Steve encouraged me, again, to stop looking for clients and

start focusing on problems. If I became a problem-solver for people, they would want to hire me. Steve even suggested that some people would beg to work with me.

I never forgot that conversation. It reinforced what I was beginning to see more clearly—that the best way to create clients wasn't through pitches, clever marketing, or even networking events. It was through solving real problems for real people. And that only happens in deep, meaningful conversations.

82

Reaching Out

In April 2015, I was having a coaching conversation with Steve when I brought up Richard Benson. Richard had been a senior leader when I worked in the corporate world. He was incredibly smart—one of the youngest leaders at his level I had ever seen. He had a reputation for pushing his teams to higher levels of performance, and I had learned so much from working under him. Despite the hierarchy, we had a good relationship, and I respected him immensely.

Nonetheless, I had been reluctant to contact him.

Perhaps it was a fear of being judged. I had reasoned that I would only reach out to people like Richard once I had 'made it'—once I had proven myself in the coaching world—rather than trying to create them as clients early on. Deep down, there was some lingering shame about being a life coach. Part of me worried that others would judge me, that they would see this as a soft profession, not a real career. I imagined that some of my former colleagues probably thought I was having a mid-life crisis.

There was no factual basis for these assumptions; no one had ever said any of these things to me. But that's the power of our thinking. I had built up an entire narrative in my head that held me back from acting.

Steve listened patiently and then encouraged me to reach out to Richard. He told me to stop making it bigger than it was and just send a message to connect. He suggested I offer to tell Richard about the kind of training I had been doing and let him know which large companies had already taken on this training. He reminded me that Dr Dicken Bettinger, someone I had spent time with and who had also mentored Steve, had gone into many organisations and helped them using his understanding of the Three Principles—with great success.

Steve laid out a few possible approaches:

- I could offer a pilot programme or suggest coming in to present for twenty minutes.
- If I wasn't confident about running an executive training programme, I could offer private coaching for a few leaders.
- I could simply start with one person as a test run.

Steve had a lot of experience working with corporates. This, in fact, was one of the reasons I had hired him. He explained that CEOs and senior leaders don't like taking leaps of faith on something untested, but if I shared which other large organisations had already undertaken Three Principles training, it wouldn't feel like a leap at all. He even suggested reaching out to other Three Principles coaches and trainers who had worked with corporations and simply asking them where they had worked, so I could reference those companies in my conversations.

This was our most uncomfortable coaching conversation to date. I had so much thinking about why I couldn't do this or how badly it would go. I kept resisting, and Steve kept cutting through my excuses. He told me that the only things in the way of my success were my own thoughts—my imagined fears of what could happen and what it would mean.

Steve was excited for me. He told me not to stop until I got into the company. I could feel my resistance, but I also knew he was right.

After the call, I sat with my discomfort and then decided to act. I knew that as a senior leader, Richard was likely interested in information about energy trends, including predictions on the price of oil as it impacted not just direct oil products but many others. My former employer had just released its annual energy outlook. I thought this could be a useful resource for him, and I made it part of my excuse for messaging him. I reached out to Richard with the following message:

> Hi Richard,
>
> Hope you are keeping well. My former employer released their annual energy outlook again last month. I sent it to you last year, and I thought it could be helpful for you and your team.
>
> [Link to energy outlook]
>
> I'd love to hear how things are going for you, and also to speak to you about what I've been up to. I've undertaken some training that has been introduced to a number of Fortune 500 and FTSE companies, such as BAE Systems, Microsoft, AIG, Boeing, and SAB Miller.
>
> While I loved working in procurement, I was so impacted by this type of training 2.5 years ago that I've gone and invested in my own training with the top professionals in this field and have been training

> others ever since. Since January this year, I am doing it full-time. I'd love to set up some time to talk to you about it.
>
> Kind Regards,
>
> Ankush

Richard's response?

Nothing.

He never replied.

I felt deflated. I started telling myself that I had burned a bridge by offering to speak to him about coaching and training. I thought, *Maybe I should have waited until I was more established before reaching out.*

But here's the thing—I had no idea why he didn't reply. He could have been busy. He could have missed the message. His inbox could have been flooded. There were a hundred possible explanations, yet I latched onto the most disempowering one: *He thinks I'm a joke.*

I created meaning out of his non-reply, even though I had no evidence that my assumptions were true. This was a powerful lesson in itself.

If I could go back and advise my younger self, I would encourage him to follow up. To send another message, even something simple like:

> Hey Richard, I wanted to follow up in case my last message got buried in your inbox. Would love to catch up and share what I've been up to. Let me know if you'd be open to a quick call.

I can't say whether a follow-up would have led to a conversation. But I do know that *avoiding* the follow-up guaranteed nothing would happen. The only reason I didn't follow up was because of my feelings around his lack of reply, which were a reflection of my thinking in the moment. What I hadn't seen was that the feelings were not *telling* me to avoid following up; I could have followed up regardless of how I was feeling.

This was further emphasised years later in 2019, when after releasing my first book I reached out to Richard again, simply asking for his address so I could send him a copy as a gift. He replied and suggested we meet. When we did, he was incredibly supportive in helping me get a contract with the major organisation where he was a senior leader.

He clearly didn't see me as a joke, but I'd spent four years avoiding following up with him (and many others too) because I'd groundlessly assumed he did.

Who could you reach out to reconnect with who could really benefit from your work?

83

A Lesson in Coaching Styles

In the early stages of my coaching career, I held onto a key piece of advice from Steve Chandler: A coach without clients is not a professional coach. My job was to fill my practice with clients. So, if someone wanted to work with me, that meant being flexible, adapting, and making it easy for people to say yes.

That mindset led me to offer a coaching package to Margaret. She was a coach herself, more experienced than me, but struggling to grow her practice. I had reached out to offer my help, and she had been open to it. We agreed on a package of 10 sessions at £250 per session.

Our sessions were a great learning experience for me. I truly admired her—she was deeply skilled with her clients, and I could see she had so much to offer. But as the coaching progressed, I noticed something. While she was gaining a lot from our conversations, she wasn't always following through with her actions.

Then, one day, she emailed me to cancel our upcoming session.

She wasn't unhappy with the coaching. In fact, she said she'd already gotten a lot from our time together. But she hadn't implemented everything we had discussed, and she wanted to complete what we had spoken about before having any more sessions.

I could have simply accepted her request and left it at that, but something told me to reach out and have a conversation—not to convince her to continue, but to genuinely reconnect and listen to what was going on for her.

When we spoke, she reiterated what she had said in her email, namely that she didn't want any more sessions until she had taken action on some of the things I had already coached her on. I suggested that instead of keeping our coaching agreement open-ended, we formally complete our work together for now. If she wanted more sessions in the future, she could reach out, and we could pick things up again. This way, she didn't feel pressured to continue before she was ready, and I could close our agreement in a way that felt clean and complete. As she was paying me session by session so there was no refund due, and her payments were up to date.

While I was eager to grow my business, I never wanted to force or convince clients to do something that didn't make sense to them. That was never the kind of coach I wanted to be. My goal was to serve powerfully and let clients choose their own path forward.

I also learned a valuable lesson from this experience, as I do with every client. With Margaret, I saw that I had given her a lot of information to help her grow her practice. Some coaches love that approach. They can't get enough new strategies and ideas. Others, however, prefer less information and need more space to take action on one thing at a time.

In my enthusiasm to help, I had overloaded her with insights and ideas. But that wasn't the best learning style for her.

This experience taught me the importance of meeting clients where they are, not where I think they should be. Margaret's hesitation to continue helped me recognise a pattern I'd been missing with other clients too. Every client is different. Some thrive on lots of new perspectives, while others need a slower, more focused approach.

The real art of coaching isn't just in what I share—it's in knowing how much to share and when to share it. I have some clients who constantly ask me for resources, whether it's in the form of books, audios or videos. They simply cannot get enough information, and I have a number of resources that I share with them. I also have clients who take bold action from any conversation we have, with great success.

I've learned to listen better when assigning resources to clients or creating agreements about the actions they'll take before our next session. If I now hear some hesitation in a client's voice before they say yes to reading a book or taking some action we have discussed, I slow down to explore what's behind the hesitation. This can be extremely useful to them, and it helps me to coach them better.

84

Momentum

Looking back, I could clearly see the shift. In the first six months of working with Steve Chandler, I had made around £12,000 in sales—double what I had made in the previous six months. Things were moving in the right direction. More than that, they were accelerating.

And of course it wasn't simply about the numbers. It was about the confidence I was building, the way I was showing up in conversations and how I was beginning to see myself as a professional coach. The old doubts weren't entirely gone, but they had less of a grip on me. More often than not, I was taking action despite them.

Steve's coaching had made a huge impact, but it wasn't just that he had given me a better system for client creation. He had also challenged the stories I was telling myself. The stories that said I had to wait until I was more experienced before reaching out to potential clients. The stories that said people wouldn't pay for my coaching. The stories that told me I needed a perfect website or a refined marketing plan before I could really succeed.

He had cut through all of that noise and brought me back to the fundamentals:

- Have powerful conversations
- Serve people deeply
- Make proposals

That was it. No gimmicks. No complicated strategies. Just a commitment to service. And it was working.

Just before the final weekend of the ACS school in April 2015, I had an important conversation with Steve. This was the final session of our six-month coaching package, and he told me that if I wanted to continue, I could do so after the school for $9,000 for another twelve sessions. He mentioned that this offer wasn't available to everyone, and I appreciated that.

I told him I wanted to continue. I had gathered momentum and it made sense to keep going.

I also signed up for his next ACS school. While the most recent cohort I'd participated in had had around twenty-five coaches, the next one would have forty or fifty. Steve assured me that it would still be a powerful experience, and that he was always looking to make the school better and better.

What really clinched the deal for me was that I could re-enrol at a lower price than the $9,000 it was for first-time attendees. I knew that many coaches had gone through the school multiple times, including Rich Litvin, and I saw this as not just an investment in my business, but also something I genuinely loved being a part of. The experience of the school and the people I met in it were invaluable.

For the first time, I could clearly see the path ahead. Coaching wasn't just something I was trying to do—it was something I *was* doing. I was running a real business. And this was just the beginning.

Looking back, I can see how important that early decision to renew really was. I could have taken a break, consolidated what I'd learned, and told myself I'd return later, but that would have killed my momentum. When you're building a coaching practice, momentum is everything. It's also fragile. It can fade without you even noticing.

I've seen the same thing happen with coaches I work with. The ones who re-enrol, sometimes more than once, are the ones who keep growing. They build layer upon layer of depth and understanding. The most successful coaches in Steve's school weren't necessarily the most talented; they were the ones who kept showing up and testing what they were learning.

Over time, I came to see that transformation isn't a single moment. It's a way of living. To experience ongoing growth, we have to invest our time, energy, and presence.

The coaches who treat their growth as a journey, not a destination, create thriving practices—not just because they learn more, but because they *become* more. Every time they revisit the work, they see something new, hear something differently, and take action from a deeper place. That's why I went through Steve's school three times. The material didn't always change, but I did.

85

Tools, not Rules

In April 2015 I took on a client whom I'll call Carlos Ramirez. He was a young man I'd met when I'd spoken in Las Vegas, at the event organised by Johnny Epstein. He was from South America, and although he really resonated with what I had shared, he told me he didn't have the money to work with me privately.

I had often heard that it's never really about the money—that if someone sees the value in what you do, they will find a way to pay for it. But I was also learning that there were no hard and fast rules in building a coaching practice. Steve would remind me time and time again, 'Ankush, this is *your* business, and you get to run it how you want.' In his ACS school, he had a mantra: TOOLS, NOT RULES. It's a mantra I've carried into my own coaching school, where we encourage coaches to use what serves them and leave behind the rest.

When Steve and I spoke about a different prospective client who was in a similar situation, he offered a perspective that stuck with me: If I genuinely desired to help this person (not out of desperation for a client, but because I felt we were a good fit and it would be mutually beneficial), then I could say something like:

'If I offered you a way to do this at half my fee, would that be something you'd be interested in?'

This wasn't something to do all the time, but rather an exception I could make when it felt right. If we were both comfortable with the agreement it could be a win-win.

Of course, sometimes prospective clients use price as a polite way to decline, so this approach tells you that, too. In such cases, offering a lower price won't change their response.

The person I had originally discussed with Steve ended up signing on for a small, $500 programme, and that experience opened my eyes. I realised I could offer the same approach to Carlos as well. As with so many coaching calls with Steve in which we talked about a specific person or situation, the advice applied far beyond that single case. This was one of those moments.

I see many coaches who don't yet have a full practice turning away clients who would be ready to work with them if there was a way to do so at a lower price. They rigidly stick to their standard fee, even when there's an opportunity to create a win-win situation. But business isn't always black and white. It's not about rules—it's about what works.

Both Carlos and the other client I had offered a lower-priced option to ended up signing up with me. More importantly, they later went on to invest even more—whether through further coaching or by attending my men's immersions. The lifetime income from these clients was far greater than the initial coaching fee.

That experience showed me something powerful: flexibility in pricing, when used intentionally and strategically, wasn't about lowering my worth—it was about creating opportunities for everyone involved. Furthermore, when I worked with the right people, those opportunities could grow into something far bigger than I had initially imagined.

Do I still do this now? No. I've had a full practice for years, and if price is really an issue for someone, I can often refer them to another coach who charges less than I do. However, many coaches who don't have a consistently full practice could benefit from having some flexibility in their pricing for the right clients.

Is there someone in your network who wants to work with you but who is hesitant due to financial concerns? Ask yourself, 'What offer could I create that would allow them to start working with me right now?'

86

Embracing Inner Peace: My Conversation with Sebastian Eck

In the spring of 2015, I had the privilege of being interviewed by Sebastian Eck for his *Peace for the World* YouTube series. Sebastian, a passionate advocate for global harmony, invited me to share my insights on achieving personal peace and its ripple effect on the broader world.

This opportunity came about because Sebastian had listened to my Relationship Series podcast, which he had found helpful. We also had some conversations where I supported him on his own journey with the Three Principles. I was only the second person to be interviewed for his series. Still, I was in esteemed company—he later interviewed some of the most respected names in the Three Principles community, including Michael Neill, Dicken Bettinger, Judith Sedgeman and Jack Pransky.

Our conversation delved into the transformative power of understanding the Three Principles: Mind, Consciousness, and Thought. I shared how recognising these Principles had profoundly impacted my life, allowing me to see that my experiences were shaped from the inside-out. This realisation brought a sense of peace and clarity that I hadn't experienced before.

Sebastian and I discussed the common misconception that external circumstances dictate our feelings. I recounted personal anecdotes illustrating that it's not the events themselves but our thoughts about them that determine our emotional state and experience of life. I had taken on board Steve's advice to share personal stories and anecdotes, as he often did in our coaching sessions. I found this more natural than trying to explain what the Three Principles were from a purely scientific perspective.

We also explored the idea that personal peace contributes to global peace. When individuals operate from a place of inner calm, their interactions become more compassionate and understanding, fostering harmonious communities. A decade on and I still see this today. I don't believe we can achieve global peace without first finding that peace within ourselves. It reminds me of the quote from Harold B. Lee: 'The most important work you will ever do will be within the walls of your own home.'

Reflecting on the interview, I was reminded of the profound simplicity of the Three Principles and their universal applicability. The conversation with Sebastian reinforced my commitment to sharing this understanding, as I witnessed its potential to transform lives and, by extension, the world.

Participating in the *Peace for the World* series was not just an opportunity to share my insights but also to deepen my own understanding of how personal transformation contributes to global harmony. While my own podcast was a way to create great content for people, I didn't speak much on it myself; instead, I created opportunities for my guests to shine. Being interviewed was different. It gave me an opportunity to share my own views, thoughts and ideas.

Interviews not only help people learn about you; they are also great to send to prospective clients as part of the enrolment process.

When someone is considering working with me, hearing me articulate my thoughts in an interview can be incredibly powerful.

This experience with Sebastian was a testament to the power of authentic dialogue in spreading messages of peace and understanding. It highlighted the importance of looking within for answers and recognising that true peace emanates from understanding the nature of our thoughts and consciousness. It was a meaningful step in my journey as a coach.

That conversation also clarified something for me. I realised that my work as a coach isn't just about helping individuals build their practices. It's about something much bigger. Every coach I work with goes on to touch hundreds or thousands of lives. Every person who finds their inner peace becomes a source of calm in their family, their workplace, their community.

In a way, coaching has become my contribution to raising consciousness in the world, one conversation at a time. It's not grandiose. It's simply what happens when we help people see who they really are.

87

A Client Who Drove Seven Hours

In April 2015, I flew to Los Angeles for the final weekend of Steve Chandler's ACS school. Once again, I took an early flight out of London Heathrow Airport on Virgin Atlantic. Thankfully, this time it was a direct flight—no layovers, no hassle. I arrived a few days early and worked from my cousin's place, taking some time to settle in before the weekend's intensive coaching experience.

I share this detail not just for context, but because it points to something I've come to realise: the effort it takes to get to something meaningful often becomes part of the transformation. Even today, clients fly in from all over the world to attend my men's immersion or the AJC coaching school. And over and over again, they tell me, it's different because of what it took to be there. I, too, have flown from the UK to Phoenix, Arizona, for my sessions with Steve Hardison several times a year. I fully recognise that many people might think I'm spending way too much money and time on this endeavour, but I welcome it as an essential investment in my own growth, and one that I know has helped me to better serve others.

One of the unexpected highlights of this trip was meeting Eva Robinson in person. Eva was a client I had first spoken to in early December of 2014. She had taken medical retirement from her job as a counsellor with Santa Clara County in California, where she had spent years helping people recover from drug and alcohol dependence.

When we first spoke, Eva had no clients but was determined to make coaching a success. She wanted to start earning money to supplement her income, and she was hungry to learn. She really wanted to coach with me, but I knew she wouldn't be able to afford my usual fees. So we had a different conversation instead. She mentioned two potential clients she was considering approaching, and I made her an offer:

'If you enrol one of them, I'll coach you.'

To be honest, I didn't expect to hear from her again.

But a few weeks later, just after attending Steve's school in Scottsdale, I had a follow-up conversation with her. She didn't just sign up one of the potential clients—she had signed up both.

I hadn't expected that. Now, I had to follow through.

I offered her a special coaching rate that was only available to her, and we got to work.

Eva quickly became my best client. She would take immediate action on whatever we spoke about. I once asked her, 'Who would you love to coach?' and she casually mentioned the checkout lady at the supermarket.

We talked about how she could enrol her, and by our next session, she had done it. Within weeks of us starting coaching, she had over ten new clients.

I was impressed. More than that, I loved working with her.

When she found out I would be in California, she told me she really wanted to meet in person. I figured it would be difficult—California is a big place, and I didn't think she lived nearby. But Eva simply asked, 'When are you free?' and I answered I could meet her for lunch one day.

And that's when she drove seven hours, leaving early in the morning, just to have lunch with me. I was blown away. She was so grateful for all the support I had given her. And the truth is, I was equally grateful for the effort she had made to meet me.

I had heard from Rich Litvin about serving clients so powerfully that they never stop talking about you. I loved that idea—the thought of making such a deep impact that a client carries it with them for years. But I hadn't expected to experience that kind of impact myself, especially not so early on in my coaching career.

To give even more context, Eva had a neurological condition that caused pain in her right hand. Driving seven hours each way for a short meeting could not have been easy. I never forgot that lunch. I was deeply touched by what she had done.

Even now, as I write about it, I feel emotional. This is why I believe coaching is not just a profession—it's a privilege. To be invited into someone's life, to help them create real change, and to witness how far they're willing to go because of the impact you've had—that is something I will always cherish.

And that is why I love what I do.

88

Freedom from Fear

The final weekend of Steve Chandler's ACS school took place in Marina Del Rey, a swanky part of Los Angeles. As I arrived at the venue, I once again couldn't help but notice how intentional Steve was with his choice of location. He never used cheap venues or second-rate hotels. And it made sense. If he was helping people create abundance in their businesses, it was only fitting that he held his events in a place reflecting that same abundance.

There was so much that stood out from Day 1, which was primarily focused on fear and worry.

Steve shared with the group how most people seek security because of their fears and worries. But then he offered a perspective I had never considered before:

Freedom from fear is the ultimate security.

What a novel thought!

Most clients, he explained, have a fear-based approach to life—and they don't even realise it. They are unaware of how the mind really works, so they chase security through external means, never seeing that true security is found in their relationship with fear itself. I had glimpses of this myself. I had lived in fear of being judged by others, of not living up to my potential, of ending up alone and so much more. This fear had driven me to try and find security in a relationship, in a job title or in my income, but it never worked. I was seeing more clearly through my exploration of the Three Principles that security cannot be found in these things—but it *can* through realising we are not our thinking. I would lose sight of this at times, but I was moving away from holding onto these attempts to find security in an external situation, a result or a person.

One of the things I loved most about Steve was how open and vulnerable he was in sharing his own stories. He spoke about his own transformation—how his mind shifted from fear when he went through recovery from alcohol addiction. Later, his perspective on fear evolved further through his work with Dr Nathaniel Branden, particularly through Branden's sentence completion technique. However, what Steve ultimately found to be the most powerful tool in his own life was something simpler:

Inquiry.

The process of questioning the belief itself.

Steve shared that, in his opinion, the best form of inquiry he had come across was the work of Byron Katie. He had attended her nine-day school and thoroughly tested her approach.

At this point in my listening, something strange happened inside me: I almost switched off. I had convinced myself that the Three Principles understanding was the most powerful approach to coaching—more effective than any other form of personal development.

How arrogant!

Almost as if he had anticipated this reaction, Steve addressed it directly. He advised everyone in the room not to dismiss something just because we weren't initially drawn to it. He encouraged us to keep an open mind. This kept me listening, albeit with some scepticism. Then, he walked us through the four questions used in

The Work by Byron Katie.[6]

Later that afternoon, he demonstrated the process brilliantly with a coach in the room who had a deep fear about her husband dying. Watching Steve guide her through the inquiry, challenging the thoughts that were causing her suffering, was a powerful experience.

What I took from the day was the power of questioning a client's thoughts (and my own).

I saw how simply asking the right questions can shift an entire belief system, how a single thought—when examined—can lose its grip on someone's life.

It was a humbling and eye-opening experience, and it reminded me that no matter how much I thought I knew, there was always more to see.

[6] Which you can learn more about at www.thework.com

89

Mastering the Art of Enquiry

Steve always emphasised that his ACS school was about client enrolment and not how to be a better coach. I nonetheless found it serving both purposes for me. The two were so intertwined—the better I became at coaching, the easier it was to enrol clients.

On the morning of Day Two, Steve gave us a fantastic exercise to illustrate the power of deep listening and questioning. We were to split into pairs; one person was assigned to be Person A and the other Person B.

Person A would share a real problem they were currently experiencing. Person B would listen. They could ask questions and relate their own experiences, but there was one rule: they were NOT allowed to give advice. After a set amount of time, we would swap roles.

I realised through this exercise just how often I still dropped into 'teaching mode' with coaching clients rather than deeply listening and asking powerful questions.

I used to believe that I wasn't great at asking coaching questions, and although some of that insecurity had faded, I still didn't feel fully confident in my ability to ask powerful questions on coaching calls. However, Steve gave us some incredible examples of how enquiry alone could create breakthroughs for clients.

One of the stories that stuck with me was about a corporate client Steve was coaching—a man who had a deep fear of losing his job. He told Steve, 'If I lost my job, I would be totally devastated.'

Steve didn't jump in with advice or try to comfort him. Instead, he questioned the language:

'Is that really true?'

To Steve's surprise, the client immediately softened and replied, 'No, not really.'

What a breakthrough! And Steve hadn't even offered a solution—he had simply questioned the client's belief. But he didn't stop there. The client admitted that 'devastated' wasn't quite accurate, so Steve asked:

'Would "uncomfortable" be a better word?'

Again, the client agreed. Steve then asked:

'Would you be so uncomfortable that you couldn't look for other work?'

Again, the answer was no. This client had gone from certainty about devastation to realising he could still take action—all without Steve giving him any advice. Steve continued:

'Would it be good if you felt uncomfortable about losing your job?'

The client paused before answering yes, because the discomfort would push him into action. Steve then enquired:

'Could you end up with a better job?'

The client suddenly saw the possibility. Yes, he could end up with a better job, despite the discomfort. This was a masterful display of coaching, using nothing but enquiry to disarm fear and shift perspective. That morning session changed the way I saw coaching. I didn't have to teach clients. I didn't have to give them advice. Sometimes, all I had to do was ask the right question—and let the client discover the answer for themselves.

I've noticed a similar pattern in my own school. Like Steve, I never designed it to teach coaches how to coach. But time and time again, I've heard from participants that just watching *me* coach, whether in person or during a laser session, has transformed the way *they* coach. They often tell me they've started going deeper, asking more powerful questions, and trusting the client's wisdom more. It reminds me that enquiry isn't something you teach through slides or modules. It's something people feel when they witness it in action.

90

The Fundamentals of Performance

On my flight to Los Angeles for the final ACS weekend, I read *A Philosopher's Notes: On Optimal Living, Creating an Authentically Awesome Life and Other Such Goodness* by Brian Johnson. Steve had gifted us copies of this book at the previous ACS weekend, and I was excited to dive in.

Brian was a modern-day philosopher known for his work on *Finding Joe*, a wonderful documentary about the hero's journey, as popularised by Joseph Campbell. He had appeared in the film alongside Deepak Chopra, Robin Sharma, and other incredible teachers.[7] There were so many nuggets in Brian's book, and I was particularly eager to read it because he was joining us in Marina Del Rey as a special guest speaker on Day Two.

Meeting him in person and hearing what he had to share was an incredible opportunity. Brian covered a lot of ground during his talk, but one thing struck me more than anything else, namely his non-negotiable fundamentals of:

- Exercise

---

[7] During the COVID-19 pandemic, the film's director, Patrick Solomon, made it available for free on YouTube, where it has since been viewed millions of times. I highly recommend every client of mine watch it.

- Sleep
- Nutrition

Listening to him talk about these areas of life was uncomfortable. At that moment in my life, I wasn't exercising at all. My sleep was okay, but I would stay up late and sleep in—completely out of sync with my circadian rhythm.

And my nutrition? Awful. I had a fast metabolism, which was a double-edged sword. It meant that my body burned carbs faster than the average person, but it also meant that I could eat poorly without gaining much weight. And I took full advantage of that. Most of my meals lacked real nutrition.

I had made a deliberate trade-off. I told myself that at this stage of my career, building my business was more important than looking after my physical health. It seemed like a reasonable deal . . . except that deep down, I judged myself for it.

I'd hoped that through my exploration of the Three Principles, I would eventually have a sudden insight—an aha moment—that would instantly shift my mindset, and I would effortlessly start eating well and exercising just like that.

That moment never came.

Brian drove the point home. He said that not exercising is like taking a depressant. He spoke about the impact of sugar, especially refined sugars, on the brain. He emphasised the importance of designing a masterful day—of having a system to ensure success.

That part was easy to understand. I already knew what to do:

- Get to bed early
- Have a good night's rest
- Wake up early and don't jump straight onto my phone or emails

- Do some exercise
- Have a prioritised to-do list and focus on the most important things first

Easy, right? Except that knowing a system isn't the same thing as *implementing* it.

It would take me years to fully embrace Brian's teachings. Even now, nearly a decade later, while I exercise four times a week, eat clean, and drink three litres of water a day, I know there's still room for improvement.

If I could go back and speak to myself in 2015, I would tell myself to pay more attention to what Brian was saying about the fundamentals. Getting these aspects of life in order would not only have helped me feel better and have more energy each day—it would have also led me to greater income, because I would have been in a better state of mind and physical health to do the work that mattered most.

91

Speaking from the Heart in Romania

I landed back at Heathrow after my trip to Los Angeles, but there was no time to rest. I didn't even have time to go home. I took an hour-long coach journey straight from Heathrow airport to London Luton Airport for my next destination: Romania.

On the surface, it all sounded glamorous—travelling to the States and then straight to Eastern Europe. And while I was deeply grateful for these opportunities, I couldn't deny that it was exhausting.

I flew on a low-cost airline and stayed in an Airbnb apartment, which was far cheaper than a hotel. The trip was not about luxury—it was about showing up and serving.

I had been invited to speak to a group of men at an annual conference run by Zan Perrion. Zan had been a mentor of mine before I started my professional coaching journey; I had taken an online course and a programme with him several years earlier. Now I had the chance to share my insights with his community. The men attending had already completed one of his programmes, which was a prerequisite to joining his online community.

There were plenty of experienced speakers at the event, most of whom had been coaching for far longer than I had. The core theme of the conference was dating and relationships. Most of the men in the room were single or dating.

I had been in a long-term relationship for over a year at this point, but I didn't consider myself a dating expert. In fact, I had never had a relationship longer than six months before I'd met my girlfriend, Yamini.

As I sat in that loft room, which was filled with men from all over Europe, I thought about what I was going to say. While I had considered my talk, I hadn't planned it—I wanted it to feel authentic and speak from my heart.

And I knew I could. This was a shift I realised had taken place in me. With all the experience I'd accumulated by this point—hundreds of coaching conversations, trainings, live events—I no longer needed hours of preparation. The best preparation I had was the life I had lived and the presence I had cultivated. I'd been getting good feedback on talks like the one I gave in Vegas, and I was becoming more and more at ease speaking in front of people.

There was no need to be impressive. Others had the more adventurous stories. Mine wasn't about being flashy, it was about being real and authentic. And instinctively, I knew that this was what would connect most.

So, I spoke about the only thing I was truly an expert on: my own journey.

I sat on a stool at the front of the room. There were thirty to forty men crammed into the space, and I began sharing. I spoke about my many failures in love: the times I had been insecure, the times I had sought validation through relationships, the times I had made mistakes.

I told them how I had once believed that my happiness depended on a woman loving me and how this misunderstanding had made me needy in relationships. I shared how much I had learned since then as I began to see through that illusion.

I offered the most important insight I had: that whatever feeling any of us were looking for in a relationship was always coming from our own thinking. No matter how convincing it looked, no partner could complete us. No interaction could build us up or tear us down. The peace and joy we were chasing were already within us.

Then, I shared about my relationship with Yamini.

I spoke of her kindness. How she didn't run at the first sign of conflict. How she spoke highly of me, lifted me, loved me in ways that no other woman ever had. She was different. What I didn't fully realise at the time, but now see so clearly, is that she was also a healing presence in my life. I told them how I wouldn't have been able to have the relationship I did with her if I hadn't first gone on my own journey of growth.

I don't remember everything I said, but I remember I ended my talk strongly, looking out at the room full of men and saying:

'I will probably end up marrying this girl.'

(And I did, but that's a story for another chapter.)

It wasn't just a throwaway line. It was a seed being planted.

What I didn't see at the time was that this talk didn't just mark a milestone in my speaking journey. It also marked a shift in how I saw Yamini. After Romania, something in me shifted. I started to consider her not just as my girlfriend, but as my potential future wife.

Without even planning it, that talk wove together everything I had been learning—about presence, about relationships, about service—and quietly opened a new chapter in my life.

92

Meeting Arthur Peters

Arthur Peters was one of the men in the room in Romania. He was a young guy with long hair, from Germany, and new to Zan Perrion's community. At the time, I had no idea that he had been particularly struck by my talk.

Arthur later told me that what stood out to him was how I appeared calm, collected, and grounded, in contrast to the other speakers, who were far more energised in their delivery. But later that evening, when we all went out together, he saw a completely different side of me—outgoing and full of energy. That contrast made him curious.

During my talk, I had offered the audience a recording of my presentation in Las Vegas earlier that year. In Vegas I'd spoken for several hours over two days, but in Romania my slot was only about thirty minutes long. So, I wanted to offer something deeper to those anyone who was interested.

Arthur was intrigued and sent me a message on Facebook:

> Hey Ankush, I loved the speech you gave and would very much like to hear the longer and deeper version. Loved to get to know you as a quiet guy and then just

> be blown away on how powerful you can get when speaking. Can't wait to talk to you again.

I sent him the files, and two weeks later, he reached out again:

> Hey Ankush, thanks again for the files. I love the principle of the self-regulating mind and will have to listen to the recording again. I am fascinated by how much I recognised in myself when you talked about your past.
>
> I would like to ask you two questions.
>
> 1. What could be a way to get a deeper understanding of these principles?
>
> 2. Would it be alright to share this recording with a group of men, as all of them are interested in growing personally? If not, could you recommend a video or article or book 'for beginners'?

I offered to jump on a short call with him the next day. We also created an agreement that he could share the audios with his group as long as they promised to actually listen to them and also not distribute them. I wanted them to value the recordings, even if they were free.

A couple of weeks later, I followed up with Arthur again and offered him a Jamie Smart audio that I had been sending to many of my clients to help them deepen their understanding of the Three Principles. He was really open to it.

I loved his enthusiasm, and a week later, I got another message from him:

> Hey Buddy, just want to let you know, I had a very full week until now. While I feel not very comfortable at all, I noticed how stressed and even anxious I would have felt during such a situation even six weeks ago.
>
> Thanks a lot for introducing me to the principles behind state of mind and taking the time for a personal call!

I wasn't chasing people to become clients, but I was paying attention to who was showing enthusiasm—who wanted more resources, and who wanted to speak with me.

Arthur was twenty-seven years old and had told me he didn't have a lot of financial resources. What he *did* have was a genuine desire to learn. He wanted to dive deeper into the Three Principles, and he read every book I suggested, listened to every audio I sent him, and was keen to coach people himself.

Within a few weeks, he had signed up for my second Powerful Men's Immersion. Taking Steve's advice, I created a payment plan of £100 a month so that he could attend. This was the most he could afford, and while I would have preferred full payment up front, I felt that Arthur was sincere and enthusiastic about the work, and frankly I liked him.

I didn't realise it at the time, but this turned out to be a brilliant decision. Not only did Arthur return as a paying client for another immersion, but he later became a part of the team that helped me deliver many immersions in the future. Years later, in 2024, he joined my coaching school too—another step in his ongoing journey of growth.

Coaching is a relationship business, and the relationships I was building at the start of my career would go on to endure and deepen in the years to come.

93

Clients Don't Pay for Me

While I was seeing success in growing my coaching practice, I also started noticing something strange. Some people would have one or two conversations with me but then wouldn't *hire* me.

Sometimes what they did was hire a colleague of mine instead. I didn't understand it.

The next time this colleague and I met, I put my ego aside and said, 'Can I ask you something? Sometimes I am speaking to someone and they don't hire me, even though it seems to me that I can really help them. Sometimes those same people go on to hire you. If we are equally capable of helping them, what are you seeing that I'm not seeing?'

He told me he'd think about it and get back to me. That evening, we spoke and the conversation really challenged me. Even though I'd said I was open to his feedback, I noticed myself getting defensive. He told me that some people weren't hiring me because I wasn't meeting them at the level where they felt truly heard.

I immediately interpreted that as meaning I needed to dial myself down, and I wasn't willing to do that. I had spent years overcoming shyness and insecurity. My confidence had been hard-earned, and I wasn't about to shrink myself just to make others comfortable. I thought he was telling me to tone down my personality, and I resisted it.

At some point in the conversation, I realised I wasn't truly listening to him. I told him: 'Right now it really looks to me like I'm right and you're wrong. But I've had many instances in my life where I was certain I was right—only to later realise I wasn't. So, I'm going to sleep on this.'

The next morning, I woke up and saw the entire conversation differently. He was right: I had been cocky and wasn't truly meeting people where they were. It wasn't about dimming myself down—it was about keeping some humility in my coaching, about keeping my heart open—even in my confidence. Because underneath it all, I still didn't feel like I was enough. I still carried a quiet fear that I didn't fully know what I was doing . . . that one day, someone would find out I was a fraud.

And that insecurity?

It leaked into my conversations with potential clients. I'd try too hard. I'd subtly position myself as the expert. I was focused on proving something rather than simply serving.

So, people didn't feel seen. They didn't feel safe. And they looked elsewhere for someone who would really listen.

I knew I had to take this to Steve Chandler. I put aside any concerns about how it would make me look, and I shared my insecurities with him. Steve, as always, didn't judge me. He never did. Instead, he reminded me:

'People aren't hiring you because you have superior wisdom. They're hiring you because they have all the wisdom they need, and when the two of you talk together, they have their own insights about their challenges.'

That hit me hard.

He went on: 'People hire a coach because he or she doesn't come across as superior to them. The coach is as much a student as the clients is.'

It was so obvious when he said it, but I had completely missed this understanding. Steve had talked about this in Los Angeles.

'All we need to do is connect with people. We don't need to impress them. Trying to be impressive often pushes people away.'

And this was exactly what I had been doing.

So many online marketers were teaching coaches that they needed to be authorities in their field, to establish their expertise. And here was Steve, telling me the opposite. It was refreshing, and it also felt true based on my own experience.

There was no trick to client enrolment. I didn't need to master my body language. I didn't need to learn conversational hypnosis. I didn't need ninja sales techniques. I simply had to continue being a student of the mind and speaking to potential clients from my heart.

Steve reminded me: 'People don't pay for you, Ankush. They pay for what happens inside of them.'

That was true then, and it remains true a decade later. It's also the foundation of what I teach in the AJC Coaching Career School. Coaches often think they need to appear as if they have it all together, to be the expert or the authority. But the truth is, clients don't hire a coach because they're perfect or impressive. They hire them because they feel deeply seen and understood—in other words, it's the connection—not the credentials—that really counts.

94

The Gold in Challenge

By mid-2015, my wonderful girlfriend, Yamini, and I had been dating for over a year. At the same time, I had been coaching full-time for six months. She had been incredibly supportive of my decision to leave my corporate job at the end of 2014. She saw how passionate I was about coaching and how unhappy I had been in my previous role.

Six months into my coaching journey, we had a conversation about how my business was going. We loved each other deeply, and I knew she was coming from a good place, as she always did. But the moment she started getting curious about the numbers, I got defensive.

Yamini was trained as an accountant, and I had always been open about my revenue with her. But this time, she wasn't just looking at the revenue. I saw her mind analysing something deeper. She asked, 'But what's the actual profit?'

She questioned whether it made sense to focus so much on revenue growth while paying less attention to my expenses. Did it really make sense to keep investing so heavily in coaching with Steve Chandler and flying back and forth to the States for ACS, so early on in my business?

Truthfully, it was a very valid question. But in that moment, I couldn't see this. I misinterpreted her intentions.

I immediately dismissed her concerns. I felt that if I just kept growing my revenue, the profits would take care of themselves. I reasoned that she didn't understand this profession, that all great coaches have to invest heavily in their growth, and that she simply didn't know what she was talking about.

But deep down, beneath my justifications and bravado, I was embarrassed. I had always been the eternal optimist, and whenever she asked about my future income, I had painted a rosy picture. More than once I had suggested that I'd be able to replace my corporate salary relatively quickly once I went full-time.

So when my actual numbers didn't match what I had confidently predicted, it was no wonder she challenged me. Looking back, I see now that I was immature about truly treating my coaching practice as a business at the time.

That's not to say I shouldn't have made those investments. I wouldn't change them—those early investments laid the foundation for all my future growth. However, had I approached my business with the wisdom I have today, I believe I could have got an even better return on those investments.

Not long after, I brought up this conversation with Steve Chandler in one of our coaching sessions. I was looking for sympathy. I wanted validation that I was making the right choices and that my girlfriend just didn't get it. But to my surprise, after listening intently, Steve asked me one simple question:

'Where is she right?'

That question stunned me. My first thought was, *Hasn't Steve heard anything I just said?* But instead of saying this out loud, I paused—and then, suddenly, I started seeing several answers:

- Her challenge was grounding me.
- It stopped me from getting carried away and spending money mindlessly on training.
- It helped me think critically about the ROI I wanted from my investments.
- It showed me that I was dating the most financially astute woman I had ever met.

What a turnaround.

Steve went further. He asked me:

'Can you come from a place of loving what she is saying?'

'Can you have zero opposition to her?'

'Can you thank her for telling you more about the numbers?'

And then he pointed out something I hadn't realised: I had a fear that if I didn't defend myself, Yamini might not respect me. Even worse, she might leave me. Looking back, that fear seems ridiculous. But in that moment, it felt absolutely real.

The Reality of Building a Business

If I may, I'd like to briefly step out of the story-telling approach I've been using in this book so far and speak directly to all the coaches reading this. I want to share something that seems especially fundamental.

While I have built a business and income far beyond what I initially set out to achieve, my early years were lean. They required significant investment into my own coaching and training. I had to learn the difference between revenue, cash flow, and profits. I now teach these financial relationships to the coaches in my school, because they are essential to understand if you want to build a truly successful practice.

Sometimes not every investment delivers an immediate positive return. It's a long-term game, and the payoff often compounds over time rather than arriving all at once. My early investments didn't guarantee anything. I still had to do the work and take action. Even then, my early growth was far slower than many people might expect. In fact, many of my coaching clients today grow their practices much more quickly than I did. And yet I see so many coaches worrying that they are moving too slowly.

My encouragement? Stay on the path. And if someone in your life is questioning what you're doing, especially in the early days, don't immediately dismiss them. Look for the gold in their challenge.

In my school, I help coaches see that they are running a business, not just practicing a craft. It's not about mindlessly spending on every new course or training. It's about making aligned investments and then doing the work to create a return. We guide coaches to balance deep service with sound business fundamentals so they can serve powerfully and build sustainable, ethical practices.

95

Possibility, not Affordability

In 2014, while supporting Jamie Smart in Norway, I met a man I'll call Timothy. He reached out in December that year, expressing interest in private coaching. By January 2015, we had our first conversation—one of my very first coaching conversations after transitioning to full-time coaching.

Following that call, I sent him a message on Facebook, along with an audio by Jamie Smart about stress, a topic we had explored on our call.

Then . . . silence.

Weeks later, I nudged him gently. He eventually replied, thanking me, saying the audio made sense, but it didn't seem like he wanted to go further. I let it go. I didn't want to be pushy.

But then, out of the blue, he messaged me again:

> Hi Ankush, How are you? I have to say that I am quite stressed at the moment. So, this is probably a good time to have a chat with you. How about some sessions as a real client?

We had another call. Again, he found it deeply impactful. He messaged me saying:

> I love it how impacted I get during our calls. The call and the rest of the evening were like a small vacation.

So I made an offer—£1,500 for a 3-month package. It was discounted from my standard £2,500 rate because I felt this would be easier for him to move ahead with. As I'd learned from Steve Chandler, a coach without clients isn't a professional coach, so I wanted to make it easy for him to say yes and for me to keep coaching. And it worked: he said yes and we started in March 2015. I felt these sessions went well, and I was sure he would want more.

In early June, he messaged me on Facebook:

> Hi Ankush, I am definitely thinking about further calls. What would be the options for those?

I was feeling confident, and when we spoke a week later, I offered a deeper engagement: £3,000 for 6 months (again, discounted from my full rate of £5,000). I saw the potential for powerful, long-term change in his life. I also suggested he could attend my next men's immersion in November which was a lower cost than the coaching, but the dates didn't work out for him as he was travelling at that time.

He paused.

> Hi Ankush, I reflected about it and I think that it makes sense for me to go at a little slower pace, maybe a little different way or also just observe a while where this has taken me so far. I decided not to continue the coaching calls now.

> I want to thank you very much for the great calls we had. And let me know when you have another event. I might join you.
>
> Thanks a lot, Buddy.

I felt deflated. I had been certain he would renew. In my mind, it was a done deal. His 'no' felt like a reflection of poor coaching on my part as well as of the increased cost for six months taking it out of his price range. I wish I could say that I saw my thinking for what it was—just thinking—but the truth is, I got really in my head about it for weeks.

I took this to my coach. Steve helped me see what I'd missed: this wasn't about the money, it was about possibility. If Timothy had truly seen what was possible for him, the investment wouldn't have been the barrier. Even if he'd won £3,000 in the lottery, he wouldn't have spent it on coaching unless he believed the experience would meaningfully change his life.

Steve told me to stop focusing on affordability and start focusing on possibility. Then he challenged me to reach out to Timothy—not to sell, but to serve. Together, we drafted a message from the heart:

> Hi Timothy—I was reflecting on our last calls and exchanges. I want you to know that I really admire your awareness and honesty. Going slower would absolutely benefit you and I see we went too fast. I would never want to push someone past their evolution. When we work together in the future, I will slow you down more than you can imagine because we are on the right path, and that is what matters.

> You're really courageous to have taken steps to look in this direction and investigate the thought-feeling connection in more detail. It takes guts to be open to that and then invest in it too. I see you as someone with a huge heart, down-to-earth and full of integrity.
>
> Take care—I really appreciated our calls and I would love to welcome you to a group event in the future.

We kept in touch, and four months later he messaged me again, straight after the second men's immersion:

> Hola Ankush,
>
> How was your event? Do you already have an idea when you will arrange the next one? I really want to be part of it and want to reserve the time slot.

Two days later, he became the first enrolee for the third men's immersion. The lesson?

A client's hesitation is rarely about the money. It's about whether they can see what's possible for them. If they don't see it, no price will feel right. If they do, affordability takes care of itself.

Possibility, not affordability.

96

Taking People off the Pedestal

In the summer of 2015, I was speaking with Steve Chandler about a potential client. He was a newly promoted director in a large corporation—confident, articulate, and, from what I could tell, earning significantly more than I was. I had only recently transitioned into full-time coaching, and while I'd worked with some paying clients, most had been younger than me or earlier in their careers. This man was different. He looked like someone who had it all figured out. And though I didn't realise it at the time, I had started to put him on a pedestal.

Beneath the surface, my thoughts were swirling: *What if he doesn't value what I have to share? What if he thinks this inside-out understanding is just fluffy, new-age nonsense? Who am I to be coaching someone like him?* I found myself comparing his outer success to my own fledgling coaching practice. I hadn't 'made it' yet. I hadn't earned the right, or so I thought. I noticed myself becoming more timid than usual—carefully choosing my words, trying to sound more professional, caught up in overthinking instead of just serving.

Steve picked up on this immediately, and in response he shared a story about a client he had once worked with: a senior VP of a global company who earned over seven figures a year.[8] On paper, this man had achieved an incredible amount in his career—far more than Steve had ever done when he'd been working in the corporate world. Steve could've simply sat in awe and wondered what I'd been wondering myself: How can I possibly help this guy?

Yet Steve hadn't put him on a pedestal. Because while this VP had reached the heights of corporate success, Steve saw the blind spots that most others missed. This VP:

- was afraid of his wife.
- was a poor communicator.
- had failed to build loyalty within his team.
- was stressed and overwhelmed.

Steve wasn't judging his client; he was simply seeing clearly. And because he saw the man's blind spots, he was able to help him. If he had put his client on a pedestal, he would've effectively increased the distance between the two of them and missed out on the fact that the client was just as human as he was.

That story struck me.

Steve helped me see that many of the potential clients I was speaking to were operating from fear—fear of making mistakes, fear of losing status, fear of being exposed as not having it all together. This was something I could help them with, no matter how successful they happened to be in the corporate world or anywhere else.

The Three Principles were still relatively unknown. And for those who had been introduced to them, the impact was often profound—transforming their relationships, their stress levels, their

[8] Steve didn't share any identifiable details, of course. He just wanted me to see something in the story.

confidence, and their overall quality of life. This understanding wasn't a magic pill, but it could be incredibly helpful. I had seen this in my own life, in the lives of my clients, and in the many others through my extensive trainings.

And the simple truth was that no one was 'above' me when it came to coaching about wisdom, the mind, and the power of thought. When I slowed down, I could see this for myself. What I had learned through my training with Jamie Smart, my sessions with Dr Keith Blevens, Chip Chipman, and my retreats with Elsie Spittle and Dicken Bettinger was beyond what 99 percent of the planet understood on these topics.

I wasn't thinking this from a place of arrogance. I was just reminding myself of the reality that I did in fact have something significant to offer—as long as I could see clearly enough not to put my clients and prospects on pedestals.

The problem was, I kept forgetting!

One of the greatest things Steve did for me was to constantly remind me of this truth. Now, I often find myself doing the same thing for other coaches including those in my school. When they tell me they feel intimidated by a potential client, I ask them:

'Who would NOT benefit from working with you and getting a deeper understanding of what you point your clients to?'

They usually pause. And then it dawns on them—they can't think of anyone. In that moment, a lightbulb goes off in their head, just like it did for me that day with Steve.

97

Launching the Coaching Group: From Frustration to Service

By the summer of 2015, I found myself increasingly disillusioned with the way the coaching profession was being spoken about online. Everywhere I looked there were countless Facebook groups, blog posts and webinars promising the latest tactics to get more clients or hit six figures as a coach. Much of the advice seemed to be recycled marketing jargon: email funnels, Facebook ads, Instagram strategies . . .

What was missing was the heart of coaching—the deep, transformative conversations that had changed my own life and the lives of those I coached.

I had been grumbling about this for months, mostly to myself, but one day in August, I found myself sharing my frustrations with Steve Chandler. I told him how angry I was that so many coaches were being misled by shiny promises and how I wished someone would offer guidance that actually helped coaches grow their practices in ways that felt aligned with the principles of service and integrity.

Steve listened patiently, as he always did. Then he asked me two simple questions:

'Do coaches need help?'

'Yes,' I replied without hesitation.

'Can you help them?'

Again, without thinking, I answered, 'Yes.'

Steve leaned back slightly, smiling in that quiet way he often did when he could see something I couldn't quite see for myself.

'What's your problem then?'

I was speechless. It felt like someone had just pulled the rug out from under all my excuses. I realised in that moment how much energy I'd been spending complaining rather than creating.

My mind raced through all the reasons I hadn't done anything yet: What if people laughed at me? What if no one joined? What if I wasn't ready? Underneath those fears, there was a quiet knowing that I had to at least try.

A few hours later, with my heart pounding, I opened Facebook and clicked the button to create a new group. I named it 'Coaching Using the Three Principles', not knowing at the time just how much impact it would end up having. (The group name was later changed to 'Coaching From the Three Principles Understanding'.)

I wrote a short welcome post, sharing why I'd started the group—to offer a professional space where coaches could support one another and focus on what really mattered: serving clients powerfully, one conversation at a time.

I invited a handful of people, expecting maybe five or ten to join in the first few days. To my surprise, the group quickly began to grow. Within a few weeks, dozens of coaches had joined and begun sharing their own frustrations and their desire to build practices based on service rather than sales gimmicks.

Shortly after launching, I received a comment from a lady who questioned my reasoning for wanting to coach coaches, especially given that I was a relatively new coach myself. She asked whether this was just a way to make money by targeting coaches. This was my worst fear—being called out. I wanted the ground to swallow me up.

I got into my head for about fifteen minutes, feeling exposed and doubting myself. But then something shifted. I returned to the computer and replied to her with as much honesty and humility as I could muster. I shared that I understood why she might question my intentions, but I was actually attempting to address the very same concerns she had. I had hired Steve Chandler and found a way to create clients that was ethical and very different from all the advice that seemed to be flooding social media for coaches. The coaches in the group seemed to really appreciate my response. That moment taught me that showing up with vulnerability and service was far more powerful than any need to prove myself.

What I remember most about those early days isn't how quickly the group grew. It's the feeling that I was finally stepping into something bigger than myself, the beginning of a sense of purpose that stretched beyond my own fears and self-doubts.

Looking back, I can see how that moment marked a shift in my life as a coach. I didn't launch the group because I was *fearless*. I launched it because I saw that *my fear wasn't a good enough reason not to serve.* This group is still active today, and that same mission has now expanded beyond the group into my work with coaches. What began as a small act of service has grown into a movement to raise the entire profession up.

This taught me one of the most valuable lessons of my journey—that the best way to dissolve fear is to simply show up and serve. When we create something from a place of genuine care for others, the impact can ripple out in ways we could never imagine.

98

The Lesson in Being Bold

I had a conversation booked with a potential client called Naomi. She was a coach who wanted to grow her practice. She had also written a book, which added to my perception of her as a serious professional. But when our scheduled call time arrived, she didn't show up. It wasn't until ten minutes later that she called in, apologising.

It felt awkward. I wanted to say something, but I hesitated. Instead, I accepted her apology and moved on. I was caught up in what Steve Chandler calls the social self—acting as I would in a casual social situation rather than a professional one. In a social setting, when someone is late, I am likely to brush it off or, at best, call attention to it with a light-hearted comment. But this wasn't just a friendly catch-up. This was meant to be a professional conversation.

I knew there was something for me to see here. So, once again, I brought it up in a session with Steve. He listened and then told me something that struck me:

'None of my clients would show up ten minutes late to a call.'

I knew that was certainly true for me. I never showed up late to my sessions with Steve, and my other clients were always on time. But why? Steve explained that it wasn't because his clients were polite; it was because they had clarity and focus. Then he reminded me of something important:

'You have nothing to lose with Naomi.'

She wasn't a client yet, and I had another session booked with her. So why not be bold? Why not tell the truth? Steve suggested we role-play. He would play the coach, and I would play Naomi, the client who had arrived late.

Steve asked, 'Are you open to coaching?'

'Yes.'

'Can I ask you a question?'

'Sure.'

'Does your life feel out of control? Because nobody I work with says they will call at 9:00 a.m. and then calls at 9:10 a.m.'

Oof. That hit me. This felt super edgy, but I could see the power in it. Steve encouraged me to be bolder, but with love.

'Imagine this is your sister, and she's hurting,' he said.

That analogy stayed with me forever. Even now, I sometimes ask myself:

'What would I do if this person in front of me was my brother or sister?'

It cuts through everything. Because even when I disagree with my siblings, I deeply love them and want the best for them. I am also more likely to find it easier to speak directly and boldly to them than I might be to a prospective client.

Another lesson came out of this: When someone is showing up late to a scheduled meeting, it's often a sign that their life is out of control. This was a humbling realisation, because I had been guilty of this many times in my own life. If I were being really honest, I hadn't felt in control for long periods of time. My system for getting things done was putting them off until the last minute, which naturally led to being late, among other problems. Not a very effective system. I was reminded of a quote I had heard before:

'How you do anything is how you do everything.'

I'd heard it from Rich Litvin, but people also attribute it to Simon Sinek, Martha Beck, and Suzanne Evans. Whoever said it first doesn't really matter. What matters is that we see the truth in it. Whatever unhelpful behaviour is showing up in one area of a person's life is likely showing up elsewhere too. And what a great avenue for exploration in coaching sessions.

Naomi showed up on time to her next calls, so I never had the occasion to engage her in the dialogue that Steve suggested. And she didn't end up signing on, though we spoke a couple more times and I shared several resources with her.

Nonetheless, the lessons from our brief exchange stayed with me. The more committed a client is to showing up on time, to engaging with resources I have sent them and to treating the coaching as important, the more beneficial the coaching is for them, and the more enjoyable it is for me to coach them. Steve had been right—as always. I hadn't had anything to lose if I'd challenged her in the first conversation, and perhaps if I had there would've been much for both of us to gain. This is something I often share with coaches in my school too: boldness can be an act of service, not aggression. When we care enough to speak the truth, we give clients a gift: a chance to see something new.

99

Rewriting My Money Story

Steve Chandler had picked up on something in our coaching sessions: I had strong beliefs about money, and they weren't positive. One day he asked me directly:

'Do you think money is vulgar?'

I didn't even hesitate.

'Yes,' I said.

I saw money as a necessary evil—something I needed to live and support myself with. But in an ideal world I wouldn't have to think about it. If money could have been taken out of the equation altogether, that would have suited me just fine.

I knew I probably wasn't the only coach who thought this way. For many of us, coaching feels noble, even spiritual—especially for me when working from the Three Principles. This doesn't seem to mix well with money.

I had a romanticised belief that if I were a good person and I served people powerfully, I would never need to sell. I wouldn't even need to look at the numbers. Somehow, all of this would just take care of itself.

I was, to put it mildly, naïve. Steve wasn't going to let me off the hook. He purchased a book for me called *Moneylove* by Jerry Gillies—second-hand, because it was out of print. When it arrived, I realised it had been published in 1978! I had never heard of it. (I learned later that it had built up a deservedly strong following in its time.)

One of the first lines in the introduction stood out:

'Thinking poor will keep you poor; thinking rich will make you rich.'

I would never have picked up this book in a library or purchased it in a bookshop. But I was a good client; if my coach thought something was important for me, I would give it a go. And I soon read something that stopped me in my tracks:

'Love and money are the same.'

What?!

This completely challenged my worldview. But the more I read, the more it started to make sense. For example, Gillies wrote:

'Statistics have shown time and again that those people who go into a business venture because they want to perform a service they love performing, or produce a product they love producing, make much more money than those who go into a business just to make money.'

This resonated with me deeply. I certainly hadn't gone into coaching just to make money. In fact, I had been prepared to make less than in my corporate career. If I could do what I loved full-time, that would be enough.

Beyond challenging my ideas about money, Gillies also wrote about financial success and self-worth. This hit home. I had always seen myself as less financially successful than many of my university friends.

I realised that I didn't feel like I deserved to be wealthy. Why? Because, as I had already admitted, wealth felt vulgar. It wasn't 'spiritual' in my eyes at that time.

But Gillies showed me something different.

Another part of the book stood out:

'Wealthy people are often very generous. Money is a flow, not something to be hoarded.'

This hit a nerve. I wasn't generous at all with money. Not at the time. It always felt like there was never enough money. Even growing up, I had learned to save every penny because it felt like resources were limited. I thought I was being smart by saving, but I hadn't seen that my lack of generosity wasn't just a result of not being wealthy—*it was also creating it.*

I considered Steve's own example. He was one of the most generous people I had ever met. And not just once. Over and over again.

After *Moneylove*, Steve recommended another book: *Money is My Friend* by Phil Laut. It built on many of the same concepts but offered a more structured approach to abundance. Like *MoneyLove*, it reinforced ideas around money and self-esteem, the idea that money isn't bad or inherently evil, and that a balanced approach to money includes giving it away.

One passage stood out:

'If you don't like your business well enough to give away your services, this may be an indication you are in the wrong business.'

That struck me enough that I often share the sentiment with coaches who are reluctant to give a potential client several hours up front before the prospective client becomes a paying one. It is a powerful reframe.

Reading these books was powerful, but Steve's actions demonstrated these principles even more clearly. He was so committed to helping me shift my money mindset that he did something else that completely blew me away. He paid for me to have two sessions with Kamin Samuels, a wealth mindset coach who was also one of his clients.

Once again, I was astounded by Steve's generosity and powerful service. This wasn't just about reading books and giving me information. Steve was doing what great coaches do: helping me transform the way I saw the world. He knew that when I changed my relationship with money, I would change everything else in my life too. This transformation didn't happen instantly, of course. Changing deeply rooted beliefs about money has been an ongoing journey, one that continues today. But having new ideas and frameworks to work from made all the difference.

Today, I encourage coaches I work with to give a percentage of their profits to a charity or cause they care about. It's not about the amount; rather, it's about breaking old patterns of lack and stepping into a mindset of generosity and flow. I also do this myself—donate a portion of the money made from my school to a charity supporting children in rural India in getting an education. This is deeply meaningful to me, because it reflects both my own roots and my commitment to creating an impact in the world beyond my own immediate work.

100

Breaking the Money Spell

Kamin Samuels is an incredible woman. She was the first African American female helicopter pilot in the Navy and had also held a senior position as Vice President of Global Web Operations at a major corporation.

When Steve Chandler paid for me to have two sessions with her, I could not have fully appreciated just how transformative they would be. Our focus was on the many invisible beliefs I had around money, including stories I'd been brought up with, like:

'Money doesn't grow on trees.'

'If you knew how hard it was to earn £1, you would value it more.'

'It takes a long time and a lot of hard work to earn money legitimately and sustainably'

I hadn't realised just how deeply ingrained these ideas were and how they had been shaping my financial reality long into adulthood—especially now, as I was trying to build my coaching business. These beliefs weren't just floating around in the background of my mind; they were silently running the show. I found myself undercharging, hesitating to make larger proposals, and creating an unconscious barrier to growing my practice too quickly. Part of me still felt like I had to take it slow and work hard to be worthy of success.

It was as if I'd been trying to create abundance while still holding on to the very beliefs that created a reality of scarcity. Kamin helped me begin to see those beliefs for what they were: not truths, but old and unhelpful ideas—passed down with love but no longer useful. And in seeing them more clearly, things began to shift.

Kamin also helped me explore my *judgments* around money—in particular about people who had money. As many of us have, I had seen examples of people who chased money and who were ego-centric, selfish, and unkind. Based on these I had unknowingly made a subconscious equation:

People who care about money = Bad people

That belief was paralysing me. On one hand, I was telling myself that money was in short supply and I wanted and needed it. On the other hand, I was judging those who had money or who were actively working to create it. In other words, even if I could *make* good money, I wouldn't be a good person if I did. It was a double bind. I couldn't win.

With Kamin's help, I started to see that I could create my own definition of success and being rich. It didn't have to be a trade-off between prosperity and happiness, or between prosperity and being a good person. This is how I had been subconsciously viewing things—as if wealth and goodness couldn't coexist. But this wasn't true. It was just a story I had been living inside without realising it.

Kamin explained something else to me. 'Comparison,' she said, 'keeps you in a box.' She advised me to be aware of whenever I fell into comparing myself to others instead of being grounded in my own path.

This landed hard, because I lived in a world of comparison—with other coaches, with friends and family, in income and lifestyle and more. And on some level, I knew that my comparison habit was actually a reflection of my own self-image—a belief that I wasn't enough. Once again, I was encountering this deep-seated thinking about myself and seeing how it was influencing my life.

My two sessions with Kamin weren't a magic pill. They didn't instantly erase all my money beliefs. But they did loosen my thinking. They opened me up to new possibilities and helped me start to see that money wasn't the enemy—it was just a tool, and my beliefs about it were shaping my experience of it.

One of the most profound shifts that came out of these conversations wasn't just about money—it was about my parents. As I uncovered how many of my money beliefs had come from my childhood, I realised that instead of feeling resentment towards them, I felt compassion. This had been a theme for me over the previous three years with the Three Principles. The more I understood about the mind, the closer I felt to my parents. They had been doing the best they could based on their thinking and upbringing, including with money.

Now I saw that I could shift my own thinking and create a new relationship and a new set of beliefs with money, in the same way I had done with my parents. This insight has proven invaluable over the years. When I work with other coaches, I'm often reminded of how invisible these money beliefs can be. We think we're struggling with marketing or pricing, when really we're wrestling with decades-old stories about what we deserve. Once you see these patterns for what they are—just thoughts, not truths—they begin to lose their grip on you.

101

Only Have Questions

It was August 2015 when a friend of mine reached out via WhatsApp. She wanted me to coach her husband. She had seen from my Facebook posts that I was now coaching and thought I might be able to help. When we got on the phone, she explained that he was unfocused and unmotivated.

I genuinely wanted to help, whether they could pay me or not. I didn't know her husband, but she was a good person and a good friend. Nonetheless, something felt off. Why was *she* asking me for support rather than him asking me? Did he want help, or was this a case where she thought he needed to change in some way?

I brought this to Steve Chandler, because I knew he'd have something to say about it. He told me that he'd had people approach him many times with a request to coach someone else—a spouse, a friend, or an employee.

Steve was always more interested in the person making the request. 'I want to understand what the problem is from their perspective,' he said. 'More often than not, the real problem isn't the person they want to refer. It's that the person asking me to coach someone else believes that person should be different than they are.'

When he reflected this back to the person, they would often say, 'I hadn't thought of it that way.'

It was a demonstration of the power of a potent coaching question. Having been asked this, the person might then be inspired to reflect inwards and perhaps discover that they weren't necessarily coming from a place of loving the other person, but instead from a place of non-acceptance.

Is it true that everyone is so open to seeing things differently? No. But in my experience, people who reach out to me to help someone close to them really do care about the other person, and most of the time they are open to seeing their role in the 'problem'.

With these examples, I saw that Steve was being far more direct than I had been in my own conversations. He wasn't worried about what people thought of him—he was concerned with helping the person in front of him. And in a situation like mine, he said he would only have questions:

- 'Why do you think your husband should be more focused?'
- 'What would be the consequence of allowing him his own path instead of pushing him down the road faster in the direction you want him to go?'
- 'What would be the downside of letting him walk his own path?'
- 'What would be the downside of really loving him?'
- 'Why is it any of your business if he's unfocused?'
- 'Is he breaking an agreement he made with you?'

Steve wasn't playing around. If I had asked these questions, it would have completely shifted the conversation. Essentially, Steve helped me see that the person I could really help was my friend. She was coming from fear, not love. And I could help her with her fear.

I ended up having another conversation with her, and she chose to not proceed with coaching at that time. In fact, she and her husband split up. Could coaching with me have saved their marriage? I will never know. I don't even have enough information to make an educated guess, but I do know that any relationship in which one person wants the other to be different is on rocky ground. If a person is open to exploring why the person they want to be different is the way they are, it can lead to powerful mind shifts and a completely different way of relating to them.

This experience with my friend taught me something important about referrals in general. The pattern I'd seen—where the real issue lies with the person making the request rather than the person they want to 'fix'—shows up in many contexts, not just marriages.

Let's say a leader has a strained relationship with their employee. They might say that their employee has 'an attitude problem'. But if the leader and I were to explore together why they think this, it might lead to them seeing things through their employee's eyes and this could lead to a change in their perspective.

None of this means that the behaviour of the employee or spouse or whoever is perfect. But often when one person has a greater understanding of the other, the relationship changes almost effortlessly without any so-called 'problem' being fixed. For example, if I feel like my spouse is really messy and I get upset by the mess around the house, and despite my constant requests, nothing changes, I may simply think my spouse has a problem with organisation. However, if I start to explore this and realise my spouse is struggling with too much to do, suddenly I stop complaining about the mess and realise they need more support from me. Similarly with an employee, their attitude problem may disappear when the leader sees they are feeling overwhelmed and underappreciated. When the leader simply makes a small gesture or two of appreciation and acknowledgement, everything can change.

Sometimes when I connect with a coach, leader, or business owner, they tell me, 'I could refer some clients to you.'

At this point I slow things down, because I want them to understand what they're referring people *to*. Coaching isn't a generic service. Every coach is different, and so is every client and even every session. They might have been coached by various coaches for decades, yet that doesn't mean they know what I can provide.

So the next time someone says, 'You could help my son, my organisation, or my friend,' remember: Slow down. Give them an experience of what you actually do. It will make the referral far more effective when it happens. And more often than not, it increases the likelihood of the referrer becoming a client themselves.

102

The Power of a Simple Invitation

I first met Igor Furdik in January 2012 at a success workshop in Las Vegas. We quickly became friends, and later that year, he invited me to visit him in Bratislava, Slovakia. I took him up on the offer, and what I experienced over those few days left a lasting impression. Igor was the most generous, kind, and hospitable person I had ever met. He showed me around the city, shared its rich history and customs, and even took me on a short drive to Vienna, Austria, one afternoon. I can still remember the incredible hot chocolate he introduced me to in Bratislava's old town. Needless to say, I had a lot of love for him.

In 2015, I reached out to Igor on Facebook, and we started having what you could call an 'innocent' conversation, by which I mean it wasn't an enrolment call or a covert way to create a client. He shared that he really wanted to help people. He'd seen that I was coaching and wanted to explore the possibility of becoming a coach himself. At the time, he was working as a project manager, but he was considering a career change.

I asked him, 'What kind of coaching do you want to do?'

He was stumped. He hadn't thought that far ahead.

Now this was my friend, not a typical potential client. I spoke with him several times, sharing Three Principles resources that I thought would help. They challenged his thinking, yet he found them useful. He hadn't enquired about hiring me, but after three or four conversations, I made a suggestion: 'I think a great next step would be for you to attend my Powerful Men's Immersion.'

I felt nervous saying it. The friendship meant more to me than any potential client relationship. I didn't want to come across as pushy. In truth, I was still being timid, despite Steve Chandler gently pointing me towards the creation of a stronger foundation from which to connect with people. But in this instance I at least made the invitation.

Igor laughed. 'I would have signed up much earlier if you had just asked!'

That was valuable feedback. I told him that my goal wasn't to convert him into a client. I only wanted him to work with me if it truly made sense for him, and if he knew exactly what he was signing up for.

I had no idea what that simple request would lead to. To date, Igor has attended *twenty-one* immersions in a row—sixteen as a client and five as a faculty member who now leads parts of the Immersion himself. What makes this work is that he's different every time he comes back, and I am different too. In fact, clients like him inspire me to keep growing, so that I'm not simply offering the same service year after year. It's become a relationship of mutual development rather than dependency.

He also attended and graduated from my AJC Coaching Career School. I never could have predicted that we would still be working together ten years later, with our relationship deeper than ever.

And all of this happened because I was willing to extend an invitation—not to make money, but because I knew it would truly serve him.

Steve Chandler worked with many long-term clients. I myself was his client for eight-and-a-half years straight, without a single break. I probably would have continued had he not retired. Years after we began working together, Steve told me that this is how sustainable coaching practices are built: through renewals and referrals.

Igor is also a great example of the power of consistency. Over the past decade, I have watched him grow and evolve in ways neither of us could have predicted. I have seen him get married, be promoted at work (he is now a Board member of an IT consultancy), and grow as a man, a husband, a father and a leader. He's even begun coaching private clients, bringing the same depth and presence to his work that he once experienced himself. He would be the first to admit that when he attended that first immersion, his mind was sped up. Now, when he walks into a room, he brings presence. He is an incredibly intelligent man, and today he carries a deep grounding in the Three Principles.

I can never predict with certainty who will become a long-term client. But one thing I do know is that I don't subscribe to the advice that coaches shouldn't work with family or friends. This approach requires careful attention to boundaries and isn't right for every relationship, but had I followed that advice categorically, I would have missed out on one of the most rewarding client relationships of my career.

103

Filling My Second Immersion

In November 2015, I was set to run my second Powerful Men's Immersion. By early September, I had already signed up seven clients—several of whom had attended the first immersion and wanted to return. This was encouraging, but I knew I still had work to do to fill the group. Fortunately, Steve Chandler had been supporting me throughout the process, offering insights and guidance in our coaching conversations.

One piece of wisdom from Steve stood out: 'No one joins a group they haven't been to.'

At first, this struck me as an odd thing to say. Of course, people sign up for things they haven't attended before—how else would events grow? But as he explained further, I realised the deeper truth behind his words.

People want an experience of a group before they commit. They need to feel what it's like to be part of it. Steve emphasised how, in today's world, people have developed high sales resistance. Most of us don't like being sold to—I certainly didn't. If a telemarketer called me, I wouldn't even let them finish their first sentence before hanging up. On the street, if someone tried to stop me to talk about saving money on my bills, I'd pick up my pace and mumble, 'Not interested.'

So how could I get potential clients to experience the immersion before actually attending?

One simple way, Steve suggested, was to run a webinar or group call and call it The Powerful Men's Immersion Webinar. The idea was straightforward: my job was simply to get people on the webinar. Once they were there, I could answer their questions and give them a taste of what the immersion was all about.

Steve shared a powerful example of how he and Rich Litvin had run an event together and then given away the entire recording of it to people who were interested in signing up for the next one they ran. Steve always led with generosity; whether through emails, audios, or event previews. he consistently gave people a real experience of his work before they signed up. I had seen this firsthand when I had attended their event the year before.

How could I apply this principle to my own immersion? Instead of just trying to sell the programme, I could share the resources and homework I'd given to attendees of the first immersion with anyone who might be a good fit for the next one. This was a shift to simply serving people first, rather than trying to convince them to sign up with little idea of what they were signing up for. It also gave me a chance to gauge their interest before having any enrolment conversations.

Of course, not everyone who received these resources ended up joining the immersion. But as Steve often reminded me, coaching is a relationship business. Serving people—even those who don't sign up—is always a good investment. He told me stories of people who hadn't joined his coaching school for two or three years but who eventually enroled because he had consistently created value for them over time.

His advice shaped how I filled that second immersion, but

more importantly, it influenced how I've approached every immersion and programme since. I now make it a personal challenge to give away as much value as possible before anyone ever pays me. This mindset always moves me into service, making the process of filling programmes feel less like selling and more like an act of generosity. And beyond being effective, it's simply a fun way to run a business.

104

Have Fun, Make Money

At the end of July 2015, things had gone a little quiet in my business. This wasn't just a feeling. In the first three months of 2015 I had invoiced nineteen clients for approximately £15,000 total, but in the second three months of 2015, I had invoiced only six clients for less than £9,000 total.

Client creation had slowed down. The energy felt a bit stagnant. I was still committed—but underneath, I could feel doubt creeping in. I wondered if this was just part of the ebb and flow . . . or if I was doing something wrong.

I brought it to Steve. Having him in my corner was invaluable, but this was one of those moments where it really stood out to me just *how* useful it was. Before hiring Steve, while I had had support through group programmes and mentors, it still felt pretty lonely building my coaching practice. With Steve by my side it was more than reassuring. It was more than knowing I wasn't alone. It was having someone on my team who could help me navigate any situation that came up. Steve lent me his cloak of confidence and experience, which enabled me to become the coach I wanted to be.

Regarding my dilemma of the sales slowing down, he listened carefully. And then he said something that shifted everything for me.

'Your business is to make money. By doing so, you'll be of maximum benefit to people.'

At first, that hit me sideways. Because, as I've already mentioned, I'd grown up with all kinds of stories about money—some conscious, some buried. And while I'd already done a lot of work to shift my beliefs, there was still a part of me that felt uneasy about openly *pursuing* money. Especially as a coach whose goal was to serve. How does one balance the idea of service with getting *paid* for that service?

Steve saw something I didn't yet: I was being timid in my proposals. I was holding back. One result of this approach was that it was *costing other people* the opportunity to truly experience the depth of what I could offer. I believed I could help people—in fact I now had years of experience proving it to myself. Yet by not extending my reach, by playing small and being overly cautious, I was limiting my own ability to help others. So I tried something new. I adopted Steve's mantra as my own: *'My business is to make money. And by doing so, I serve at the highest level.'*

With that in mind, I began to look for ethical, creative, in-service ways to get paid. Not from a place of desperation or a need to force things, but from a place of fun. Of play. Of curiosity. For example: A man from India reached out to me. I knew that the 'old' version of Ankush would have dismissed him—assuming he couldn't afford to work with me. But this time, I created a one-off coaching agreement with him for £100. Then I had an idea with one of my clients that led to our co-creation of a small group programme. That brought in $600 USD. Another coach wanted to work with me but wasn't ready to commit to a full package, so I offered 45-minute sessions at £250 each.

Then a referral came in. A client in Canada. We started with twenty-minute coaching sessions at $100 CAD. I'd never coached in that way before. But it worked. It served him, and it served me. I gave him a book to read in between every session; one of those books was *Somebody Should Have Told Us* by Jack Pransky, which was all about the Three Principles. After reading that, this client stopped smoking! That never would have happened if I hadn't gotten creative in how we worked together. These were all exercises in simplicity, freedom and fun. I was open to experimenting in ways that felt light and which also led to money creation. Service, money and fun, all rolled into one.

And then something beautiful happened: I created my biggest client to date. This was someone I'd already worked with. He had attended both my *Powerful Men's Intensive* and the first *Men's Immersion* I had ever run, and we'd had a few coaching conversations. We had stayed in touch after the first immersion, and he'd been really impacted by our interactions. He had expressed an interest in getting his own coaching business up and running, but he was also interested in other potential career options. I continued to serve him, share resources that I thought might be helpful, offer advice when asked and even have occasional conversations with him between April and August. I wasn't doing this to 'get' him as a client but just to help. There was no indication that he would reach out to sign up for coaching.

Then in mid-August he asked for a conversation about us working together, and he said yes to a six-month coaching agreement for £6,500. I was ecstatic. Not just because of the money—but because I now *saw* the connection.

When I make money a game, when I stay in service and get creative and light-hearted, my business flourishes. When I take money too seriously, it feels heavy, hard and restrictive. That kind of energy drags me, and consequently my business, down.

Steve was incredibly supportive throughout this period—always encouraging, always believing in me, and always reminding me that creating clients and making money doesn't have to feel like work. In fact, it can feel like fun. That summer I didn't just make money—I *changed my relationship with it.*

And I changed my business in the process. This is what I want for every coach I work with: to experience that creating money can be as fun, light, and creative as the coaching itself.

105

Coaching Is an Active Investment

By September 2015, I was seven calls in to my second coaching agreement with Steve Chandler. We'd been working together for a year at that point. The coaching had been excellent. I was growing, creating more, and learning a lot—but it was also taking longer than I'd expected to see the return I had imagined when I first signed up. By this point I'd earned under £34,000 in coaching income since January 2015. This was a big improvement from 2014 where I had earned just over £10,000 in the entire year. However, I was now also investing more time and money than ever into the business.

These were not small investments for me; my agreement with Steve was twelve calls for nine thousand dollars. I was feeling grateful, no question. Steve had been kind, supportive, and generous. Not only had my sales more than tripled but I was also more skilful as a coach and as an enroler of new clients. Lots was going well, but underneath that, there was also a quiet uncertainty. I found myself wondering: *Can I do more with this opportunity?*

So I asked him directly,

'Steve, how do I make the most of my investment coaching with you?

'He didn't hesitate. 'You create your return. Just like I did when I worked with Steve Hardison. I didn't leave it to chance. I played an *active* role in my coaching. I used to show up to sessions with Hardison and say things like, 'I need to make $200,000—let's go.'

He gave me an example. At one point he had a client—a multiple six-figure coach who was nearing the end of their agreement. Steve didn't know if the client would renew. And instead of just waiting to see what would happen, he brought the situation to Hardison.

Together, they redesigned what the next year of coaching could look like for that client—and *created* the renewal. Their joint brainstorming took into account the work that Steve had already done with the client, and rather than just have Chandler do his best and hope that the client renewed, they took a more active approach. They saw the outcome he wanted—the client to renew—and they created a compelling vision and structure for the client that he said yes to.

The power of this approach wasn't just coming from Hardison. Chandler wasn't passive. He wasn't waiting to see what Hardison would deliver. He was *creating* the return he wanted in the space that he and Hardison co-created. Chandler took an active, integral role in his own coaching. In fact, *he was guiding his coach to help him get the return he wanted.*

This landed very deeply for me.

Up until that point, I'd mostly been showing up to sessions with Steve and sharing whatever was going on in the moment. I didn't always have a clear intention. And because Steve had such a stellar reputation for helping coaches grow their businesses ethically, I trusted that it would all work out. To be fair—it had. But I saw something new that day.

I could take an even more *intentional* role in my own coaching. I could create the return I wanted. I could stop *hoping* for a breakthrough and start *designing* one. I began coming to sessions more prepared, asking myself before each call, 'What would bring the biggest return on this conversation?'

For example, one powerful tool Steve gave me was something he called 'Game Film.' If I had a prospective client on the verge of signing up, I'd bring that upcoming conversation into our session. We'd dissect it—what I could say or not say, what I could look for and what I might miss. Often during the course of such conversations, Steve would offer one insight, one shift in perspective or approach and I'd apply it. Time and again, it would lead to the client saying yes.

What it took was my coming to the session fully focused on what I wanted to create in that session. In the past I might've approached a conversation with Steve simply with a vague desire to make more money or attract a certain client. I might even subtly allow Steve to lead the conversation because I wasn't quite clear on what I wanted to talk about or where I wanted to focus. These discussions were still valuable, and they usually led to insights that had a positive impact on my coaching business.

But when I upleveled my conversations with him I came to our sessions armed with very specific goals—just as he had done in his example with Hardison: 'I need to make $200,000—let's go.' The difference was that there was nothing vague about this intentional approach. I chose what to focus on, and that's what we did. This brought both Steve's and my own full attention to play. And it's this laser-focus that can create immediate breakthroughs.

How did I choose what to focus on? One technique was to make a list of all the potential clients that I was currently communicating with who hadn't yet signed up. I would then look at the list and choose the one that I needed the most support with. It became obvious that if I brought all of my potential clients into my coaching sessions, I would invariably make more money. And the more intentional I was, the better. When I'd started working with Steve, I would bring up the conversation that seemed 'easier' or less edgy first. This wasn't the best use of our session. Yet focusing on the potential client I needed most support with first changed everything.

This is an example of 'you get back what you put in.' When, as a client, I approach a coaching conversation with only vague ideas of what I would like to accomplish, it's like I'm bringing maybe 10 percent focus to the conversation. But if I know what I want to accomplish, I enter the room with 100 percent to give, and my coach and I can dive right in and make immediate progress.

Today I teach this to my own clients—especially the coaches I mentor. I see this in action all the time. I have had clients create their investment back within two weeks of signing up with me—sometimes before we even officially begin. The key is that *they take an active role in creating the return.* The clients who experience the greatest results are the ones who know what return they want, communicate it clearly, and then use the resources available to them to create it. Coaching is not something that's *done to you.* It's a co-creation. A powerful partnership. You get out what you put into it. I highlight this right from the start with new clients when we go through our coaching agreement. I want them to see just how much agency they have in making this the best investment of their life.

If I show up with 100 percent of my energy, skill, and presence, but they only show up with 10 percent? They'll only get a fraction of the transformation they could've had. But if we both show up at 100 percent, not passive, but fully active, fully alive, we create miracles.

I don't say that lightly. Your return on coaching is created by the participation, intention, and the energy you bring into your sessions. When approached with this understanding—with full intention and attention—coaching becomes the most powerful investment someone can make in their business, their life, their relationships and their leadership.

106

Serve, Even if They Don't Sign Up

In September 2015, I was preparing for my second *Powerful Men's Immersion*. The first one had sold out, and I was determined to replicate that success. But as we edged closer to the November event, I still had three spaces left.

The pressure was quietly building. Of course, I wanted it to fill. I felt a sense of urgency and, if I'm honest, a touch of fear that it might not. So, I brought the issue to my coaching session with Steve Chandler. He listened and then gave me one of the most powerful lessons I've ever received on filling a group—or building anything, for that matter.

'Serve them,' he said, *'even if they don't sign up.'*

He explained how he and Maurice Bassett, who was the Director of Steve's school, would pour themselves into serving potential clients. Not to manipulate them or close a sale, but to *genuinely serve*. So much so that even if someone didn't join the school that year—or the year after—they often came back later. Not because of a clever funnel or sales strategy, but because of the value they'd already received.

I loved this. It resonated with me immediately. This was the kind of coach I wanted to be: service before profit. Integrity before income. And it was a way of being I was already aiming to bring into every aspect of my practice. So I decided to put it into practice immediately. Instead of pushing harder to fill those final three spaces, I focused on serving the people I was already talking to. I had several conversations scheduled with potential attendees, and rather than trying to convince them to sign up, I coached them. I asked the deeper questions Steve had given me and shared what I honestly saw.

Before the immersion started in November, all three remaining spaces were filled—not through closing sales calls, but through people experiencing what it was actually like to work with me.

Nonetheless, a part of me still wondered: 'Could it really be that simple? Just serve . . . and people will eventually say yes?' It sounded almost too good to be true, but I was in. I trusted Steve, and I trusted the spirit of what he was pointing to. This wasn't a tactic, it was a way of being.

But there was another dimension to Steve's advice, which became apparent when he challenged me to risk being a jerk. I had spent much of my life trying to be the good guy, the nice, polite guy who didn't rock the boat. Steve knew that about me—he probably knew that about a lot of people, since many of us have that people-pleasing urge inside us.

I knew what he meant. Growing up, I didn't feel close to my siblings and I struggled to make friends. I was bullied in my teens. I came to believe that if I wanted connection, I had to *please* people: teachers, parents, friends, girls, bosses. So, I shaped myself to fit what I thought they wanted.

When I became a coach, then, it was no surprise that I carried some of that forward. I was friendly, kind and helpful. Sometimes, when I felt particularly brave, I could be a little blunt, but that's about as far as it went. Steve now was inviting me into something more refined and courageous. To that end, he offered me a couple of simple questions to use in my conversations with potential clients:

- 'Can I be really open and truthful with you?'
- 'Are you open to hearing me share what I see?'

These weren't clever questions, but neither were they superficial ones. They were invitations into real service. Because if I truly care about someone, I won't just try to create rapport with them or hope they like me. I'll speak to them as their coach with the intention of serving them right away, and not waiting until after they've signed with me or joined my group.

Steve was saying: 'Show them *now*. Coach them *now*. Let them feel it.'

When someone experiences what it's like to be coached powerfully, with love and truth—they remember it. And that moment plants a seed that might grow immediately . . . or years later.

Despite already understanding this to a degree, I often still held back in initial conversations, thinking it best to wait for someone to hire me before I really showed them what coaching with me could be like. It was another year or so before this lesson fully landed in my bones. But the seed had already started to take root.

I began showing up differently, more boldly, more like a coach. My attempts to win people over faded, and I started telling the truth, with heart. And the results were immediately apparent. The entire tone of my conversations changed. The energy shifted. It was like we moved from surface-level dialogue into what was *really* going on for the client.

I remember one man who was struggling in his relationships. He had all kinds of stories about why things weren't working, but what I saw—and eventually reflected back to him—was how timid he was being with the women he liked. And it wasn't just in dating; it was showing up in his career too. When I shared this directly, with love, it cut through the layers of excuse and hiding. He felt it. And something opened up. But I've learned that this kind of directness isn't always appropriate or helpful. It requires reading the person and the situation carefully. As I learned from Dr Mark Howard's audio (discussed earlier), rapport is the currency we use to allow us to be direct. The more direct you want to be with a client, the deeper the rapport needs to be first. Otherwise it can fall flat and not be useful. Some clients prefer a softer or slower approach—not because they're broken or damaged, but simply because that's what serves them best in the moment. The key is developing the judgment to know when directness serves and when a gentler touch is what's called for.

It's no coincidence, really. I had to shift into being more direct *myself* in order to see this more clearly in *him*—and to express it. If I'm being timid in my coaching, I can't help others see where they're being the same way in their lives.

Today, I share this same lesson with the coaches I mentor. Most of them are big-hearted and care deeply about people. That's why they got into this business in the first place. But as was once the case with me, they are risk-averse when it comes to possibly offending someone. They're afraid of coming across as arrogant. And so they do what many of us do when trying to be liked: pull their punches.

We get timid. We soften the truth. We back away from sharing the insights that will help our clients the most. And in doing so, *we rob them of the value they came for*. Love isn't always soft and gentle. It can be direct and bold, too.

Over the years, many of my clients have told me: 'I didn't like what you said at the time, but I'm so glad you said it.' That's the paradox of loving service. Sometimes, it stings before it heals.

But when I speak from love, and I hope I always do, it tends to land. I had an outstanding teacher for this in Steve Chandler; it's what he was modelling for me all along. Leadership, truth and love—right from the start. And funnily enough, when you serve people like that, they're more likely to sign up.

'Love is the intention. Truth is the method.'

~ Steve Hardison

107

Share Your Story

In September 2015, I was getting ready to fly to Chicago for a few days with Steve Chandler's Advanced Client Systems school.

I was excited. Every time I was with other coaches in the school, I felt like I truly belonged. There was a spirit of togetherness, of generosity, and of genuine support that ran through the community. None of this was an accident—Steve had set out to create it intentionally, and he had succeeded. He didn't just run a coaching programme—he built a culture. A place where people were encouraged to lift each other up, to celebrate each other's wins, and to grow together.

This left a lasting impression on me, both inside and out. That experience shaped how I now run my own programmes—from the Powerful Men's Immersions to the AJC Coaching Career School. Over the years, I've heard countless people reflect on how connected and safe they feel in those rooms. And I know that came from Steve. It was a part of his DNA. Now I've made it part of mine.

In a coaching session just before that trip, I told Steve I'd be heading out to Chicago soon. He paused, then asked, 'Why haven't you shared that on Facebook?'

This caught me off guard. I'd always considered myself a pretty open person. I was younger than many coaches I knew, and I was far more comfortable on social media than most. If anything, I expected Steve to tell me to spend *less* time on social media—not to post more.

But he wasn't criticising me; he was pointing to something I'd missed. 'There are coaches in your group who would love to attend ACS but can't,' he said. 'Let them see what you're doing. Let them see your commitment. Show them that you're not just dabbling in this profession. You're all in.'

He was right. I wasn't hiding anything on purpose. I had simply taken the experience for granted. I didn't realise how meaningful my story might be to someone else.

I'd always had a growth mindset. It first took root in my early teens when I joined a youth group for young Hindu boys in the UK. It helped me build confidence and showed me I didn't have to live by default. That seed grew stronger when I was nineteen and studying at Aston University in Birmingham. I discovered personal development books and I was immediately hooked. Throughout my twenties, I devoured anything that could help me grow.

So, when Steve encouraged me to share this moment, it wasn't about self-promotion—it was about showing others what was possible. It was about letting them in.

Accordingly, on 24th September I posted:

> Getting ready for my flight to the good old US of A to meet some familiar faces from the ACS and some new ones too. Three days of learning and sharing with the best in the world. Look out Mr. Steve Chandler—you've got another Brit incoming.

It was a simple post but it marked a shift. That post reminded me that sharing your story builds connection. And this profession of coaching is a relationship business. Since then, I've shared my story more and more.

When I published my first book in 2019, I included stories from my own life; I was honest, real and sometimes vulnerable. And the feedback was incredible. People didn't just enjoy the book; they told me they could see themselves in it. It helped them feel connected to me, and to their own journey.

That's why this book you're reading focuses on my early years as a coach—not just the somewhat more polished successes I've been blessed with more recently. I wanted to show the messiness, the uncertainty, the lessons in real-time—because so many coaches assume that if someone is doing well now, it must've been easy for them.

It wasn't. And I'm no exception. I'm not an enigma. I'm just someone who kept showing up and sharing the truth of it all. These days, I regularly encourage coaches to do the same.

One of them, Angi Scott, wrote a book called *The Coaching Blueprint* about her first two years in my coaching school. I know it's going to help people, not just coaches. It will raise her profile, yes, but more importantly, it will connect her to others in a way nothing else could. Because that's what stories do. They connect, inspire, build trust . . . and remind people they're not alone.

I often say that sharing your story isn't about showing off. It's about showing up. This isn't just true in business. Sometimes I'll coach someone who longs for a deeper relationship with their spouse. They'll tell me how much they love their partner and how amazing they are—and also how much they long for greater connection. So I ask:

'Have you told them that?'

More often than not, the answer is, 'Not in so many words.'

In other words—no. So many people hold back, never sharing what's in their heart. They think they're protecting themselves, but really they're missing the opportunity to create deeper connections.

We humans have always passed on wisdom through stories. I still love hearing them from my parents about their youth, their lives . . . everything. And I know my son lights up when Yamini or I tell him stories about my childhood.

Stories are how we connect. How we teach. How we love. And if you're a coach (or a human being) reading this, please: Don't hold back!

Let people see the path you're walking. Not the perfect version, but the true one. Because somewhere out there, someone needs your story—to believe in their own.

108

What Are You Waiting For?

By September 2015, I'd recorded over twenty-five interviews for my podcast, *The Relationship Series*, which I had started in 2014.

The conversations were still centred around the Three Principles. I interviewed some of the most experienced psychologists, teachers, and practitioners in that field—many of whom had been involved in the understanding for decades. There were very few coaches among them, but they were all deeply steeped in the work of Sydney Banks.

The podcast had begun as a way to serve and learn—and it was working. The conversations were powerful, the reach was growing, and I was building relationships with people I had previously only known from books or conference stages.

There was one person I hadn't asked yet: Dr George Pransky. George was a psychologist who had been one of Sydney Banks' earliest students. He'd essentially been around since the beginning of the Three Principles movement, and I'd heard he was one of the most financially successful practitioners of the work.

I'd met him briefly in 2013 when he was a speaker at a Three Principles Conference in London. He was clearly well-respected. People looked up to him. Yet even though I'd already interviewed many of his peers, I felt intimidated about asking him to be on my podcast.

I didn't have a personal connection with him. I hadn't worked with him. And as I considered the matter a little more closely, I caught myself putting him on a pedestal. Around this time I had a conversation with a former client of mine, Henk Kok, who told me with great excitement that he had interviewed George for a podcast he was running for artists and creatives.

'Wait,' I said, astonished. 'You interviewed George Pransky?'

'Yeah,' Henk said. 'I just asked. And he said yes.'

That landed hard. Here was one of *my* clients—someone I had coached—interviewing a man I'd admired from afar and whom I had hesitated to reach out to. It was humbling, and also energising. The natural next question occurred to me: *What am I waiting for?*

I still felt a flicker of hesitation when I sat down to email George. But I'd been in this position before, and I'd learned not to overthink it. So I wrote an email, hit send . . .

. . . and George said yes.

From our very first exchange, he was warm, kind, and incredibly open, the very qualities I'd seen in the most successful coaches I'd met in ACS. These were people who had done really well *and* who were still deeply generous.

When we recorded the interview, a few more things stood out. George was remarkably present and giving. But what really struck me was that he had taken the time to read my website before we spoke. I was not aware of any other guest who had done that.

In fact, he'd read it well enough to ask me at one point, 'Why haven't you mentioned Sydney Banks on your website?'

The question caught me off guard. I felt a bit embarrassed, not because I'd been hiding anything, but because I realised I'd overlooked something that mattered. I assured George I had deep respect for Syd's work and was more than happy to add an acknowledgement. George even offered to help me with the wording. I was moved by his care and attention.

That conversation turned into a two-part episode—and it became the most listened-to interview in the entire series, with over 17,000 views on YouTube alone. Beyond the numbers, though, it deepened my understanding of a concept I had already started to learn: that the people we put on pedestals are just people. Yes, George was a pioneer. But he was also approachable, generous, and very human.

When I treat others as peers (not idols) everything changes. Something shifts internally. I stop performing or trying to impress the other person and instead start connecting and get into rapport more easily. I no longer need to prove anything, and in that space, the real magic occurs.

This was something I saw in Steve Hardison too. He didn't put anyone above him. Because of that, he moved through the world with a kind of freedom. If someone seemed unreachable, Steve picked up the phone. He just saw a person—not a pedestal. That was part of what made him so powerful.

When we let people down from the pedestals we've placed them on, something within us can shift. We realise we don't need to be 'more important' than we are to approach the George Pranskys in our lives—we just need to be willing. If we're with a client or someone else we can serve, we don't need anyone else's permission to show up for them—just our own, along with our willingness to serve.

It's easy to forget this when we're starting out, or when we're looking up to someone we admire. But courage often looks like a quiet email or a question asked, even when your voice is shaking.

Courage can be simply showing up when you feel like shrinking back.

That moment with Henk wasn't the last time he inspired me either. A few years later, *he* wrote his first book—*before I wrote mine*. It was the nudge I needed. Seeing him do it lit something up in me, and it helped me give myself permission to finally start writing my own. This is one reason why maintaining relationships with colleagues is so valuable in a profession that can feel lonely. We can use each other as inspiration, support, and sometimes just the reminder that we're not alone in this work.

Sometimes the inspiration we're waiting for doesn't come from those ahead of us. It comes from those we've walked beside.

109

Interviewing My Coach for the First Time

Later in September 2015, I did something that scared me just enough to know I was on the right track. I interviewed my coach, Steve Chandler, for the Facebook group I had created for coaches.

I was both excited and nervous. Steve was one of the most respected coaches in the profession. He was direct, bold and funny, and he didn't sugarcoat anything. I loved that about him, but I wasn't sure how others, especially those from the Three Principles community, would respond. Some coaches in that world preferred a softer style, one with more space and less edge. Steve wasn't harsh, but he didn't hide. He spoke plainly. He had a grounded sense of humour and an unwavering commitment to truth. I trusted him completely. Still . . . this was my group. My reputation. And I was about to put a spotlight on my own coach.

The intention behind the interview was simple: to serve. When I had initially created that Facebook group, I'd wanted it to be the most valuable free resource for coaches anywhere online. I was frustrated by the marketing hype that had crept into the coaching world—people selling expensive programmes to coaches without delivering real results. I'd seen too many well-meaning coaches spend thousands and walk away discouraged and confused. I wanted to offer the opposite: real conversations, real value, real honesty.

So who better to interview than Steve Chandler? However, I was really nervous. I was going live with Steve and I had no idea how it was going to be received. I still carried a fear of being judged by others, and in a way, I was bringing two worlds together: the Three Principles community, which was more reflective, and the Chandler world, which more direct and unapologetically practical.

Steve opened the interview with his usual dry humour, deadpan and wry, which made me laugh but didn't quite settle my nerves. I'd love to say I relaxed after a few minutes, but honestly, it took longer than that.

Steve was calm and laid-back, but he didn't pull punches. He was honest. He was serving. And even though it didn't feel like I was being coached in public, I definitely felt vulnerable. I wasn't hiding, and neither was he.

We didn't dive into the Three Principles directly, though Steve did mention being mentored by people like Dicken Bettinger. What struck me was how different he was from me at the time, with my nervous energy. He wasn't trying to impress anyone. He was just honest, sharing what had worked in his practice, what he'd learned the hard way, and what he knew to be true. There was a clarity and confidence to it that I wanted to develop in myself.

The conversation was wide-ranging, touching on a number of subjects that Steve and I had explored in my individual coaching sessions, and often going deeper into them. I listened to everything Steve said that day like it was meant for me, because in a very real way it was. I was still early on in my journey and had yet to fully own the truth that I was running a business—and that this business was meant to be profitable.

Steve kept pointing me back to that truth when he said things like:

- 'When someone pays for coaching, they open up to greater change.'
- 'Coaching isn't therapy—it's creation.'
- 'You don't need to give your time away to everyone, but you do need to serve.'

In the second part of the interview, he took things deeper. He talked about how love and building a prosperous coaching practice go hand in hand. That love isn't just softness or approval—it's being willing to serve deeply, even when it's uncomfortable to do so. *Fierce* love. The kind that sometimes looks like setting boundaries, challenging someone, or speaking truth when it's inconvenient. Love, Steve said, is not timid. It turns over tables. It speaks directly. It wakes people up. And that, too, is what powerful coaching does.

He said something that sticks with me to this day: 'If someone says they got everything they needed in one free session, what they're really saying is: "I didn't experience you as powerful enough to want *more*."'

Steve also reminded us that there is no 'pyramid scheme' in coaching. Coaches coaching other coaches is how the craft evolves—just like doctors are trained by other doctors. What matters most is that you're good. That you make a real difference in people's lives, and that you're willing to get better every day.

He challenged the obsession with websites, personal branding, and being visible, observing that, 'People don't hire you because you've been on Oprah. They hire you because you helped them or someone they know.'

The moment that surprised me most in the interview was how

candid he was about money. Without flinching, he said that his high standard for taking on clients included one simple question: Do they have the money to pay me?

He said this without apology or softening. In fact, the whole interview was filled with his grounded, stripped-back wisdom. It all landed powerfully with me, and from the feedback I received afterwards, it resonated with the group as well.

The interview wasn't just well received—it was loved.

People posted comments like:

- 'This was brilliant—thank you for sharing Steve with us.'
- 'Wow—I didn't know Steve had a connection with the Three Principles. That's really helpful!'
- 'This really made me think differently about coaching and money.'

That interview has now been one of the most viewed on my YouTube channel. But more importantly, it marked a turning point for me personally. For the first time, I wasn't just a coach—I was starting to become a leader in the coaching world. People were approaching my work for deeper understanding and support on their own journey. I don't say this from ego—obviously my success was supported by people like Steve appearing on my channel, and by learning from countless others. I just felt like I was settling into the process of being a coach and supporting others doing the same. By bringing Steve to the group, I wasn't just sharing wisdom—I was saying, 'This is who I learn from. This is what I believe in. This is the kind of coach I want to be.'

Looking back now, I see that interviewing Steve wasn't just

about content. It was about *commitment*. It was about stepping into visibility, leadership, and service—even when I was nervous—and elevating the conversation for coaches who were tired of fluff and hungry for truth.

It was about becoming the kind of coach and man I wanted to be. That interview planted a seed, and this book is one of the many things that grew from it. What I was starting to realise back then was that building a coaching practice isn't really about getting or attracting clients. It's about how much love and service you're willing to bring to your work, even when you're worried about being judged for it. Even when you're not sure you're good enough yet. Steve showed me that day what it looked like to just show up and serve. I'm still learning. As Steve Hardison would say, this is a mountain without a top!

110

Falling Even More in Love with the Profession

At the end of September, I flew to Chicago. It was a very different city from Phoenix. The weather was colder, for one thing. But it felt like a proper city: tall buildings, bustling streets, and a skyline that looked like it belonged on a postcard.

I completely misjudged the distance from the airport to the hotel. In Arizona, an Uber cost me around $20. This time? $124. That stung. But the hotel itself was stunning—smack bang in the middle of downtown, surrounded by skyscrapers and the energy of the Windy City.

Steve once explained what a powerful decision it was to hold the ACS in venues like this; it was high-end with a price tag to match. He was modeling something important: coaches deserve to occupy these spaces.

This lesson was one I took to heart for my Immersions and my school. Today, the venue I choose for my coaching school is directly in the heart of London. It's the kind of venue which used to intimidate me because it was grand and, frankly, expensive. Now I love calling this hotel my second home.

In Chicago, I had no issues with thinking I didn't belong. Being in the midst of this community only deepened my love for the profession. This was my second time through the ACS. When Steve welcomed us returning students, he made a point that stuck with me: '*You're* not coming back to the same school because you're not the same person who left. ' He mentioned that some of the most successful coaches had done the programme multiple times—Rich Litvin had done it four times. It wasn't a coincidence, Steve said, that the coaches who kept coming back were often the ones making the most money. That's exactly why I was there—to stay on the path.

The air buzzed with excitement. People had travelled from all over the States, and a few of us from even further afield. Familiar faces greeted me: Melissa Ford, Gary Mahler, Jason Goldberg, Lisa Giruzzi, Karen Davis, Robert Diaz. It felt like a reunion of people who were all committed to the same journey. Alongside the familiar faces were some new ones too—coaches who were joining this larger cohort of the ACS for the first time. It felt expansive. A growing community of committed professionals. And although the jetlag kicked in hard by the afternoon—I was something like six hours ahead on UK time—I was still energised to be there.

Steve started strong, going straight to the heart of things. 'This programme is about making money,' he said. He wasn't being crass, just clear. After all, the name of the programme was Advanced Client Systems, and its aim was to show coaches how to create a prosperous coaching practice through profound, powerful service. This message wove through everything we learned that weekend.

Steve is fond of distinctions—those powerful black-and-white insights that have the power to rewire how you think. One that really stood out that day was the 'Giver versus Taker' distinction. Steve told us how he used to be a Taker. He'd think of coaching as taking someone's time, as bothering them, and, ultimately, as trying to take their money. But then something in him shifted. He started reaching out to people as someone who could serve them, someone like a paramedic helping out in a crisis. The paramedic isn't superior to the receiver; they're simply someone who can help in that moment. This was the state of Giver. Someone who is present and has something to offer. In terms of coaching, the prospective client can choose whether or not to take what is being offered; the coach's job is simply to give the experience of coaching.

I myself had definitely felt like a Taker quite often as I was building my practice. I understood and practiced the idea of service at some level, but when I wanted a client it was sometimes challenging to detach myself from what I wanted and just fully give through service. In other words, I hadn't completely transitioned into seeing myself as a Giver. But I trusted and believed in Steve. So even if I didn't feel it fully yet, I was now aware of and open to the distinction he was making. And that was enough.

Steve introduced another powerful distinction: Connection versus Perfection. Connection builds trust. It's the greatest thing we have as coaches. But perfection? That's rooted in fear. It drives people away. So many coaches, myself included, often think we need to get it 'right': Ask the right questions, do it the 'Three Principles way,' give the best answers . . . But our job isn't to be perfect. It's to help. To connect.

As Steve told us, 'You can be wrong. Don't use that as a reason to hold back.' He challenged us to act as if this was the last time we'd ever speak to a prospective client. Or the last time we'd give a talk. What would we say if this was our only shot? 'You don't need to come across as superior,' he said. 'Come in with a worse story than theirs. *The most powerful client attractor is how effective you are as a coach.*'

Every coach starts at zero. No one skips any numbers. Even

Steve Hardison, who'd had, among other formative experiences, hundreds of hours with Werner Erhard and years of practise coaching in corporate settings before going solo. Even he had to grow as a coach. Hearing this was liberating. Steve Chandler's great gift was to help me shift my relationship with the coaching profession. For so long it had felt like an impenetrable riddle, a dark and mysterious art; suddenly it became approachable, tangible, doable. The path ahead grew ever clearer.

He gave us ways to raise our effectiveness as a coach: Attend programmes. Read. Listen to audios. But more importantly, be coachable. Be honest about your fears. Slow down. Re-read your last twenty emails and discover ways to improve your communications. Be curious about what your client really wants. Don't ask what's *wrong* with you as a coach—ask what you can bring to the table in order to serve your client.

Another point brought about a shift in the way I see people. Steve pointed out that 'We can never move someone from unsuccessful to successful. Only from successful to more successful.' Our job as coaches is to find what is already working in our clients' lives and build on it. Everyone is doing the best they can. Many clients come into coaching overlooking or minimising the success they have already achieved. However, when a client recognises what *has* been working, it's a much stronger base on which to build. This is something all my coaches have helped me with. They pointed me to what was working, what I had achieved and built on that.

For example, imagine a client comes to me, 'I never stick to anything. I start things but then don't keep at them.' I can ask questions and explore where they *have* actually stuck to things. It could be as basic as learning to walk and talk. They probably didn't give up there. Often there are more recent examples of success. This isn't simply reframing their problems but helping people to not over-dramatise them. It was not lost on me that this didn't only apply to the clients we coach but to us as coaches too. If you had to make a list of all your accomplishments in an area where you would like to grow, that list would probably be longer than you realise.

111

Just Coach

The next morning in Chicago, Steve Chandler took us deeper. He had a way of expressing ideas that cut through complexity to create understandings of great clarity and simplicity.

Steve began the day by challenging a belief many of us held—that coaching was 50 percent business and selling, and 50 percent actual coaching. The former, most of us believed, was the hard part.

Steve introduced us to a new paradigm.

What if your entire business was *just coaching*?

This wasn't just a clever soundbite. He meant it. He walked us through an example: imagine you have four sessions on your calendar—two with existing clients and two with prospective clients. Steve's suggestion was to *treat all four the same*. Coach in every session. Let the prospective clients *experience* what it's like to work with you. They don't have to imagine or guess what it's like to be your client. They live it. They can make their decision about signing up with you with a precise understanding of what they're signing up for.

It was a brilliant suggestion that felt right because it aligned with the idea of pure service. Don't hold back till money has exchanged hands. Serve first and always. Steve was showing us this was possible not just as a practice but as a business model as well. I'd already been coaching a lot and finding ways to sign up clients, but this 'just coach' principle began to melt away whatever residual tendencies I had to fall into 'sales mode.' *No selling. Just coaching.*

Steve also encouraged us to let go of the idea of 'worthiness'—for the simple reason that you can never truly know if you're worthy. Who decides? What score do you get? It's nebulous. Made-up. But *usefulness*? That's tangible. You can measure it. Was this conversation useful? Is this resource useful? Would this coaching be useful to your client?

For my own part, I was still comparing myself to Jamie Smart and my Three Principles mentors. And in *my* mind I always came up short. A feeling of personal worthiness was something I was chasing without even realising it, and this subtly (or not so subtly) impacted my ability both to connect with people and to raise my fees. If I wasn't 'worthy' then why should I reach out to anyone, much less charge them for coaching?

Yet Steve's distinction gave me permission to drop that question and show up fearlessly when reaching out to existing and prospective clients. It focused more on service and less on outcomes. Whether someone took me up on an offer didn't matter—it was about helping. My focus wasn't on proving myself worthy, but on developing the *service muscle*. My job wasn't to manage what people thought of me or even what I thought of *myself* in terms of worthiness. My job was simply to serve.

Steve shared an example from his own coaching with Steve Hardison. Hardison had asked him, 'If you could have anything you wanted in your life, what would it be?'

Steve said, '$400k.'

Hardison replied, 'Which person would pay you that *and* have it be worth it to them?' The exchange led to Steve creating a client who paid him $400k. If Chandler had got into thinking about whether he was worthy to sign up a $400k client, he probably would have not created this revenue for his coaching practice. Focusing on creating something that was truly useful for the client created a client paying him this fee, which was far higher than he usually charged.

At that time, Hardison charged $150k a year to work with him (and in some cases, even $1,000,000, because he understood that for some clients, $150k wasn't enough to generate deep commitment). Pricing wasn't about worthiness; it was about usefulness and the value of our services. In this case, the price helped create a degree of commitment the client would not have had otherwise. That commitment is part of what made coaching with Hardison really useful for those who work with him. It wasn't about whether Hardison was worthy of $150k or $1m per client. It was the value he was creating for his clients. Worthiness is simply an idea and cannot be tangibly measured.

That story cemented everything Steve was teaching. It wasn't abstract theory. It was lived experience. He told us he could distil the entire ACS programme into this one thing: **Just coach.**

You don't need to be known. You don't even need to believe fully in coaching or yourself—aka whether or not you are worthy. You just need to jump in and test it. And the more you test it, the more you'll see for yourself. Because the experience of coaching *sells* the coaching. This is still true for me a decade after attending that weekend. I am far more experienced and skilled as a coach, but the only thing that matters to someone who would hire me is whether I can be useful in helping them create whatever they want to create.

People have no idea whether I can truly help them until they experience my coaching.

One more powerful phrase from that weekend still sticks with me: 'Your greatest weakness can turn into your greatest strength.'

That was me. I used to struggle connecting with people. I was caught in comparison, overthinking, trying to get it right, managing how others perceived me, wondering if I was good enough. Of course, part of me still carried on in this vein even after this ACS weekend, but something shifted. The weekend was a turning point in how I saw myself and how I practised as a coach.

Now, connection is one of my greatest gifts. I connect effortlessly with people from all around the world. Today, I teach my clients in my coaching school: Stop obsessing over yourself. Stop asking if you're worthy. Ask instead: *Can I be useful today?* Go out and help someone. Serve. Take action, however messy.

That's what changes everything: stop proving your worth, start being useful. Just coach.

112

Event-Action

I didn't know at the time just how powerful the Event-Action distinction would turn out to be. It came on the afternoon of Day 2 in Chicago, almost as an afterthought, a final insight in a day full of powerful distinctions from Steve Chandler's book *Crazy Good.*

It didn't feel like a big deal in the moment, but looking back now, it was the seed that helped me fall in love with my intuition and start acting on it.

Event-action came from Steve Hardison. The essence of it is simple: the longer you take to act after an event, the less powerful and effective that action becomes—because life happens in between. Things change. Energy fades. People get distracted. The impact dissipates.

Steve gave us a straightforward example: Imagine a prospective client tells you they want to work with you. That's the *event.* You tell them you'll send over your proposal. That's the *action.*

If you send the proposal an hour later, or even the same day, you're in sync with the moment. But if you wait three days? The energy has shifted. The clarity they felt in the moment may have dissolved. Something else may have caught their attention. Life happened.

The thing to remember is that the event isn't always something external, like a coaching conversation. It could be internal, within yourself—coming in the form of a thought, a nudge, a whisper from the soul. What some people call intuition and others the voice of God.

One example of how I started putting this awareness into action is that if I woke up in the morning and the thought of a former client popped into my mind, I'd message them. Sometimes they'd respond, 'How did you know I was just thinking of you?' Other times I'd get an idea to send a resource to someone I hadn't spoken to in months, and they'd reply, 'This is exactly what I needed.' I didn't know. But the Universe did. And I followed its nudge.

I've used this in creating programmes too. I'll get a wild idea—to launch something new, to invite a guest faculty member who normally says no, to write a post that comes through me in the moment—and I act. I don't wait. Because I've learned that if I wait, the moment passes. I start questioning. Doubting. Talking myself out of it. But if I act, magic happens.

This is one of the most powerful and underrated distinctions I've learned in my coaching journey, not to mention my life. Of course, not *every* inspired action yields a viral hit or a new client. My Business Series podcast didn't become an overnight success, and many of the people I've reached out to never hired me. But every action taught me something. Every time I acted, I learned, refined, and grew.

What I didn't realise then is that this is a muscle. You need to do the reps. When you do, your relationship to intuition, to life itself, changes. I've built a team around me now to help implement faster, but the core principle remains: Act fast. Don't delay. Don't second-guess. Just move.

Steve Hardison later deepened this understanding in me. He

taught me that if I wanted to live by intuition, I couldn't question it. I had to honour it by acting immediately. That's how you turn intuition into your superpower. I see this clearly in my work with other coaches. The clients who experience the biggest growth—both financially and in themselves—are the ones who take swift action after a conversation, a coaching weekend, an online masterclass, or even from watching a laser-coaching session.

Whilst it happens less often, I still catch myself waiting sometimes. Waiting to feel more ready, more experienced, more certain. But I've learned that the feeling passes when I act. The muscle only grows when I use it.

Because, as Werner Erhard famously said: 'Life is a game in which there are no rules except the ones you make—and you can't play if you don't act.'

I've watched this play out hundreds of times now, both in my own life and with my clients. The ones who grow the most aren't the ones who wait until they're ready. They're the ones who act when the nudge comes, even when they're scared.

113

Day 3 In Chicago

As usual, by Day 3 of the ACS weekend, I was a little tired. Not just from the intensity of the work inside the room, but from the richness of the connections outside it. Every morning I'd get up early and head to breakfast to eat with some of the other coaches. It became a bit of a ritual. I didn't want to miss a single moment. There was something sacred about those mornings: the camaraderie, the laughter and the deep conversations.

Jason Goldberg was often there, and without fail he would have me laughing hard over some ridiculous story. I'd forget I was tired and the buzz would return. I never felt like that going to school as a kid. This wasn't education. This was something else entirely.

The morning of that third session started with Steve Chandler saying:

'The future you create has infinitely more power over the quality and success of your life than your past (which has passed).'

This landed deeply. Not because it was new to me, but because of who I was now, where I was, and what I was ready to hear. Up until that point, so much of my life had been shaped by a quiet story running in the background: I was an underachiever. I'd never quite live up to my potential. I was weaker than others. I wasn't enough.

I didn't walk into the ACS room consciously thinking these

things, but that's the nature of stories: we don't always realise we're carrying them until someone offers us a mirror. Steve held that mirror gently but firmly. And as he spoke, I began to drop pieces of that identity. It was a healing process; I could feel something inside me soften and re-form.

This is what Day 3 became for me: not just a classroom or a coaching intensive, but a space of reinvention. It's hard to pinpoint exactly how or when the shift happened. It had something to do with the energy, the room, the feeling . . . Something also to do with what I absorbed simply being around Steve and the other coaches.

But shifts like these happened every ACS weekend. When I left them, I felt like a professional. Not just 'some guy with a coaching business,' but someone who was part of a noble profession. One that could pay well, yes—but more than that, one that could truly serve and uplift people.

As I reflected on the weekend while flying home, something else Steve had said came to me:

'Sometimes to learn something, you have to create it.'

I felt like I belonged in the world I was creating. I wasn't pretending. I was investing in myself to be around the best in the world, and I could feel the powerful results of this growing inside me. I was a builder. A creator. A man who had a choice. The younger version of me—the boy who sometimes felt like life was happening to him—needed to hear Steve's observation to grow into the role of creator. To understand that the future was still wide open. It didn't matter what I'd been or what had happened. I could build something different from this moment forward.

Steve's words landed because I was ready to hear them. That's what Day 3 was for me, and more.

Nowadays I see this same spirit alive in the work I do with

coaches in my school. When they leave our live weekends they don't just feel inspired; they feel transformed. Many step into a deeper sense of belonging and purpose, seeing themselves not simply as people running a business, but as part of something bigger: a movement to raise the standard of our profession. They return home carrying that sense of mission into their conversations and into the lives of their clients.

The experience of Day 3 was another step away from who I thought I was and towards who I was becoming.

114

The Gift of Slowness

In October 2015, I made a last-minute decision to attend a retreat that would turn out to change not just the way I saw life, but the way I ran every Men's Immersion from that day forward.

The retreat was hosted by Tikkun, the educational branch of a North London-based Jewish charity that had been quietly doing something extraordinary: offering low-cost, high-integrity Three Principles events to the public. And this one was different. This one featured Chip and Jan Chipman.

Chip had been mentoring me for some time as part of Jamie Smart's Clarity Advanced Training. His presence, humility, and unwavering grounding in the Principles had already had a deep impact on me. I'd heard he and Jan were coming to London, and although the retreat wasn't expensive, I'd been watching my costs carefully. I wasn't sure I'd go.

A month before the retreat, I sent them an email just after midnight:

> Hi Jan and Chip,
>
> It's past midnight here and before going to bed I wanted to send you both a message. I've been reading *Paradigm Shift* by Jack Pransky, which describes

a lot of the history of what happened in the past forty years with the Principles. I didn't know what to expect but it really was enlightening. Something occurred to me while reading it—George points out that you were very successful in bringing this understanding into the business world, that you were able to support yourselves through your work, that you were close to Syd, and that you didn't seem to get caught up in the politics.

This didn't seem like a coincidence to me. I just felt a deep appreciation for you both and for being who you are. I feel really privileged that we spent some time together and in that lovely space. I'm most likely not coming to Salt Spring Island this year as I'm watching the costs, but I hear you are going to be in London in October. I'd love to meet you and I might join you for the immersion event.

Just reflecting that life (as they might have said in the 70s) is a real trip! Love you both,

Ankush

I told myself I'd attend if a new client signed up. And just days before the retreat, one did. Money came in. A door opened. And I stepped through it.

The retreat was held at De Vere Hunton Park—a beautiful hotel set in stunning grounds. From the moment I arrived, something felt different. There was no rush, no pressure. No overpacked schedule. Long lunches. Breaks where we were invited—sometimes gently nudged—to go for a walk. It was the complete opposite of every training I had attended before, which typically tried to pack as much value and information into every available minute. Chip and Jan did the opposite.

They knew something I had yet to learn fully: space is not a break from the learning. It *is* the learning.

One night, I lay in the small single bed of the Airbnb I'd booked—just a spare room in someone's nearby house. It was quiet. Still. And without any prompting, I had what I can only describe as the mother of all insights.

I can't remember what I was thinking about before it happened. But suddenly, it hit me like lightning through my nervous system: *Everything I feel is coming from my thinking.*

Everything.

Every moment in the past.

Every moment to come.

Every experience of life.

All of it is being created through Thought.

It was as if an insight I'd had many times before now landed on a deeper floor of the building. I felt weightless, joyful, peaceful, like I was walking on air. Even now, years later, just remembering it brings a smile to my face. I knew better than to try to hold onto it—insight is like a bird that lands gently on your shoulder and flies off just as freely. But it had touched me, and I would never be quite the same.

I shared what had happened with several people, including Terry Rubenstein and Steve Adair, both of whom were deeply immersed in sharing the Principles through their own coaching and training. They understood. We spoke the same language. It felt like I had come home.

And strangely, something else happened that weekend. People

I'd never met began coming up to me and asking, 'Are you Ankush Jain?'

At first, I was caught off guard. Apparently, they'd been listening to my *Relationship Series* podcast—and loving it. I felt humbled, a little awkward, and quietly proud. These people knew more about me than I knew about them. And I realised: you never really know who's listening. Who you're touching. Whose life you might be impacting, even if you never hear about it.

I joked that I'd become 'Three Principles' famous. But it was more than a joke. It was a gentle nudge from the universe to keep going.

Maybe the biggest gift of all was the walks. Every walk we took slowed me down—not just physically, but mentally. I found myself actually *being* where I was. Listening. Taking in the beauty of the grounds. Not rushing toward the next insight, the next takeaway, the next achievement. Just being with others. With the moment. With life.

This was a gift I had almost never given myself. In my world of filling every moment, to-do lists, this retreat offered me stillness—the good kind. Space to breathe. Time to just be. A chance to meet myself again.

That weekend didn't just deepen my grounding in the Three Principles. It transformed how I ran my own Immersions from then on. I stopped filling up every minute. I let the room breathe. I began to honour silence as part of the work. And I trusted something far greater than my own content to guide people home. Years later, this slowing-down approach also shaped the live weekends in my school. I ensure that we have time for breaks and long lunches. We finish by 5:30pm and don't carry on late, like some trainings I have attended. Many coaches tell me those breaks are some of the top moments of the school where they get to connect with their colleagues in a relaxed way.

All because I said yes—at the last possible moment—to a quiet invitation to slow down.

115

The Ashram Talk

It was a crisp October evening in 2015 when I returned to the Jain Ashram in Birmingham—only this time, I wasn't coming to sit at the back and listen to a lecture from a visiting monk or enjoy the food (they always had hot vegetarian samosas!). I was coming to speak.

Arvind Jain, the president at the time, had seen some of my coaching posts on social media and invited me to talk to the community. Perhaps he wanted to engage more young people, and he thought my message might resonate. I was nervous, but I knew I had to say yes. The only way to get more comfortable with speaking to groups was to speak to more groups.

For context, Jainism is one of the oldest religions in the world. It originated in India and emphasises non-violence, self-discipline, and seeking liberation through inner transformation. The ashram in Birmingham wasn't just a place of worship—it was a community hub. My grandfather had helped build it, and my parents were still active members of the committee. I had been there countless times for Diwali fireworks, prayer services, and cultural events. It was home.

That night, I stepped into the ashram wrapped in nervous anticipation. The building was almost always cold when you first arrived, but on this night, thankfully, it was warm. It wasn't packed like it could be during a big festival, but there were quite a few people who had turned up to hear me speak.

I looked around and saw so many familiar faces. Aunties and uncles. My mum and dad. People I respected. People I feared would dismiss me. I wasn't a monk. I wasn't a scholar. I was a coach speaking about something most of them had never heard of—'The Three Principles.'

I began by sharing my story—how I left the corporate world, including a successful job in London, and transitioned into coaching full time.

My heart was thumping. Not because I didn't believe in what I was about to share, but because this was a kind of 'coming out' for me. I'd spoken in Las Vegas and Bucharest, but here I felt more vulnerable. Here, there were no strangers. There was no hiding. And yet, as I began, something settled in me. I wasn't there to impress. I was there to serve. To share. To offer something from the heart.

I spoke about how our experience of life comes from thought, not circumstance. About separate realities—how no two people live in the same world, even when sitting side by side. About psychological innocence—the understanding that people are always doing the best they can, given the thinking that looks real to them.

To bring this home, I told a personal story about an upsetting email I once received. At the time, it had really rattled me. But when I came back to it a few days later, in a different state of mind, the same words read like a different message. Nothing had changed in the email but my thinking had shifted.

To my surprise, the room didn't grow cold. The audience leaned in. Heads nodded. Eyes widened. And at the end, people came up to me and thanked me for the talk. People I never expected to be interested—elders, family friends, even my own relatives—came up to ask questions, to understand more.

'What's this thing you do again?'

'How does it help people?'

'Could you speak to my son?'

I mentioned a paid event I was running with Gabriela Maldonado—a chance to go deeper for those who were interested. But there was no hard sell. Just an open door. While no-one became a private client, some of them did sign up to the event I was running with her.

And that was enough. That night helped me be more visible and more comfortable as a coach. I also recorded the talk, which became a helpful resource I could share with clients and potential clients in the future.

It was the first time many of them saw me not as the kid they once knew, but as a man with something to say. And it was also the first time I fully saw what I did as sacred—not 'just' a career, not just coaching, but a modern-day form of pointing people towards the truth—something our sages and scriptures have done for centuries.

I learned that you never know who's ready to hear what you know to be true.

116

A Collaboration That Brought out the Fun in Me

When I first met Gabriela Maldonado Montano, I had no idea what I was getting into.

We were scheduled to record an episode for my podcast series on relationships, and I'd been told by a mutual contact that she was someone worth speaking to. What I hadn't been told was that within minutes of starting our conversation, I'd be in fits of laughter. There was an ease, a lightness, and a sense of joy between us that felt rare. By the end of that conversation, I knew I wanted to create something with her. Before I could even say it myself, she said, 'Let's do an event together.'

We were both in. We decided to run a live event in Birmingham, preceded by a series of five free webinars on relationships. We called the series *Rediscover the Fun in Your Relationship*. It was playful, light-hearted, and deeply aligned with who Gabriela was. She had a motto: 'If it's not fun, I'm not doing it.' And she meant it. Gabriela brought out the part of me that I often left behind—the fun, mischievous, childlike part. The part that didn't take everything so seriously.

In the weeks leading up to the event, we ran those five webinars together. We didn't rehearse or plan much—we just showed up and talked. We joked, we teased each other, we reflected on love, dating, connection, and compatibility. And we laughed. A lot. The kind of laughter that leaves you feeling lighter just for having been around it. It felt effortless, like we'd been doing this together for years. We were so in sync, so on the same page, that it never felt like work.

The night before the event, Gabriela and her husband came to my parents' house for dinner. My mum made a beautiful Indian meal, the kind that only comes from someone who cooks from a space of love and tradition in their bones. My parents were warm and generous, and Gabriela and her husband were visibly touched. It meant a lot to me to bring these two parts of my world together—my family and my professional life—and see them connect so naturally. My mum still talks about that evening.

The next day was the event itself. I was nervous, of course. I always was in those days. But it was also exciting. It felt like something real, something I was meant to do. One of my clients was in charge of recording the event on my dad's digital video camera. So the same camera that had probably captured birthday parties and family holidays was now capturing me leading a room of people alongside Gabriela, an experienced teacher. My parents were in the audience. So was Yamini.

What I remember most vividly about that day wasn't the talk itself—it was the look on Yamini's face afterwards. She was proud. Not just politely supportive, but genuinely impressed by the man she saw in front of the room. The leader. The one people looked up to. Something deep had shifted. Yamini saw me differently that night, and I saw myself differently too. I felt I had earned some respect from her for what I did. That meant a lot to me.

Professionally, the event wasn't a massive financial success.

We didn't sell hundreds of tickets or pack out a venue. But it didn't matter.

What mattered was that together we'd created, from a single idea, something real, something fun. And that Yamini had seen me step into it with confidence and joy.

Working with Gabriela showed me something I'd forgotten: connection doesn't always have to be deep and serious. Sometimes the lightness is what creates intimacy. The laughter, the silliness, the ease—that's real too. Maybe even more real, because it's harder to fake. I realised I could bring more of this into my practice. Steve had been showing me this all along—that being a coach didn't mean being serious all the time.

117

The Proposal

The weekend of the second Powerful Men's Immersion was already special. I had just come off the high of delivering the event with Gabriela Maldonado Montano, and now this Immersion had a new kind of energy to it. Something was shifting in me, and as a result I was being seen differently by others—and more importantly, by myself.

It was in my hotel room after Day 2 of the immersion that the thought landed: I was going to propose to Yamini.

We had already planned a short trip away to the Loire Valley in early December. I thought to myself, *What better time? What better place?* That night, I opened my laptop and began searching for the perfect spot to propose. I stumbled onto a forum where someone mentioned a romantic chateau-turned-hotel in the Loire Valley called Château de la Tortinière. It looked like something out of a fairytale. One of the rooms was in a turret. I was sold.

I booked it for three nights.

Then, for good measure, I booked a cheap hotel nearby and sent Yamini the confirmation for that one before cancelling it. She had no idea what was really waiting for her.

A few days later, on the 11th of November, I had a coaching call with Steve Chandler. I debated whether to bring it up. It wasn't my usual kind of coaching request, but something told me to share it, and I'm so glad I did; that session became one of my favourite calls with Steve.

He told me, 'Make it as romantic as you can. If you do it right, she'll want to talk about it for the rest of her life.'

He was right. Steve always talked about *client astonishment*—the idea that we go above and beyond for our clients in a way that leaves them feeling cherished and amazed. Why wouldn't I do that for the woman I loved?

He told me the proposal needed an element of surprise. Something dramatic and unexpected. Flowers. Music. Emotion. He encouraged me not to be afraid of making a fool of myself. He reminded me that in both love and coaching, real connection often lies on the other side of risk. Of course, proposals don't need grand gestures—some of the most meaningful ones are quiet and simple. For us, this felt right. Steve also suggested I write a handwritten letter, one page in length, to be given *after* she said yes. In it I would explain why I wanted to marry her. 'She'll keep it forever,' he said. I believed him.

Initially, I thought I'd propose on the last day of the trip. But Steve turned that on its head. 'Do it as soon as you arrive,' he said. 'Before you even open your bags. Then the rest of the trip becomes a celebration. She'll feel like you couldn't wait another minute.'

And then, as always, Steve shared a personal story. When he proposed to his wife Kathy, it was an ambush. She thought they were just coming home to feed the cat. Instead, she walked in to find flowers everywhere, and when she turned around, Steve was down on one knee.

I loved that. Soon after, I drove down to the Jewellery Quarter in Birmingham and had a custom ring made. A single, high-quality diamond, elegant and timeless. Although I wasn't yet earning what I had been in the corporate world, I knew this was a moment that only comes once. I was investing in a memory, in a milestone, in her. It wasn't about the money or appearances. It was about creating an experience Yamini would never forget.

I rented the best car they had available at Tours airport, though I skipped the upgraded seats on the flight out, just to keep her off the scent. I'd also asked her dad for permission beforehand. That mattered to Yamini, and I wanted to honour that.

Keeping it all a surprise wasn't easy. Yamini was a fraud investigator by profession, after all. I had to tell a few playful fibs along the way. Like when she questioned the car size and I told her we must've had a free upgrade. As we drove toward Tours, she pointed out when we missed the turnoff for the hotel she thought we were going to. I just smiled and said, 'I think we're on the right path.'

When we arrived at Château de la Tortinière, the staff were in on it. They were beaming as we checked in. I had arranged for forty-eight long-stem roses and a bottle of champagne to be waiting in the room. Yamini was puzzled but hadn't quite figured it out yet. Then, in that turret room, I played *our song*. We danced. And just as the lyrics said, 'All that's left for me to do is pop the question,' I got down on one knee.

Everything stopped. This was what I had been building towards for weeks. Her eyes widened. She was definitely surprised. I could see the weight of the moment land in her body. And then, after a short pause that felt a lot longer than it actually was . . . she said yes.

Afterwards, I called my parents. They had been waiting with bated breath to hear the news. I asked them to keep it quiet so we could savour the moment a little longer. Within minutes, relatives from India began calling. Clearly, not everyone found it easy to sit on the news, and honestly, I loved that they were so excited they couldn't hold it in.

The next few days were magical. We explored the grounds, took photos, ate incredible food, and let ourselves be completely present with each other. She loved the hotel. She kept the handwritten letter. And I felt proud. Proud not just to be in love with her, but to be the man who had created an experience she would never forget.

I didn't want to be the 'poor artist' stereotype. I wanted to be a leader, someone who created extraordinary experiences for us. And in that moment, I was.

118

A Full Practice Takes Years, Doesn't It?

In January 2016, I posted something that felt like a milestone. A marker in the ground. A signal, not just to others, but to myself, that this path I'd chosen was working.

Just over three years after I started coaching, and only twelve months into doing it full time, I had finished 2015 with a full practice. My calendar was booked up. I had clients every day. Both my Powerful Men's Immersions had sold out and I was already planning the next one. I'd just proposed to Yamini, and she had said yes. Our parents had met. The wedding was later that year. Life was good.

What struck me most wasn't the money, or even the fullness of my schedule—it was the shift in how I *felt*. I was proud. Happy. I was doing work that mattered, and people were responding.

I wasn't chasing my dream anymore. I was *living* it.

And I wanted others to know this was possible for them too.

Because if someone else had told me this story as their own, a part of me would have probably said, 'Lucky you.' That's often how it looks when someone else gets what we're striving for—like they had something we didn't. Some secret. Some edge.

But I can say this now with honesty: there was no secret. No shortcut. What I had was a solid commitment and an excellent mentor who helped me keep showing up when things felt uncertain. Steve Chandler and his school were my secret weapon. I leaned on him during the wobbles. He helped me stay grounded and move forward. And I did. One conversation at a time. One courageous action after another.

Years later, I found myself on the other side of this journey, supporting coaches. I see the same doubts and hopes I once had, and I watch coaches transform as they learn to create clients one conversation at a time. It has become one of the most rewarding parts of my life seeing them build their own thriving practices—not by trying to impress, but by serving powerfully.

What surprises many people is how ordinary the path was. I wasn't a marketing expert. I didn't have a huge email list. I didn't have a slick website or run Facebook ads (I still don't). I didn't present myself as a guru or hide behind polished branding. I was just a man who had been impacted by the Principles and who wanted to serve others by sharing what I'd seen. That's it. In that Facebook post, I wrote:

> There is nothing special about me. I don't consider myself an expert in the Principles. I'm a very ordinary bloke who was deeply impacted personally and who would love others to get a glimpse of them too.

Looking back now, I wouldn't change that line. If anything, I'd add one thing: 'I trusted my gut, and I took action.'

Even when I was scared. Even when I doubted myself. Even when it looked like it might not work. I didn't wait until I was fearless—*I just stopped letting fear decide what I did next.* If you're reading this and wondering if it's possible for you: **This is very**

doable.

It doesn't happen overnight. It took years of service, of mistakes, of learning and trying again. But it happened. It takes consistency. It takes a willingness to serve. It takes a willingness to get uncomfortable. But it works. And when it does—when the calls are booked and the calendar fills and the conversations are real and deep and transformational—there's no better feeling. You're not just making a living. You're making a difference that ripples out in ways you can't fully measure.

That's what matters most. I closed that post in 2016 by saying:

> I'd love nothing more than all the coaches here to have waiting lists of people wanting to work with them. Because it's a great way for these wonderful Principles to get out into the world.

Nearly a decade later, that desire has only grown stronger. And now, as this book draws to a close, I want to leave you with this:

I started off coaching, and within a few years, I filled my practice.

I didn't do it by trying to be impressive.

I did it by being of service.

And if I can do that, you can too.

Let's keep going. Let's keep serving.

And let's transform this profession—together.

119

I'll Meet You There

It was late 2015, and Steve Chandler had made it clear: he wouldn't be taking on any more coaching clients in the coming year. He was pouring himself into the writing and release of *Death Wish*, a book on addiction, recovery, and freedom that was deeply personal to him. He was committed, focused—and unavailable.

I didn't like that answer. I still had a few sessions left in our agreement, but I didn't want them to be our last. So I asked him: 'What would it take for you to make an exception for me?'

He replied without hesitation: 'A million dollars.'

It was a bold number. Perhaps meant to end the conversation. But I leaned in with a smile and said, 'Well . . . we've got three sessions left to make that million.'

I wasn't trying to be clever. I was being earnest, in my own cheeky way. I didn't believe I'd earn a million in that time, but I did believe in possibility. And I was planting a seed, hoping something might shift. Then, weeks later, completely out of the blue, an email from Steve landed in my inbox. It wasn't a warm-hearted 'Let's keep working together.' It was concise, direct, and firm. He'd made an exception. There were conditions. It was clearly a one-time continuation—not a new agreement. But the door was open.

I was overjoyed, and I responded immediately to say yes,

wiring the funds before anything could change. I wasn't going to miss that window. But I added something in my reply. I said,

> Let's play at a higher level. I know we've done great work, but I believe there's more in the tank. I want to move towards world-class—in my coaching, in my prosperity, and in how I show up in this relationship.

His reply was simple. One sentence.

> I'll meet you at any level you choose to play at… and you can tell me what that means to you.

That line hit me hard. It shifted everything between us. I realised he wasn't there to pull greatness out of me. He wasn't going to 'coach harder.' This wasn't about him. It was about me.

If I wanted to play at a higher level, it had to begin with how I showed up:

- More honest.
- More vulnerable.
- More coachable.
- More committed.

That exchange didn't just raise the bar for that year. It raised the standard for every year that followed. Because becoming more coachable wasn't a one-time decision. It became a practice. Each time I renewed with Steve, I saw a new layer. I saw where I was still hiding. Still playing it safe. Still intellectualising instead of revealing. Still bringing 'strong' topics instead of true ones.

And each year, I recommitted to meeting him at a deeper level—because the invitation was always open. That one sentence—

'I'll meet you at any level you choose to play at'—became both a mirror and an invitation, showing me where I was and where I could go. A compass. A challenge. A gift.

And I've been walking towards it ever since.

THE END

Further Resources

Throughout this book I have shared stories, principles, and practices that have shaped my journey as a coach and human being. If something here resonated with you and you'd like to go deeper, here are some of the books and resources that have been invaluable to me as I grew my coaching practice.

Sydney Banks

The teacher and author who first articulated the Three Principles understanding. His books are simple yet profound explorations of the nature of Mind, Consciousness and Thought:

- ***The Enlightened Gardener*** – A story that illustrates the simplicity of the Principles through everyday conversation.
- ***The Enlightened Gardener Revisited*** – A continuation of the dialogue, exploring deeper layers of the same wisdom.
- ***Second Chance*** – A spiritual novel about hope, renewal and insight.
- ***In Quest of the Pearl*** – A parable on the search for truth and awakening.
- ***The Missing Link*** – A concise articulation of the Three Principles in everyday language.
- ***Dear Liza*** – A novel that gently conveys the life-changing power of thought.

Jamie Smart

- ***Clarity Activator*** – An excellent resource for experiencing insight-driven clarity in your own life: jamiesmart.com/pcp06
- ***Clarity: Clear Mind, Better Performance, Bigger Results*** – a book on how clarity of mind transforms both wellbeing and performance.

Steve Chandler

- ***The Prosperous Coach*** (2nd Edition, with Rich Litvin) – A foundational book for coaches who want to build a thriving, service-led practice.
- ***CREATOR*** – On shifting from victim to creator in every area of life.
- ***How to Get Clients*** – Practical strategies for building a sustainable coaching practice.
- ***Crazy Good*** – Stories and insights into creating a life filled with joy and impact.
- ***37 Ways to Boost Your Coaching Practice*** – Short, actionable strategies for growing as a coach.
- ***Wealth Warrior*** – A book on transforming your relationship with money and service.
- ***The Power of Systems*** – How simple systems create freedom, consistency and momentum.

Essential Reading for Coaches

- ***The Coaching Blueprint*** by Angi Scott – a thoughtful and practical guide for coaches who want to build with integrity and depth, based on her experience through attending the AJC Coaching Career School three times
- ***How to Get the Most Out of Coaching*** by Karen Davis and Alex Mill – a must-read guide for clients and coaches alike to maximise the value of a coaching relationship
- ***Lessons from My Coach*** by Amir Karkouti – reflections and insights from a powerful coach and teacher
- ***Living Service*** by Melissa Ford – on making coaching a way of being rather than just a profession
- ***Mastery*** by George Leonard – a classic exploration of the path of lifelong growth and practice
- ***Overcoming Underearning*** by Barbara Stanny – a transformative look at money, value, and self-worth
- ***The Ultimate Coach*** by Amy Hardison – ostensibly about my mentor Steve Hardison, but ultimately about the reader's own capacity for transformation and Being
- ***Mental Toughness Mantras*** by Chris Dorris – short, potent reminders for resilience, courage, and focus
- ***Sweet Sharing*** by Ankush Jain – my first book, written to help readers rediscover their true selves beneath the noise of everyday life

Acknowledgments

I am deeply grateful to the people whose love, wisdom, and presence have shaped both this book and who I've become.

To **Yamini**, my wife, for marrying me without any guarantee that this profession would ever make us a penny. Your love, patience, and belief in me have been my anchor. Thank you for proofreading, for standing beside me in all seasons, and for walking beside me through all of this. I fall in love with you more each day. You're brilliant, kind, an incredible mother, and the best gym partner I could ask for.

To **Sydney Banks**, although we never met, your simple articulation of the Three Principles changed the entire experience of my life. Through your books, videos, audios, and students, I saw for the first time the power of Thought in shaping human experience. Without what you saw, none of this would exist.

To **Steve Chandler**, this man is an angel. Without you I would likely never have stayed in this profession, let alone become successful. Your fingerprints are all over my work. You modeled love, kindness, generosity, and taking responsibility. You were there for me in my lowest moments, believing in me when I could not. In our years together, you helped me grow my business, but far more importantly, you helped me become a better man, a better husband, and a better father. This book would not exist without you.

To **Steve Hardison**, The Ultimate Coach, my coach for nearly four years. You expanded my mind beyond what I thought possible, completely reshaped my self-image, and helped me see that what I could do in this life could be far greater than I imagined. You guided me to think and play bigger while dropping ego and loving more. You showed me the difference between being a coach and doing coaching, and even created a system with me that enabled this book to be completed. I cannot overstate your impact. It has been one of the greatest blessings of my life to work with you.

To **Jamie Smart**, who first pointed me to the Three Principles and supported my first steps as a coach. I deeply value our friendship. Thank you for diligently reading this book for errors and for your continued support. Without your training, none of this journey would have begun.

To **Sydney's students and the teachers who followed**—Keith Blevens and Valda Monroe, Dicken Bettinger, Chip and Jan Chipman, Elsie Spittle, Mark Howard, Cathy Casey—your love, mentoring, and guidance have deepened my grounding and opened my heart. Chip's presence continues to live on in me, and I am profoundly grateful for his legacy.

To **Chantal Burns**, for your friendship and wisdom in shaping my writing.

To **Garret Kramer**, for your early teaching and inspiration.

To **John Epstein**, for helping me redefine success in ways that bless my life.

To **Zan Perrion**, for inspiring me to live more boldly.

To **Abdul Amin**, for first introducing me to personal development and your ongoing friendship.

To **Henk Kok**, for inspiring me to finally start my first book and for your continued friendship.

To all of my **clients**—private, those in the AJC Coaching Career School, and the men who have joined my Immersions. Every agreement has been sacred. Your courage and openness have taught me more than you know.

To my **colleagues and mentors around the world** who have walked alongside me in service of raising consciousness.

To **Chris Nelson**, my editor, for your care, diligence, and excellence in shaping this book into its final form.

To **Rose Latham**, for diligently reading the proof copy and doing a full spell and grammar check when this book needed it most. From client to Director of Client Astonishment at AJC, you've been brilliant every step of the way. I'm incredibly lucky to have you in my corner.

To **Felipe Bernardo**, Director of Operations and Creativity at AJC, who has been a godsend over the years. You helped me find the right subtitle, coordinated the cover design with Jefté on your team, and support me in countless ways that never make it onto the page. Your pursuit of excellence inspires me daily. You're a kindred spirit, and I'm deeply grateful.

And finally, to **my parents**, for their love, encouragement, and unwavering support.

This book is the result of countless people who have shaped my life and work. I am forever grateful.

About the Author

As a shy teenager in the UK, Ankush Jain joined a youth group, where he first discovered the beginnings of confidence and leadership. That early spark grew when, at nineteen, he stumbled into the world of personal development. The next decade became an obsession with books, seminars, courses and videos. This was more than a hobby. He wanted to know: *What am I really capable of?*

Yet coaching was never something he considered as a career. He told himself it didn't pay well. Besides, he had the safety of the corporate world. Or so it seemed. His identity was tied to job titles, company cars, and salary brackets. Around him, family and friends were doctors, lawyers and accountants from prestigious universities. He feared that if he left and failed, he'd prove everyone right—that he didn't measure up.

What changed everything was realising this wasn't just about a career. It was a calling. Even if it meant making less money or being judged, Ankush knew he couldn't keep living a life designed by someone else's expectations.

That leap set him on a path of transformation. Earlier mentors like Zan Perrion and Johnny Epstein introduced him to ideas about mastery, service and generosity. Jamie Smart introduced him to the Three Principles, and Dr Keith Blevens later strengthened that understanding in ways that deepened his foundation. Steve Chandler became his first long-term coach, and later Steve Hardison reshaped his self-image in ways he couldn't have imagined.

Through his own practice, Ankush discovered that coaching at its highest is sacred. Its impact ripples out across generations. He stands for powerful, life-changing conversations rooted in service, love, and connection. He stands against gimmicks, hustle and chasing income at the expense of true transformation. His mission is clear: to raise the consciousness of the planet by transforming the coaching profession into one that is as well-paid and well respected as any other profession.

Outside of coaching, Ankush's greatest joy is his family. His wife, Yamini, is both partner and teacher, and his son Raunak is his biggest blessing. He treasures friendships, community and the everyday miracle of being human. When he isn't serving clients, you might find him in the gym, experimenting with essential oils or dancing to bhangra music.

Ankush is the founder of the AJC Coaching Career School, creator of the Powerful Men's Immersion and the author of *Sweet Sharing: Rediscovering the REAL You*. His proudest moments are when clients tell him the coaching they've received through his work gave them far more than they came for.

If you take just one thing from his story, let it be this: Ankush is a human being, just like you. His journey is proof that you can create a life of freedom, love and service, no matter where you start. He hopes his work helps you see what's possible for you.

Continue Your Journey: The AJC Coaching Career School

If this book resonated with you, you already know that building a meaningful coaching practice isn't about gimmicks or the latest sales tactic.

It's about who you are *being* as you serve, and how that shapes everything you *do*.

The **AJC Coaching Career School** is more than a professional programme to help you grow your income. It is a six-month development experience for those who are committed to taking the coaching profession forward while growing their income in the process. By joining, you become part of a global community of world-class coaches that lovingly supports you and doesn't let you play small when you feel like shrinking.

At AJC, we go beyond teaching you how to fill your practice or improve your skills. Those things will happen, but they are by-products of something far more powerful: becoming part of a movement that is raising the standard of coaching worldwide.

Here, you will:

- Learn how to create your ideal clients through genuine connection and deep service.
- Build a prosperous, sustainable practice that reflects your values and have fun along the way.
- Become the kind of coach clients trust, refer to their network and want to hire again and again—not just learn enrolment techniques.
- Step into your innate leadership potential and help shape the future of our profession alongside other dedicated coaches.

This isn't about learning to convince people to hire you. It's about developing the certainty that you can create the income you want by doing your best work.

Graduates have gone on to lead their own communities, write bestselling books, host world-class retreats and mentor others. Not because they learned new techniques, but because they saw themselves differently. They dropped the thinking that they couldn't, that they had to wait, or that they weren't good enough.

Client Experience

"When I look back at the key moments that helped me build a thriving, oversubscribed coaching business, both trace directly back to Ankush Jain. The first came when Ankush invited me to stop treating coaching like a glorified hobby and start treating it like a real business. Committing to a consistent number of conversations each week became the foundation and quickly changed the trajectory of everything that followed.

The second moment came when my practice was half full and I found myself resisting Ankush's advice to lower my fees. I had convinced myself that doing so would make me feel like a lesser coach... like I was failing. But when I finally took the leap, the opposite happened. I felt like an incredible bargain, and I knew anyone who didn't say yes at my new rate was missing out. That shift in mindset changed how I showed up—more confident, more grounded and more certain of the value I bring. Within six weeks, I was fully booked and I've never looked back.

Ankush always said something magical happens on the other side of full, and he couldn't have been more right. Since then, my business has grown year over year. Today it's built on renewals, referrals and real results. The AJC approach works because it's grounded in reality, not hype. It's been the foundation for everything I've created."

—**Deryl Sweeney**, Multiple six-figure coach and AJC Graduate

"Very few coaches can effectively teach the systems and secrets that lead to prosperity in this profession as well as Ankush Jain."

—**Steve Chandler,** Author of *The Prosperous Coach*

Exclusive Bonuses for Attendees

When you enrol, you will gain immediate access to a collection of exclusive resources designed to deepen your learning and accelerate your growth. These are not available anywhere else:

- **A never-before-seen video with Steve Chandler** on *Coaching as a Career*, recorded exclusively for AJC students.
- **Access to "The Coaching Library"**, Ankush's comprehensive online programme packed with practical guidance and tools.
- **A copy of** *Sweet Sharing* **by Ankush Jain**, a reminder of what true transformation looks like from the inside out.
- **A rare two-hour masterclass with Steve Hardison, The Ultimate Coach**, recorded in 2024 exclusively for AJC students. It is an unforgettable exploration of presence, creation and being.

Those who sign up early also receive access to **bonus practical pre-school webinars**, providing extra insight and momentum before the school begins.

Several coaches each year make back their entire tuition investment **before the first live weekend** simply by applying what they learn from these bonus resources and webinars.

All of this exists to support one goal: helping you build a thriving practice and lead the next evolution of this profession.

If you are ready to join a movement of coaches committed to mastery, service and transformation, visit the link below or reach out directly.

Learn more: www.ankushjain.co.uk/ajc

Or email **info@ankushjain.co.uk** to begin a conversation or request the school brochure.

Let's build the coaching profession we want to see in the world—one which is as respectable and well-paid as any other.

Also by Ankush Jain

In *Sweet Sharing: Rediscovering the REAL You,* Ankush Jain uncovers the hidden beliefs and misunderstandings that keep us from experiencing life to the fullest—and shows us how to free ourselves from them. Using stories from his own life and from the lives of his clients, Ankush gently points us towards a transformative understanding of how the mind really works and invites us to rediscover who we truly are.

"Without ego promises, this book, like its author, quietly *delivers.* A 'Sweet Sharing' indeed! It is transcendent in its simplicity, honesty and humility."

~ **Keith Blevens, Ph.D.,** Clinical Psychologist, Three Principles educator, trainer and consultant

"*Sweet Sharing* is a beautiful, personal journey of Understanding. Ankush helps us find the wisdom to resolve everyday human issues.

I recommend this book to any human being that wants to discover their own wisdom, love, and understanding."

~ **Mark Howard, Ph.D.,** Clinical Psychologist, Three Principles educator, trainer and consultant

"*Sweet Sharing* is personal yet universal; simple yet deep. The stories and insights in this book show how transformation happens naturally when we wake up to how our human experience works. Ankush's stories will entertain you, and what he shares about how the mind works just might change your life."

~ **Amy Johnson, Ph.D.,** author of *The Little Book of Big Change: The No-Willpower Approach to Breaking Any Habit* and creator of The Little School of Big Change

Printed in Dunstable, United Kingdom

79347057R00268